Curtains

TOM JOKINEN

Curtains

ADVENTURES OF AN UNDERTAKER-IN-TRAINING

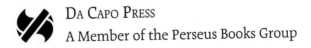

DA CAPO PRESS
A Member of the Perseus Books Group

Cataloging-in-Publication data for this book
is available from the Library of Congress.

First Da Capo Press edition 2010
Reprinted by arrangement with Random House Canada
ISBN: 978-0-306-81891-2
LCCN: 2010920629

Published by Da Capo Press
A Member of the Perseus Books Group
www.dacapopress.com
Da Capo Press books are available at special discounts for bulk
purchases in the U.S. by corporations, institutions, and other organizations.
For more information, please contact the Special Markets Department at the
Perseus Books Group, 2300 Chestnut Street, Suite 200, Philadelphia, PA 19103,
or call (800) 810-4145, ext. 5000, or e-mail special.markets@perseusbooks.com.

10 9 8 7 6 5 4 3 2 1

For Annie

Has your life been a failure?
Let's make your death a success!

—Jean Teulé, "The Suicide Shop"

————————

Books . . . are tombstones.

—Antonin Artaud

Contents

Prologue

wo rules for picking up a body at the hospital, known as a "removal": (1) Make sure it's the right one. This business, when you shake it down to first principles, is the burial or cremation of the dead, two relatively irreversible acts. Mistakes are frowned upon. Please check the ID tag carefully; and (2) Never stop for food on the way back to the funeral home when you're "carrying," not even at a drive-thru. It's bad for the brand, and is apt to put other drive-thru-ers off their doughnuts.

I'm anxious about my first removal at Seven Oaks Hospital, which has, I'm told, a finicky loading dock that makes getting the stretcher into the van a game of brute strength and faith. And my stretcher technique is poor. I know this. I've practised a few times with an empty stretcher, shuffling it in and out of the van at the crematorium. The stretcher has collapsing legs that fold under on the way in, and fall back into place on the way out. The trick is to make sure the legs snap back when you pull it out, to listen for the telltale click that says the legs are locked in place. Everyone talks about the *click*. If you don't hear the *click*, you'll be picking your body up off the floor. In industry jargon, this is considered "undignified," and dignity is an even bigger deal in funeral service than not going through the drive-thru with a dead body.

For the Seven Oaks gig, Glenn comes with me as a spotter. Glenn is younger than me; he runs his uncle Neil's crematorium and in his off time he plays rugby and tends nighttime bar at the Pasta La Vista restaurant on Kenaston Boulevard. He's not an undertaker: though Neil agreed to sponsor him at the embalming school, Glenn said he didn't want to spend his life stuffing cotton into orifices, thank you. But he's worked the technical side of funeral service since high school, during which time he's removed and cremated and buried scores of dead people, and sold "pre-need" funeral insurance to a few of the living.

At Seven Oaks, there's a hallway at the back near the loading dock, where the undertakers gather every day to pick up their cargo. Here they chat about the weather and hockey and chew nicotine gum while they wait for Security to unlock the Silver Doors like they are waiting for Walmart to open. Every hospital in Winnipeg has its Silver Doors, a gentle nickname for the morgue, only at Seven Oaks the entrance is neither silver nor plural: it's just a door. It could be the entry to a janitor's closet. Glenn makes small talk with a red-faced undertaker from another firm who wears a baseball jacket and tie, and tells us about the time he pulled the short straw and got the oversized body, a "hernia case" that took up two gurneys and nearly flipped off the stretcher on the way into the van. The mood is light, courteous. Me, I'm rehearsing stretcher moves in my head. My track record with mechanical objects is spotty. Once, while trying to fix a bicycle chain, I got a knot in it—which a mechanic told me was impossible until he saw it.

Security arrives, bored. We follow him into a small office. A wastebasket in the corner is full of latex gloves, and there's a baptismal font of Purell hand sanitizer on the wall. He checks our paperwork. Death is a bureaucratic event. No one is allowed to die unless the right forms are signed and cross-checked by a high-school dropout with a lot of keys. Then he opens another door, and I feel the cold breeze and smell what smells like a refrigerator that needs a box of baking soda. It's dark in this second, even smaller room, and I can make out a few gurneys set at odd angles. I expect big stainless steel drawers, but here, every cop procedural and scare-'em-straight after-school special I've ever watched has betrayed me. No drawers. The dead are on the gurneys, wrapped tight in white plastic from head to feet like frozen turkeys, packing tape around their necks and ankles. Four of them, identical. No toe tags even. Which one is ours?

Glenn and the red-faced undertaker commence shopping. Each body has a file card taped to its shin, an impression of its plastic hospital ID in purple ink.

"Bingo."

Glenn has a match. Then, the other undertaker finds his. Glenn gives him a hand loading out and leaves me to "check for valuables."

Here the job is to inspect the corpse's hands for jewellery, rings and bracelets, and to double-check the hospital wristband while I'm there. To do this I have to feel for the hands through the plastic and rip a hole in the shroud to get at them. I want to do this, to show I'm able, but in fact I'd rather cut off my own thumb with tin snips than hold hands with the dead.

They're folded on his belly. The plastic is thick, but I tear a gap. His hands are big, like he built things outdoors. They're yellow and cold, the nails white and trimmed too short. No rings, the wristband matches, and he has an IV lead taped to his wrist still red with dried blood. The moment seems to call for a gesture and all I can come up with is to give his hands a light squeeze. This is a lonely way to end up, wrapped in plastic in a room full of strangers, and if I think about it, and I'd rather not, I'll end up in a cold room too, one day, maybe holding hands with a trainee undertaker who I hope will have better stretcher technique than me. Just not today, not next week, please, not for a while.

He slides on like a charm: shoulders and butt first, then the legs swing over. I brace the stretcher with my hip so it doesn't roll away. We strap him in with seat belts and cover him with the cloth sham, on which the name *Neil Bardal Inc.* is embroidered, since you never miss an opportunity to fly the company colours. Gloves come off, hands are ritually Purell'd, and we head for the loading dock, leaving the last two wallflower corpses in the dark, still waiting for their rides. The dock turns out to be mismatched for the height of the van, but with Glenn ready to catch whatever falls, me or the stretcher, I'm able to aim, trigger the collapsing legs when they hit the bumper and then let gravity do the rest. The body is now in the truck. I lock the stretcher in place with a cotter pin, so it doesn't roll out the back on the highway back to the crematorium like in a *Flintstones* episode, and we're off.

Glenn once "removed" a body at a seniors complex in Winnipeg. It was Halloween. When he got there the corpse was still in the bed where it died. He strapped the body to the stretcher, and on the way out, the doors of the elevator opened onto a costume party, staff and residents dressed like Disney characters. What could he do? He had to slalom his stretcher through the wheelchairs, those in the crowd alternately wondering who was under the cloth and whether they would be next. A nurse dressed as Snow White scowled. Glenn might as well have been carrying a scythe. This, he says, is why the Silver Doors are always in the back of the hospital with the laundry bags and medical waste. People don't want to know. There's a time, from when someone dies to when they magically pop up at the funeral or the cemetery or as a bag of ashes, that remains a black hole, invisible to the rest of the world, and everyone's happy with the arrangement. We in funeral service cover the gap. People pay us to keep to ourselves what goes on there.

The body in the back passes wind when the van hits a bump. It happens, Glenn says. He opens the window.

At the crematorium, I hop out to finish the job and haul on the stretcher—but it won't budge. Forgot the cotter pin. Second try, the stretcher rolls free, and I listen for the *click*. The first set of legs locks in place, then the others drop, clickless, but it's too late—the head end of the stretcher smacks the bumper on its way to the pavement, which it hits with a *whang* like an aluminum baseball bat. If he wasn't already dead, I've killed him. I pull back the cot cover to discover that the man's hands are still folded comfortably on his belly. He's past caring.

"It happens," says Jon, the boss's son, who comes to my aid.

But I can feel the impact still humming in my hands. Dignity, I say to myself. I'm afraid it doesn't come naturally to me.

One

The Factory

The sociologist Zygmunt Bauman says that humans are the only creatures who know they're going to die, and even worse, they *know* they know it, and it's not something they can "unknow." All they can do is distract themselves, briefly, like you might mask the smell of burnt food by spraying the kitchen with Lysol. The main reason I'm here, working as a trainee in Neil Bardal's funeral home in Winnipeg, in my ham-fisted, dignity-challenged way, is to figure out if the screwball rituals we perform and the industry that's evolved to support them are part of the Lysol, or if in fact the way we handle death, with caskets and trinkets and stone markers, is our way of facing up, finally, to the smell. Not that I think that by being mindful of death we can lead richer lives. A life "forgetful of death," Bauman says, "life lived as meaningful and worth living, life alive with purpose instead of being crushed and incapacitated by purposelessness—is a formidable human achievement." I'm with him, and Epicurus too, who said that there's no need to fear the oblivion after we're gone if we never cared about the oblivion that came before we were born. Cheer up. Death obsessing is for boozy existentialists and bad poets.

Which prompts a bony question: why do we each spend up to $10,000—for most, the third-biggest cash outlay in our lives after a house and a car, according to Jessica Mitford, who wrote *The American Way of Death*—on funerals?

Neil Bardal says we need the ritual to know the person who's died. We need to see the body, we want the proof: we're empirical, modern, enlightened souls who benefit from looking at death when it comes, standing up to sing and pray in its presence. Neil's my boss. He's a third-generation undertaker, his oldest son Eirik is an undertaker, and Jon, the youngest, works at the crematorium (although, like his cousin Glenn, he's not keen on it and is studying to be an electrician instead of an undertaker). Neil's sister Jean answers the phones and his wife Annette does the books. There are four other funeral directors on staff, and in flush times they sponsor trainees. That's where I come in. Neil has agreed to take me on as a paid intern (plus free dry cleaning and a company golf shirt) if I agree to hump caskets and flowers, set up chairs at service, mop floors, wash the hearse, help the directors do what they do, and otherwise participate in the day-to-day rituals that families need, even if we don't agree on what constitutes an empirical, modern, enlightened response to death. Full disclosure: when I die, I've asked to be left in a blue bin at the curb on recycling day.

The funeral chapel is downtown in a strip-mall on Aubrey Street, ten minutes from my house, but the crematorium is a long bus ride away, near the airport, the last building on Notre Dame Avenue before Winnipeg turns into plenty of flat, treeless nothing. From the street there's little to betray its purpose: could be an insurance office, until you see the hearse parked in the side lot and the stone slab in the walkway inscribed ASK NOT FOR WHOM THE BELL TOLLS. Could be a very frank insurance office. Inside I meet Jon. He has his father's sad eyes and he yawns a lot.

My internship starts with a slapdash tour, beginning in what Jon calls the Committal Space, a faux living room with faux colonial furniture, faux plants, and prints of other faux plants on the walls. Each end table has a box of Kleenex with a single, perfectly teased-out tissue, and on one there's also a picture frame, empty, which gives me a chill. There's something unwholesome about an empty picture frame. The Committal Space is where the family gathers to "view" the body before cremation: there's a nook for the casket, and a brocade curtain for privacy. At the back of the nook is a heavy armoire with a bronze sculpture of a horse. The room is cold and clean, and smells of Endust; it reminds me of the living rooms of kids I knew whose parents had some kind of preservation fetish and declared the good furniture off limits. The horse is a nice touch, a bit of whimsy, but the horse turns out to be an urn: the ashes go inside the wooden base. The Chinese lantern next to it is an urn too, and so is the little blue porcelain teddy bear holding an umbrella, designed for infants. I don't want to touch anything in here lest it contain someone.

Not only can you view the body before cremation in this room, you can also watch the main event, car-wash style, through a window separating the Committal Space from the working side of the crematorium. When Jon snaps open the blinds, I'm face to face with a monster machine, one of the facility's two "retorts," which looks like an over-designed Soviet-era East German pizza oven, with a fat stainless-steel chimney growing out of its head and a small glass porthole in its black iron door. A single unblinking eye. This is Retort Two. She's fussy, tends to belch black smoke and burn out of control when dealing with the heavier bodies, which the Bardals prefer to assign to Number One, an older, less temperamental machine. Number Two prefers thin, elderly bodies without much fat.

This whole place is built like a theatre: a public space up front, with its living room set, and a backstage where all the magic happens. Only Neil's broken the fourth wall, encouraging people to bear witness, to see the event through to the end, which is both noble and oddly post-modern. Jon admits most Winnipeg families prefer not to watch, unlike in England, where watching is the norm. But if you're into it, Neil's the only open-window cremator in town.

Backstage presents a different vibe than front-of-house. Twenty degrees Fahrenheit hotter, and noisier. As soon as Jon opens the connecting door I hear the low rumble and feel the dry heat. We pass Number Two's backside and all her ductwork, stop at the sort table, where the remains—shattered bits of bone and whatever else survives two hours at 1,600 degrees Fahrenheit in the retort (casket hinges, pants zippers, artificial knees and hips)—sit to cool before human is separated from non-human. They use a magnet to pick out the metal artifacts and then sort through the pile by hand, chucking out anything that doesn't look white and bony. Then it all goes into a sturdy blender, which turns everything to powder.

Jon hands me a plastic bag full of a recent customer: it's about the size and heft of a two-pound bag of cornmeal, clearly labelled with name and number, since at this point we all look very much the same. I sneeze. It's dusty at the sort table; there's a thin white film on everything, on the heavy black vacuum hose that hangs over the table, on a Remembrance Day poppy stuck to a bulletin board, inside the blender. People dust.

To get to Number One I follow Jon down a dark hallway lined with medieval instruments: long-handled iron hooks and brooms with steel bristles, and a winch affair, an upside-down L-shaped bracket with three blue canvas straps for getting a body into a casket without wrenching your back. Number One is in action, and I feel the rumbling of its burners in my chest. Jon explains the routine: body comes in from the hospital, it's transferred to a cardboard box and stored in the cooler, waiting for its place in the cremation queue. Or, if it's going to be embalmed or "prepped" for what Jessica Mitford called the full-fig funeral (viewing, visitation, open-casket service at the chapel or church) it goes onto a gurney and into the prep room, the door to which is always locked, to keep civilians and wayward deliverymen from walking in on an embalming-in-progress. This is a full-service operation: some bodies are cremated, some are prepped, some are even prepped *then* cremated, an act, if you'll forgive me a one-time use of the term, of overkill. It all depends what the family wants. If you want a full-fig funeral followed by cremation, you get it.

If you buy a casket for the service, the casket goes into the retort: the Bardals don't reuse them. Some funeral homes rent caskets for the funeral–cremation combo. The casket is a shell with a collapsible door at the foot end, through which slides the body in an MDF (medium-density fibreboard) liner: the body goes in for the service, comes out for the cremation. The shell goes back into rotation.

The rental fee is usually the wholesale cost of the casket, so the unit pays for itself after its first outing: factoring in depreciation (nicks and scrapes), the undertaker may get fifteen or twenty uses out of it before the casket is retired. Neil doesn't carry rentals, he doesn't like the concept. "Same concept as shoes at a bowling alley," he says. If you just want to scatter at the lake, the body might go straight into a cardboard box off the van and into the retort, and you can pick up the ashes the next day. Every former soul that comes in through the garage door is assigned a number: it's written in Sharpie on their cardboard box and the corpse's wristband, not unlike the wristbands they issue at raves and folk festivals.

We pass another doorway, through which I can see a young woman brushing an older woman's hair. The older woman is lying on a gurney in a blue dress and clunky black shoes. The younger woman smiles and waves at us, then goes back to work, cradling the older woman's hair in the palm of her hand, pulling the brush gently so it doesn't snag. There are two other women on gurneys, both dressed in skirts and cardigans as if they were going out for afternoon tea with the third. One clutches a purse. It's a quiet, domestic scene. They look so still and benign that there's no reason my heart should be racing, but it is, and I back away from the doorway. It's the stillness that scares me. Even sleeping people have some animating spark, you can sense it, and if you watch them for long enough you'll see it too, a twitch or an itchy earlobe scratched. These women are empty. Well dressed and nicely groomed, but done.

Jon flips the cover off the peephole on Retort One so I can have a peek. The man's body is on its back in the chamber, hands at its side, feet pointing ten o'clock, two o'clock. The orange and blue fire roars from the roof of the retort like water from a firehose, hitting the chest, and I can see another jet farther down the chamber, and bits of fly-ash circling in the turbulence. The body is black, and the bones glow in the way a burning piece of firewood glows if you blow on it hard. There's no smell, but I can feel a draft on my ear as an air current rushes past me, through the porthole, into the chamber.

"The head burns slowly, the heart burns slowly," Jon says.

Hanging on the wall next to the retort are two iron hooks. When the body no longer looks like a body, when all that's left are scattered bones and a black mass the size of a pumpkin, Jon feeds the longer of the two hooks through the porthole and rakes everything into a pile under the gas jet, to finish the job. Then he opens the door a crack to let the bones cool, and I can see the stone wall of the retort and the pieces, a hip ball-joint, a jaw, glowing red.

We break for lunch and I scrub my hands and forearms in the bathroom and rinse my mouth with Scope until my gums sting. I tell myself I'll get used to it, like the others who work here. And I know I'll lick the primal uneasiness that drove me from a room full of harmless little old dead ladies, but right now I can't imagine ever getting used to the violence of the retort.

I find Jon and the young woman in the arrangement room having lunch. I have brought a sandwich from home, but my appetite left me somewhere around the baby urn. Jon eats a pizza sub and leafs through *Maxim* magazine. Natalie—I can call her Nat—used to work at Shoppers Drug Mart, where she sold cosmetics before she became a funeral director. Her hometown is St. Claude, a French farming community south of Portage la Prairie, which has both a dairy museum and the world's second-largest smokable pipe, 20 feet long and weighing 430 pounds. Nat's lunch is a microwaved pork chop that she saws with a plastic knife, holding her fork in her fist the way a child does. She is the chief embalmer. Jon flashes her the *Maxim* centrefold, who wears a leather bikini.

"Nice," she says, not looking up.

There's a stack of funeral trade magazines here too: *American Cemetery* and *Canadian Funeral News*, no centrefolds, but Dodge chemicals has a full-page ad in *CFN* for Plasdopake, an embalming fluid that looks alarmingly like orange soda, and promises "fine tissue texture, glowing color undertones and faultless preservation." It's a "humectant-type arterial wholly free of circulation-clogging animal fat precipitation," with a skull-and-crossbones on the label. I remind myself to drink only tap water at the new job, never anything from the fridge.

I meet Annette, Neil's wife, who shakes my hand loosely. I smile, she doesn't. My impression of her impression of me is that I'm an interloper whose motives for nosing around her family business are still unknown and are presumed muckrakey. She's a skilled hairstylist who still works on corpses from time to time when things get busy, but her daily job is as office manager. Not only is she the boss's wife and business partner but she's responsible for cutting the paycheques, so I promise myself I'll be nice to Annette, even though, so far, she scares me half to death.

That afternoon both retorts are roaring, and Nat has a job for me: helping her dress another of her endless supply of old ladies. I tell her, so she knows, that I sometimes have trouble dressing myself (button alignment issues), but she says there's nothing to it. The arms and legs will be a bit stiff, but don't be shy about man-handling them: the dead are uncooperative, but they respond to gravity and brute force, a kind of mortuary tough-love. Have I ever dressed another person? she asks. I don't have kids, but there was that incident in college involving tequila and a grad student, and certainly I've known people who respond only to gravity and brute force, but otherwise all I can do is follow her lead.

The lady is wrapped in a flannel sheet, her face and hands goopy with Kalon skin cream to keep them from drying out. She's also green. Not sickly peaked green in the cheeks, but forest green, an artifact of the embalming chemicals reacting with the jaundice she had before she ended up here. This will be covered up by makeup, but for now she looks like The Hulk.

We take turns, alternately rolling the woman to one side and then the other, scooting up her hose and skirt in stages, then the bra and blouse. It's a funeral director's job to counsel families on clothing for their dead: find something with a high collar (to cover the incision near the neck where the embalming chemicals went in) and please send underwear. Turns out most people don't think of it. "I won't bury anyone without underwear," Nat says.

They keep a bag of spares. Once they had an apprentice who was so firm on the matter, she used to raid Neil's office for boxers and socks, where she knew he always kept a change of clothes for services ("Do you know how many people are buried in my clothes in Brookside cemetery?" he told me). Most men are laid to rest in suits and ties, and it's got to the point that Nat can only tie a tie from above. When her boyfriend Robbie needs his tie done, she makes him lie down. "I had this dream once," she says. "I was dressing my uncle, and he wasn't even dead."

She shows me how to roll a corpse without dropping it: grab a wrist and a hip and hug tight, being careful not to be too rough with the bare skin, which has a tendency to slip.

"Slip?" I ask.

Come off. Bodies that have been dead a few days before embalming accumulate little bubbles of gas under the skin, which can cause the skin to slip off like wet saran wrap if you're not gentle. Our lady is still quite sturdy and fresh, but I do as I'm told, hug a hip and pull. Her goopy left hand is hard to hang on to, and as a result she slides more than rolls, to the edge of the gurney, where gravity's waiting. I hug tighter, and now we're face-to-green-face. This must be embarrassing for her, that's all I can think. And I'm sorry. I'm sorry she's green, and half naked, and in the arms of a hapless stranger when she'd rather be alive and home watching *Wheel of Fortune*.

The blouse is next, which requires wrestling with an elbow that won't unbend: it's like dressing a tree. When I lay her flat, her hand slaps me on the chest. Fair enough.

To stick to the skin, real makeup needs heat, which the dead no longer have. Mortician's makeup is more like paint. The green woman needs a heavy base, but for most corpses, Nat just adds a bit of colour to those spots on the face that naturally respond to sun (tip of the nose, forehead between the eyes, cheeks) and then works it in with a gloved finger. Lips are painted purple, which looks more natural than red on a dead person. Nat has a trade client named Reg, a local undertaker on Erin Street, behind a sports bar. He subcontracts her as an embalmer, instead of carrying the overhead of maintaining his own prep room. Reg likes a lot of purple on his corpses' lips, even the men.

Nat steps back to examine her work, then adds a layer of powder, and blows lightly on the woman's face to remove the excess. I can smell Nat's peppermint gum. Then she grabs my hands and holds them against the woman's scalp.

"Feel that?"

"What?"

I do feel something, two knotty bumps over her temples.

"Horns!" Nat whispers, wide-eyed. I pull my hands back. "Must be from the cancer, poor thing."

Cut into conceptual bite-sized pieces, all this might one day, like Jon says, be easier to swallow: the dead put on their pantyhose one leg at a time like the rest of us. But there's something black and malevolent breathing in here too, behind that rumbling noise. Call it uncanny. For Freud, that feeling of vertigo when the rational and irrational collide is uncanny: he says there's nothing more uncanny than a dead body. We're still savages on the subject, informed by pre-modern ideas that "whoever dies becomes the enemy of the survivor, intent on carrying him off to share his new existence," even as we know, rationally, that they're just spent biology: dead meat. Freud also says that if we repress these primitive fears they'll sneak back to haunt us later as neurotic symptoms. But I think repression is underrated. I have the feeling it'll be my most valuable friend here at the death factory.

When Glenn comes back from a removal with a small cardboard box, we gather around to see what he's brought. Natalie opens it. Inside is an infant, blue-grey. She lifts it up. It's still wearing a Muppets diaper.

"Aww," she says, "I can't wait to start having kids."

Neil has an electric piano in his office. To relax he plays ragtime, slowly, the way Scott Joplin said it should be played. On his desk is a copy of Rheinhold's sculpture of a philosophizing ape holding a human skull, a humble charm against hubris, a memento mori: if we think we're indestructible, at the top of the food chain, nature has other ideas. When Neil was an apprentice, his father and uncle ran a conservative funeral home: they embalmed everything that came through the door. Cremation was a fad for pointy-headed university professors and Unitarians, until Jessica Mitford wrote "that book" in the early '60s and the fad evolved into a social trend. But it wasn't until twenty-five years ago that Neil finally embraced cremation and became what the mainstream industry calls a "bake-and-shaker," a lower-cost provider of a cleaner, more manageable, less Gothic and scatterable end product. Although he still believes in the therapeutic power of a well-embalmed body, you can't fight a social revolution. Especially now, with the baby boomers idling in their Humvees at the lip of the chasm—76 million of them have already left their muddy tire-tracks in every other intersection of the economy, from pop culture to fashion to the derivative markets (well done there) to yoga and the ovo-lacto frozen dinner-treat industry, and are now facing a guaranteed 100 percent death rate. They'll want something different from their grandparents' church services.

"The traditional funeral is gone," Neil says, "and it's never coming back."

Two

A WAY OF LIFE LIKE ANY OTHER

A week into the job, I come home at night in the dark (in Winnipeg, in the winter, the sun goes down soon after it comes up, sometimes before). I shower for longer than I need to, and wash my work clothes separately to keep crematorium dust out of the towels and sheets. My wife, Annie, wants to know what it's like, but in my head it sounds like a fairy tale: the dead come from a magic place called the Silver Doors, from which they're whisked into boxes or made to drink potions that turn them from yellow to green, then they're painted pink and purple and powdered, and some are baked in an oven where they are turned into flour by special death-fairies. I am now a death-fairy. Instead of telling her all this, I just use up her hand lotion and watch Werner Herzog movies to cheer myself up.

Annie and I live in the Wolseley neighbourhood of Winnipeg,

known as the "granola belt" for its progressive politics and its high batik-wall-hanging-to-resident ratio. There are two organic grocers at the same intersection, a bakery that sells bread made from grass and spelt muffin-pucks (and awesome whole-wheat cinnamon rolls), and a cobbler who wears an unironic leather apron and fixes Birkenstock after Birkenstock. I came here from Toronto three years ago so Annie and I could live in the same postal code for a change (she's from Winnipeg), to work at CBC Radio, a government job with a pension. I'd taken a month's leave to dabble in death-care. Neil and I have an understanding: if I want to stay longer, I can. But that would mean quitting the radio job, and leaning on Annie's salary (she's a union lawyer) to keep us fed and watered.

Winnipeg is a city where neighbours will notice if I park a hearse in front of the house (as opposed to Toronto, where you could park a hearse, set it on fire, and they'll only complain to the city about the smoke). In February the air is full of ice crystals that you're expected to breathe. On a map, Winnipeg is the geographical centre of the continent. If North America were an LP record, Winnipeg would be the spindle. It's also a practical place to die. There are thirty-eight funeral homes here—more funeral homes than Starbucks outlets. Freud would've been happy here, as much as Freud ever was. Study the place and you'll see that as well as being a rusty railway hub, the Chicago of Canada, Winnipeg is a hub for the uncanny return of the repressed, in particular the forgotten-but-never-gone dead.

From 1918 to 1934, Thomas Glendenning Hamilton, a doctor and member of the Manitoba Legislature, conducted secret scientific experiments into the existence of life after death, by logging and photographing hundreds of seances. The glass-plate pictures he took, of spinning tables and mediums with ectoplasm flying out of their noses, are in the archives of the University of Manitoba. The pictures are chilling (even if the ectoplasm, that wet, sticky, snotty manifestation of otherworldly spirits, looks like cheesecloth), and for a time, Winnipeg was known as the "ectoplasm capital of the world." Sir Arthur Conan Doyle, whose Sherlock Holmes represented modern man's triumph over mystery through the empirical study of physical clues, came to see Hamilton's seances for himself (and according to one medium's report, he returned to the city years later, or rather his spirit did, after his earthly death). Local filmmaker Guy Maddin's first film, called *The Dead Father*, is a black, neurotic and autobiographical comedy about a man who comes back from the grave, annoyed, in plaid shorts and a golf shirt, to lie down on his dining room table as if it were his funeral bier and pester his family. Maddin has also written about Garbage Hill, a former dump and the only hill in this prairie city, where kids go tobogganing in the winter, only to be surprised by bits of trash and car parts that work their way up through the frost. He claims he once slid down the hill and was speared by a set of deer antlers his own father had thrown away decades before. Meanwhile, east of Garbage Hill, the Red River has been biting away at its banks under Elmwood cemetery, threatening to expose old graves. In 1997, the city had to move 105 caskets before they fell into the muddy water.

And my first winter in Winnipeg, the newspapers covered the disappearance of a local deejay named Grandmasta Sanchez, who worked at the Village Cabaret nightclub in Osborne Village. Fourteen months he was missing, until they found his mummified body where they'd least expected to: jammed between two walls of the very nightclub where he'd played his last shift. It was determined he'd crawled in there by himself and suffocated ("positional asphyxiation," police called it), and if not for a recent smoking ban that allowed long-hidden smells to surface, they might never have found him. I'd like to say I was surprised when, a few years later, at a nightclub just down the street from the Village Cabaret, another body turned up, this time wedged into the ductwork (the dead man was presumed to be a thief who hid out until patrons left but got stuck).

In Winnipeg, the dead and the discarded come back: they refuse to stay hidden.

Cemeteries and funerals, the way French historian Philippe Ariès sees it, are social constructs to keep nature, the hostile world of worms and decay, separate from a civilized life of flat-screen TVs and microwave chapatis. Look at it this way: we evolved, beautifully, from monkeys into type-A control freaks, with a system (government, laws, religion, organized labour and technology) designed to overcome nature. And for the most part, we pulled it off. There are only two weak spots where chaos sneaks in, wild, wet and savage, reminding us we're doomed animals: sex and death. So we devised taboos to deal with the former, to take away its power, and ritual to weaken the chaotic impact of the latter.

To let off communal steam, we devised orgies, bacchanalia, All Souls feasts; Ariès says that graveyard parties were so common in medieval France that by 1231, the Church councils had to ban dancing, juggling, theatre and mummery in cemeteries under threat of excommunication. Meanwhile, how the two circles of sex and death intersected was the business of poetry and porn, and the subject of apocryphal stories of men who got erections when they were hanged.

This worked fine until the Enlightenment and later, when we "found ourselves," pre-California-New-Age-style, and funerals were less about confirming the collective permanence of the social order and more about me me me, which peaked with the Gothic sob-fests of the nineteenth century. The Church, which used to own ritual, had to cede to the private sector, which could make up ritual as it went along. The fantasy of redemption and immortality, out of which Darwin was kicking the stuffing, gave way to a market-place solution to death, the purchase of things: rings and brooches made from the hair of dead loved ones, the memento mori, and burial robes, badges and gloves for the pallbearers (the gloves were to be left on the lid of the casket and buried with it). Neil Bardal says his grandfather sold memorial clothing, pants and dresses and shoes that split at the back for a more comfortable fit (on the corpse); for an extra five dollars he'd squirt an onion into the eyes of the horse that pulled the coach so it looked like the animal was crying. Death got more elaborate and personal. And more private.

But the dead themselves became a nuisance. Urban cemeteries were thought to be the source of some fusty miasma that made city folk sick, so the dead were segregated to suburban park cemeteries, where families could visit if they had the car fare, bring flowers: the sanatorium model, a kind of refugee facility with nice trees and stonework. The whole puzzle of how we deal with death comes down to that nasty poser: what to do with what's left behind? Awe of the dead was giving way to modern science's mis-guided itchiness about hygiene. People just kept digging holes, farther and farther away from the living. Soon, as Geoffrey Gorer pointed out, the Victorian fussiness over sex and its fascination with death switched places. Sex came panting out of the closet, and death, and all its trappings, went in: it was best managed in the dark, preferably after a few stiff drinks.

Henry James got so fed up with the privatization and apartheid of death that in 1895 he published a story called "The Altar of the Dead," in which his character George Stransom builds a shrine of candles in a London church to his growing list of dead friends. In his journals, James says Stransom is "struck with the way they are forgotten, are unhallowed—unhonoured, neglected, shoved out of sight; allowed to become so much more dead, even, than the fate that has overtaken them has made them." Without the comfort of a community, he invents his own private religion, one candle at a time, for the "worship of the Dead," until he has a blazing do-it-yourself memorial, which of course won't be complete until there's "just one more" candle: Stransom's own. But who'll tend the altar when *he's* gone?

I know this story, or a version of it: the story of how we ache to remember or to be remembered. I heard it as a kid. I prefer not to think about it, but there's a memory itch I can barely reach.

I had a grandfather who fought in Spain with the International Brigades, killing fascists and blowing up rail lines while the Nazis test-drove their military hardware for the other big war that followed. He never discussed it. He never discussed anything. They were Finns, he and my grandmother (he was her third husband: the second was buried in Mount Pleasant cemetery in Toronto when I was still an infant, and the first, I have no idea what happened to him). Finns, especially Red Finns of their generation, had neither the language nor the inclination for chit-chat. Bertolt Brecht once said the Finns he knew, most of whom also spoke Swedish, were uncommunicative in two languages. There's a story of two Finns in a bar drinking vodka. A half hour passes in silence, glasses are emptied.

"Do you want another?" the first Finn says.

"Are we here to talk or are we here to drink?" says the second.

My grandfather had only two things to say about Spain: One, it's possible to survive for weeks by eating toothpaste. And two, the worst thing Franco's fascists did was to bury the enemy, the Republican soldiers, in unmarked graves. The victors got monuments. The rest were left unhallowed, unhonoured, neglected, shoved out of sight.

I have two pictures of my grandmother, taken years apart. In one she's sitting on the grass, wearing orange culottes and cat's-eye glasses, her expression neutral, looking at the camera. She's holding flowers, and she's on a grave in Mount Pleasant, her second husband's. A shrub barely clears the top of the granite headstone. In the second picture, the shrub is taller, but there's no grandmother now, just the headstone, with her name on it. She's under the grass on which she once sat. The framing is almost identical, as if they'd been taken seconds apart. I used to play a game with the pictures, flipping them like cartoon cards: now she's alive, now she's not, above ground, below ground, the disappearing grandmother. But what struck me when I got older and lined them up side by side was how little I knew about what had happened in the years in between. Maybe she saved a girl from drowning or fell in love with a Hungarian prince, but probably not. I know she lived in a house with the man who'd once survived on toothpaste, they had a floor lamp made from a rifle, and she cleaned other people's homes for money. Other than that, there's just the picture of her on the grave, waiting to get in.

The lesson, or the one I invented, said that life was a series of unconnected, disappointing and treacherous events, the goal of which was to acquire enough property, six by six feet of it, for a decent burial and a headstone with your name on it. Death wasn't something to fear, it was something to aspire to, after the troubling business that came before it, of which there was little need to speak. Folklore says the only time a Finn ever feels joy is when he's imagining his own funeral: the flowers, the people who'll come and the nice things they'll say, the coffee and cardamom *pulla*, the hymn from Sibelius's *Finlandia* and tango on accordion. A quiet, dignified ending, the payoff. As Herodotus (Greek, but in spirit a Finn) says in *The Histories*: call no man happy until he is dead. At that point life takes on the glow of retrospection: it sucked, really, but as we remember me now, it had its moments. Read it this way: life is chaos, but the funeral narrative makes sense of it.

Some families, all they aspire to is leather furniture. My Finnish version lived in the blazing light of the Altar of the Dead.

Growing up, I rejected this absurd Nordic death wish and came to see the funeral as a wrong-headed act of vanity. Does this mean I'm just covering up my own fear that life is hopeless and death is a delicious release, and the best party is the last one? I circle it and circle it, but I can't get any closer to understanding it, other than to take a stab, make a Solomonic compromise: both life and death are absurd. But . . . what I know is that when I'm alone, I feel a bony finger tapping my thick forehead and then a voice with a Finnish accent says: What's your smart-ass alternative? To just disappear? Without a remainder? It can't be done. In death you're a cold, physical problem that must be dealt with.

The voice gets louder the older I get. This may go some way towards explaining why I took a job at a funeral home: to get a closer look at what I may be fated to never figure out: why we do what we do when someone dies, and how we handle the leftovers.

Three

"ALL THAT MALARKEY"

> Gradually, almost imperceptibly, over the years the funeral men have constructed their own grotesque cloud-cuckoo-land where the trappings of Gracious Living are transformed, as in a nightmare, into the trappings of Gracious Dying . . .
>
> —**Jessica Mitford,** *The American Way of Death Revisited*

*I*n "that book," as Neil calls it, Jessica Mitford asked a similar question: What constitutes a nice, decent funeral, and why on earth is it all so expensive? Nobody expected her book to be a hit, least of all the undertakers, or Mitford herself, who figured she'd sell a few copies to Berkeley profs and the cardiganned members of the San Francisco Bay Area funeral society, arguably the least sexy of the anti-commercial rabble-rousers on the West Coast in the '60s, who were lobbying for more access to low-cost, no-fuss cremation. But *The American Way of Death*, published in 1963 (and again, as *Revisited*, in 1996), was a knockout success. Bobby Kennedy said "that girl's book" influenced the choices he made for his brother's funeral. It's why he chose a simple casket and kept it closed (and in the end, JFK did for funerals what he had done for men's hats: he changed fashion). *TAWD* empowered consumers otherwise too embarrassed to ask questions about a taboo transaction; for the industry it was a kidney punch. The undertakers called Mitford by just the one name, hissing it out: *Jessss-ica*. She was thrilled. In America, she said, only the super-famous get single-name status, like Cher and Madonna.

They heckled her at conferences. They called her a communist. Of course I'm a communist, she smiled.

"How much money did you make on *The American Way of Death?*" they asked her.

"Absolute tons," she said. "So much I can't even count it—it made my fortune."

They tore out their hair.

And all she'd done, she said, was consult their own literature and sales pamphlets, use their own words to make her case: that far from being an honour-bound tradition, the modern funeral was a recent invention, not much older than she was, a luxury item hooked to some vague promise of "grief therapy," with products aimed not at meeting consumer demand but at defining it. The casket, the vault (with a 3/8-inch reinforced concrete inner liner, "Guaranteed by Good Housekeeping"—guaranteed against what she never dared to ask), the makeup and funeral clothing, "all that malarkey," were the tools of high-pressure sales disguised as good works. Where funeral men believed in the "Beautiful Memory Picture" provided by a well-prepared body, as a means to repairing the mental health of the survivors, Mitford saw embalming as a way to "make the corpse presentable for viewing in a suitably costly container." And only North Americans still did it. This was no small point. As a Brit, she admitted this was as much about taste, or lack of it, as it was about economics (and H.L. Mencken said, "No good American ever seriously questions an English judgment on an aesthetic question." Although, as theologian Thomas Long points out, it's too bad Mitford didn't live long enough to see the Diana funeral, and the row of horrified royals watching Elton John sing "Candle in the Wind").

If, as the industry's own rhetoric said, the funeral was a "drama" in which "emotional catharsis or release is provided through ceremony," then why did we pay to have the star of that drama "sprayed, sliced, pierced, pickled, trussed, trimmed, creamed, waxed, painted, rouged, and neatly dressed" before plowing him underground?

The questions had been asked before. Bertram Puckle for one said that while "almost all our present [customs] have their origin in stupid pagan superstitions, they have none the less an interest of their own to record," which he did, with cool pictures, in 1926 in *Funeral Customs: Their Origin and Development*. But not as colourfully as Mitford asked them. What had once belonged to the Church—ritual, and rites of passage—she called out as a meaningless commodity, the way Andy Warhol said art wasn't art anymore, it was soup cans. Warhol made his soup cans the year before the Mitford book came out. Culturally, her timing was spot on.

The book was her husband Bob Treuhaft's idea. At first she thought, if there's muck to rake, surely the pharmaceutical and automotive industries are meatier targets. Why pick on the poor gruesome undertakers? But Treuhaft, an activist and union lawyer, saw that when working men died, their hard-won death benefits, for which they might've walked the picket line, and which were intended for their widows and families, wound up in the hands of the funeral director. "These people seem to know exactly how much a warehouse worker gets, and how much an office secretary," he said, and they set their prices to match.

He did the fieldwork—sat in on an embalming, went undercover to price property at the famous Forest Lawn cemetery in Glendale, California (taking his friend, the actress Julie Andrews, to play his wife)—while Jessica studied the ads from the Practical Burial Footwear Company of Columbus, Ohio, and did her sums: the "formula pricing" of a mainstream funeral, she discovered, was based on a markup of 400 to 900 percent of the wholesale cost of a casket.

In *TAWD* she cites Wilbert Krieger's 1951 template for a successful casket showroom. The product—your steels, your hardwoods, your cheaper cloth numbers, he said—should be arranged in a broad semicircle, with a path leading from the least expensive to the most expensive, left to right, the natural inclination for shoppers and lost travellers, since 85 percent of us are right-handed. This is called the Avenue of Approach, and encourages families to "pick cherries" from the top of the tree. To the left are the low-end caskets, on what Krieger calls Resistance Lane. Some will push hard against the current into Resistance Lane, but most consumers will find themselves stopping midway along the Avenue, in the heart of generous-markup-land. To the civilian, a casket showroom looks like a random array of boxes. In fact it knows more about you and your commercial habits than you do.

Readers loved the book (my favourite entry in the index is the one for "caskets and coffins, burping"). It confirmed what they already suspected about a creepy underground brotherhood, worse than Masons. The undertakers fought back, or tried. It got dirty. They called Jessica anti-Christian (when the red-baiting flopped) and they said she was grinding a personal axe, that she hadn't grappled with the grief of losing her own son, who was hit by a bus in 1955, and that now she was swinging at the closest target (she never responded to that one).

At the time, Neil was a young undertaker, and he saw more than a few family funeral home owners call it quits. "Maybe it would've happened without her, but it was the start of the end of the family business. People panicked, they sold. She created a buyer's market for the new corporate chains who bought up all these funeral homes" from motivated, panicky sellers. (This is Neil's analysis, but even if it's only half true, it's wickedly ironic: the publicly traded corporate funeral chains were her broadest targets, with their higher-than-average prices and their covenant with shareholders to boost market value and keep up with the Dow Joneses—no way to run a funeral home, according to Mitford.)

Still, he says, if he and his mates had done any kind of self-analysis, they'd have seen the cracks in their own shell. As an embalming student he used to brag about doing two preps at the same time, and lightning-quick twenty-minute family arrangements to get the volume through the door. "We figured people trusted us. But to be honest, I was taking shortcuts. She woke us up." He speaks with neither contempt nor reverence about Jessica Mitford. To him she's just a fact of life, like the weather.

But her attack on embalming did sting.

Neil was taught, by his father and his uncle, that if they lost embalming they'd lose everything: No body to show, no casket.

No casket, no hearse and then no chapel, and soon enough they'd be an overdressed pickup and removal service for the blasted cremators. And that was the Mitford message: drop the morbid corpse fetish and cremate your dead, liberate yourself from the *thanatos*-industrial complex. Cremation is clean and takes time pressure out of the economic equation: no rush to make snap decisions and get the body in the ground before it turns. Even the Episcopal Church said, "The body has served its sacramental purpose, that of housing the personality of the individual. . . . The remains are not a person; they are rather like discarded clothing." Bake, shake, be done with it. The message stuck. Now the cremation rate is over 50 percent in some Canadian provinces including Manitoba (where, when Neil started in 1962, it barely topped 2 percent), higher in B.C. (over 90 percent on Vancouver Island), and 60 percent or more in Nevada and Arizona, in the lucrative grey-belt, all part of the legacy of *The American Way of Death*.

Turns out the industry made the "best of a bad job," as Mitford put it in the update of the book published in the 1990s. They pushed urns and cremation-specific wood and pressboard caskets, discouraged scattering (or as the English clergymen preferred, "strewing") in favour of urn burial, niches in graveyard walls and mausolea, and bronze plaques for the niches. Cremation didn't have to mean cheap. In fact, with a casket, embalming, two nights of visitation in the chapel followed by a church service, cremation, an urn and burial of the urn in a cemetery, you could make more money cremating than by providing a traditional burial.

When Mitford died in 1996, just before *Revisited* came out, she was cremated and her ashes were "strewn" at sea. Her mourners held a party in San Francisco at Delancey Street, a halfway house for cons and addicts founded by her and Bob Treuhaft. There was a New Orleans marching band and a cortège led by four horses in black plumage, the most ironic funeral ever held in the Bay Area. The bill for the cremation, the only taste the industry got that day, was $490.

To me, the heart of the debate she left behind is a nagging question: what is the body, anyway? Is it charged, mystical, something to be marked and honoured with ceremony and balm, or is it "discarded clothing"? Her answer might've been: you decide. You figure out your own emotional cost and come up with a price—just don't leave it to the band of gentlemen who sell product in the name of hygiene, tradition and pop psychology.

The year after she died, an editorial in *The Director*, one of the funeral trade magazines, had this to say: "The importance of the memory picture created by the properly embalmed and restored loved one is something we must never lose sight of and never be ashamed to ask permission to do. . . . Hold your head high, take care in the work you do and be proud to be an embalmer."

The battle for hearts and minds (literally) continued.

Four

I'm Sorry for Your Loss, but You've Mistaken Me for Someone Who Knows What He's Doing

The downtown chapel of Neil Bardal Inc. used to be a bakery. Neil leased it, tore out the ovens, put in stucco and pink carpeting and a glass-front Coca-Cola fridge to hold snacks for receptions, and a casket showroom. It's on Aubrey Street between a Domino's Pizza and a pediatrician's office, and when the main door opens it dings like at a 7-Eleven. The chapel is Richard's turf. He's been with Neil the longest of all the funeral directors, since the '80s, before which he sold auto parts. Neil says widows love Richard; they want to pinch his cheeks and bake for him. Wiry, boyish, a bit tightly wound, he views the undertaker's role as therapist this way: grief therapy is bullshit. The only therapy he provides is to make sure the limo shows up when it's supposed to, the right hole is opened at the cemetery and the right music is played at the service. He manages logistics for families who are otherwise preoccupied. There's no false sympathy and hand-holding, which is how the corporate undertakers mostly play it. They want to be your friend. He wants to be your funeral director.

The C. family, recently bereaved, has come to make arrangements. Mother can't speak English but daughter translates, son says nothing, and another young man, presumably the daughter's boyfriend, spends the conference fetching her Kleenex. It's her father who died. Mother wears a cardigan held closed with a safety pin and carries a canvas shopping bag, and wants, it turns out, after some back and forth, a nice decent burial.

"Would you like a viewing?" Richard says.

The daughter looks to her mother, who shrugs.

"What's a viewing?" the daughter says.

"It's completely optional."

Which is true. But realizing he needs to back up a step, he explains the concept. The body is displayed in an open casket, and people come to pay their respects. There may be prayers, also completely optional.

"How is this different from the funeral?" she says.

"Usually it's the day before."

"And is he there?"

"Who?"

"My father."

Richard considers this.

"Yes," he says. "Yes. Of course."

They agree to the viewing.

It emerges that the family has a plot at Brookside, and Richard notes it on his tick-sheet, along with facts relevant to the provincial department of records: where the man was born, names of his parents, where he worked. Richard's tone is firm and neutral. When the daughter cries, he stops the conference until she's finished. Then, with dates set and details ticked, he leads us from the arrangement room, past the Coke fridge, to the casket showroom.

There is a difference between a casket and a coffin. A casket has a round, swelled-top lid, and is sturdier and more furniture-ish than a coffin, which is a simpler box, hexagonal and tapered, common in Europe and vampire stories and Halloween store displays. We only carry caskets. They're open, to show off the interior fabrics. Some are quilted, some are velveteen, some have design flourishes: three birds and the legend "Going Home" stitched on the underside of the lid. The hardwoods gleam under the pot lights. They're arranged in a broad arc with a narrow shopper's path between them à la Krieger's Avenue of Approach. In a corner to the left (Resistance Lane) are two covered in chintz cloth, known in the local trade as Mennonite Specials. At the end of the lane there is something that looks like a tipped-over dresser, which turns out to have been made by a local craftsman in his garage. Except for the handyman's special, these are brand-name caskets: Batesville, Victoriaville, Colonial.

Richard stands back while the daughter and mother touch the caskets. They run their hands along the swing-bar handles, tug on fabrics. The mother picks up the pillow from an Octagon Oak and considers it.

"That's a ladies' casket," Richard says. Ladies' caskets are more tapered, with chamfered edges, therefore considered more "slimming." Like wearing vertical stripes.

Mother wants something simple. It's just going in the ground, she says, through the daughter. They become enamoured of a

Colonial with a deeper grain than the Octagon Oak. It sits on a pedestal. As they tap and tug, it occurs to me that they must know that we know that they don't have a clue what they're doing, and why should they? They might as well be buying a nuclear reactor for all the foreknowledge they bring to the transaction. This pretending-to-shop is part of the ritual, the dance. How do you decide which one? Colour? Finish? Handling and durability? City versus highway mileage? The steel caskets have rubber gaskets along the rim, and are known as "sealers." According to the manufacturer, the gasket "resists" water and foreign elements (things that live underground), although you can't hold back nature for long, certainly not with a simple rubber ring (in the old days, "sealer" caskets walled into mausolea had a tendency to explode from the gases produced by anaerobic bacteria, which thrive in the very conditions the gaskets create: no airflow, no oxygen. Only later did casket makers develop "burping" technology, which allows for gas to escape, as with Tupperware. We don't get into this with the C. family).

They settle on the Colonial and a vault to match. The vault is a concrete grave liner with an optional plaque or insignia on the lid. Too heavy to display in the showroom, these are represented by miniature mock-ups, big enough to bury a Barbie doll. The son is confused by the little vault, until Richard explains it's just a model.

In the office, Richard's quick estimate, not including cemetery expenses (headstone and the cost of opening and closing the grave are Brookside's bite), comes to $7,680, which he rounds up to $7,900 to provide wiggle room. Then, if the final bill is less than the esti-mate, they'll feel like they got a deal.

"I need a Monticello for Brookside for Monday," he says on the phone to his rep at the vault-maker. "What do you put on there for a Chinese person? Looks like two tadpoles swimming in circles? That's it. Give me one of those."

Understand your families, Richard says. Know where the power lies. The mother was the power. He kept eye contact with her even though she couldn't understand his language. The son was wallpaper, and the boyfriend was just the get-the-Kleenex guy, non-factors both. Sometimes you get a family member who shouldn't be there, often a sister or sister-in-law who just buried a husband and now she's an expert. Stick to your tick-sheet, and focus on the power. This is how to keep an arrangement on track instead of unravelling into a two-hour chaotic hem-haw session. There's no trick to sales: the room does the work. The Colonial is the most popular casket in the room, and three-quarters of all clients buy it. The place where it sits is what Richard calls the "sweet spot."

The old-timers had tricks. If a customer wound up in Resistance Lane in front of a cloth casket, the salesman might demonstrate its "solid workmanship" by punching or even stepping on the pillow, then lead him to a more expensive hardwood or steel. At this point the customer couldn't erase the mental image of the salesman stepping on the pillow, and by extension the loved one's face, and bought whatever came next. That's called up-selling, and it's unethical. Richard's casket prices are based on 2.5 times markup on wholesale cost, or else a "perceived value" (a cherrywood might be more than 2.5-times wholesale, a Colonial might be less, whatever the local market will bear, otherwise known as a "wild guess"), with the above-average caskets at the peak of the sales curve. Most big-item shoppers, whether it's for refrigerators or caskets, consider themselves above-average. They don't need to be pushed.

I'm still stuck thinking about this "sealer" business, and the whole concept of protection. The body's in the ground. The ground is full of water and things that crawl and bacteria that, presumably, are nature's ally in the grand messy cycle of renewal. Why are we fighting this lopsided battle?

"It's true," Richard says, "a steel casket will probably rust at some point." But some have a feature, called cathodic protection, a gizmo used on automobiles and on pipelines too: it's a bar that sits under the casket to sacrificially attract the rust. You have the same bar inside your hot water heater at home, he says, to keep it from rusting. There are also nice design features, like casket corners that are like porcelain charms, stuck to the casket with magnets. If mom was a gardener you might want casket corners that look like a terra cotta pot with flowers growing out of it, or if dad was a musician, a little doodad that looks like a scroll of sheet music. "There's four of them, one in each corner," he says, "and they come off before the casket is buried. You give them to the family, they can frame them with mom's picture. Keepsakes."

Fine, I say. But you're still putting the body, the embalmed body, into a steel casket with a rubber gasket and a cathodic bar to keep away rust, and then the works go into a vault. What exactly are we protecting?

"Well," he says, "the idea is if the casket ever had to be disinterred for some reason, and it comes up from time to time if there's been a tragic death, where there's a real need to keep the body preserved should things change technologically down the road, well then, it's important. One example, down in the States, some-one was murdered and the funeral home and the state had the foresight to protect the body as best they could, so when it was exhumed they were able to do a more thorough post-mortem examination and found proof of the murder, and they were able to tie it to someone."

"But most of us aren't murdered," I say, not a hundred per-cent confident in my facts but close enough for the purpose of the debate.

"It's a cultural choice," Richard says. "It's up to the family's belief structures, not mine. I have trouble with it too. But I have to provide, as a funeral director, the things that people want. It's how people feel about the body and what it needs to do, the idea of being resurrected, to be whole again."

Back in the showroom alone, I imagine myself in the shoppers' shoes. Which one best suits the lifestyle to which I'm accus-tomed, or the deathstyle to which I aspire? The top-of-the-line Champagne "sealer" is sweet, but showy: there's a small drawer in the lower half of the lid, a "Memory Safe" drawer, for keep-sakes, maybe an iPhone, car keys. The hardwoods, including a Harvest Oak with a sheaf of real wheat sewn into the lid fabric (popular with farm families), have homespun charm, but the steels come with a limited, pre-interment fifty-year manufactur-er's warranty against the elements.

I hear a sound that seems to come from behind the Champagne casket. A muffled sound, like a baby crying.

Then someone behind me.

I jump. It's Eirik, the boss's eldest son.

"It's needle day, at the pediatrician next door," he says.

With the C. family now gone, we set up for the afternoon service. It's sparsely attended. My job is to point mourners at the coat rack, the guest book, the chairs. I wear the only suit I've ever owned where the jacket and pants match: Italian design, made in Turkey, probably one-size-fits-all, possibly flammable. The guests are apprehensive but well behaved. They smile thin-lipped half-smiles when I hand them memorial brochures with the order of service, but don't look me in the eye. Ladies sign the guest book for their husbands. A little girl in snow boots walks on her heels so as not to mess up the pink carpet. Richard lights twin candles at either end of the closed casket (another Colonial) and then cedes to the minister, hustling back to the office, where he joins Shannon, the junior funeral director, to work the phones. My perch is at the threshold between the office and the chapel. I can follow the action on both sides.

"She always carried Life Savers or Chiclets," the pastor is saying. "With her pristine Pepsodent smile, Lord, she has so many times been the rope that binds us together. We celebrate her life with great joy."

The guests look at their shoes.

In the office, Richard books a grave at Chapel Lawn, while Shannon whispers to a customer on the phone. "However it's convenient for yourself," she says. "And do you happen to have her particulars, her social insurance number, and whom her parents may have been so we can have that information at the time of her untimely death?"

The pastor says: "She was a rock. She could tell a spellbinding story or involve herself in conversation on any topic. Life is short, compared to the life of a tree."

If the funeral is meant as an instrument of spiritual and emotional renewal, and transcendence over death and the chaos of nature, or as Milton said in *Paradise Lost*, to "justify the ways of God to man," then someone forgot to tell these people. The room is tense, breathless. A man in jeans and a parka in the back row yawns. When the eulogy is done, Richard hits the CD player and "Red River Valley" plays over the sound system, and no one in the chapel moves. To my left, in the reception area, away from the view of the crowd, I can see Neil and Helen, the hostess who prepares the food and serves the coffee. They're dancing.

This, I take it, is Funeral 101: developing a detached engagement with technical details and zero or minimal engagement with the emotional ones. There's a logic to it. Carnies don't get whipped up about riding The Zipper, cabbies don't get involved in *why* people want to go to the airport. Here, funerals happen, then more funerals happen. Tomorrow there'll be another one. After the service is done, a man approaches me and asks if he'll get a ticket if he parks on the road, and I have to admit I don't know. Another man in a red shirt and cream tie asks for the bathroom and I lead him the wrong way, through the private family room to the reception area, where we have to start again. This adds up to me already flunking Funeral 101: I have zero engagement with technical details.

After coffee and some strained mingling, Neil leads a short procession of cars to Brookside cemetery. I'm tagged to drive the hearse. A Cadillac Superior funeral coach, barely a year old, it's a $100,000 machine that I tell myself I won't wrap around a utility pole as long as I keep my eyes on Neil's four-way flashers. The front end alone covers a car-length, and it has the turning radius of a commercial fishing trawler. The seats are low to the ground. If I open the door I can touch the road, but I don't. In my rear-view all I see is the casket and a pile of white roses. There's not a sound from the outside world. Traffic stays out of our way. It's a heady moment, sensing this new, unfamiliar authority in my black suit, Ryders wraparound sunglasses and a vehicle worth more than my house in Wolseley.

At the cemetery gates we wait for the sexton, who leads us in a pickup truck to the grave. The grounds are snow-covered, until we get to the hole that is bordered by AstroTurf so nobody slips and falls in. Once parked, I scoot to the back and open the door for the pallbearers. Neil tells them to slide and lift so that they're not surprised by the weight. They carry the casket head first, facing the stone, and lay it on the straps of the Device, a steel rack that, once engaged, will lower the casket into the grave. The pastor says a few words and then, seemingly inspired, Neil picks up a flower and hands it to one of the women in the family. Then everyone gets one. A man at the back of a small knot of people puts his white rose in his mouth and executes a quick tango move. It's like the air's been let out of this overinflated event: shoulders relax and people start chatting and laughing. It's over. Once the last civilian car is out of sight, the sexton lowers the casket into the hole and chucks the AstroTurf into the pickup truck. The casket is never lowered in front of the mourners. It's considered too real.

And so my life goes for the first weeks, flipping from the chapel on Aubrey Street to the Factory. The suit stays at Aubrey, my work clothes at the crematorium, me in one or the other depending on personnel needs. Glenn whips me into military order at the Factory, sending me on removals where I can work on my stretcher skills and to the car wash to keep the coach and cars muck- and road-salt-free. All vehicles are to be kept topped up with fuel, like the Cold War bomber fleet (to avoid running out in the middle of a procession), and with earth. We keep a Gerber baby-food jar of dirt in the glove box of each vehicle for ceremonial sprinkling at graveside. The jars are supplied by a bag of C-I-L potting soil in the shed, actual grave dirt apparently being too dirty. At the Factory, when I pass by, I keep an eye on the locked door of the prep room (sign says ALWAYS KNOCK BEFORE ENTERING! NO EXCEPTIONS!) where all I see, through the ventilation grate at the bottom, are Nat's blue paper booties sliding back and forth. I'm in no rush to get in there. There are floors to swab and bodies to burn.

We take delivery from one of our "trade clients" (local undertakers who hire us to cremate their dead) of an elderly, birdlike lady wrapped in a crocheted quilt. Straight from a seniors home, she arrives without the standard hospital plastic shroud. Her head is cocked up and to the right, as if she were listening for a faint sound, and her hands clutch the quilt. Glenn asks the undertaker who brought the body if we're to cremate the quilt as well. He shrugs.

"Maybe you should check," Glenn says, and the undertaker takes his cell phone outside.

Glenn shows me how to search for a pacemaker or defibrillator, either of which, if left in the body, might explode in the retort and damage the brick interior, or the cremationist if he happens to be peeking into the porthole when it goes off. I feel around the top of her bony chest for anything the shape and size of a box of wooden matches. She's clean.

The trade undertaker returns and gives us a double thumbs-up: the family wants the quilt to go with the body into the fire. It was hers. She made it.

The body goes into a cardboard box on an electric scissor-lift, which whines when Glenn raises it to the height of the open retort. Then, aided by a set of steel rollers, he slides the box in and shuts the door. First step: light the box. This is done by turning on the gas jets for a few seconds until the container ignites, and then leaving it and the quilt and other bedclothes to burn away on their own. A secondary chamber under the retort will deal with smoke and combustible gases, so that the chimney on the roof won't belch black, which is considered bad form (like lowering the casket into the ground: too much reality for passersby).

"That's getting a pretty good roll on it now," Glenn says, studying his work through the peephole, and then giving me a turn.

She's covered in slow, swimming, watery orange and blue flames. It's hypnotic but horrible. There's no smell. Fans suck all the smoke and gas into the bottom chamber. When Glenn turns the main jets back on, we watch the temperature rise, past 1,000 degrees, then 1,200. Air intake and gas levels are carefully controlled so she doesn't blaze out of control. Each body is different. You have to watch, and adjust. I can see her rib cage now. This is a good sign, I'm told. We can walk away from the machine for a spell now that the fat's burned off, since there's little remaining threat of heavy smoke and flare-outs. With her size she'll be done and sweepable in ninety minutes.

It's an odd relief that each corpse has its idiosyncrasies in the retort. The big and fat call for vigilance, some measure of babying and fiddling with the airflow and gas, while the small and reedy, like our little quilt lady, are more independent and can be left alone without fear they'll burn out of control. What they ate and stored around the waistline, how fit they were, whether they had strong long-bones, the femurs and humeri, from a lifetime of manual labour – it's all relevant to the cremationist. Some bodies will raise their arms in the retort like they're hailing a cab, a result of tendons contracting in the intense heat: what an odd relief that, even in death, we find ways to express ourselves.

Just under two hours and a lunch later, we open the heavy door to reveal her scattered skeleton, pieces of white bone blown around by the powerful gas jets. I sweep out the remains with the heavy steel broom. To get at the corners, I have to reach into the hot retort and sweep by hand, wearing suede gloves, until everything that looks bony and human and white is in the pan.

She has no artificial joints, but at the sort table, the magnet picks up a couple of black screws and staples, leftovers of a burned casket from a previous cremation. Her bridgework, three false brown teeth in a sooty plate, survived the fire. Fillings do not. Gold and mercury sublimate to gas and go up the chimney. Glenn demonstrates technique, flicking bits of black and yellow stone fragments from the floor of the retort into the slag box, and the bone shards into a pile. He picks up a ball joint, maybe the hip. I find another and do the same. It's light like a macaroon, and crumbles in my grip. A fat black vacuum hose hangs over the table on a garret, to suck up the dust.

"You can go mental," Glenn says. "You could work on a sort for days. Don't. Just use your common sense, get as much of the crap out as you can." The goal in the end is to have a white powder. It's part of Neil's brand, having the whitest cremated remains in Winnipeg.

"What's this?" I say, poking at a hard green glob the size of a pencil eraser.

"I don't know. But every cremation, we get one or two."

Without evidence to the contrary, I decide it must be the soul.

Five

LOVE YOUR HAIR, WHO'S YOUR EMBALMER?

*T*o get to the Silver Doors at St. Boniface General Hospital I rattle the stretcher down a long corridor, always empty of people but full of discarded hospital gear: iron bed frames, armless armchairs, IV racks. At St. B the Silver Doors can handle a dozen or more plastic-wrapped corpses comfortably. The security guard has waxy yellow smoker's hair and a lot of questions about working in a crematorium.

"The teeth," he says. "What do you do with them?"

"What do you mean?" I say, checking name tags.

"The *teeth*," he says, and then taps his own in case I'm fuzzy on the concept. "Gold teeth. You pull them out, no?"

"Why would we do that?"

"For the gold."

My corpse is tall, his feet hanging past the end of the

gurney. I rip a hole in the plastic sheet and check for jewellery.

"We don't pull out any teeth," I say, but the guard smiles and winks, picturing me, I can tell, with a pair of pliers and my foot on someone's jaw. This is how people see us, if in fact I'm an "us" yet. Gothic weirdos and alchemists, the so-called Dismal Traders, with a bucket full of teeth we put under our pillows to hose the Tooth Fairy.

"I guess I'll have to take out my own," he says.

"That's probably a good idea."

At the Factory, pulling out the stretcher with the tall man strapped into it, I trigger the collapsing legs just as I was taught, forgetting that I was taught to trigger the collapsing legs on the way into the van, not on the way out. Collapsing the legs on the way out is bad. I know this from experience. The stretcher drops, head first, again, hitting the floor, leaving me to stand with the foot-end in my hands while Jon rushes out to see what all the noise is about. This turns out to be a company record: two dropped bodies by a single funeral assistant in a supporting role. Maybe I'll get a plaque on the wall of the lunchroom.

Nat tells me to change into scrubs and meet her in the prep room, and to put some Blistex under my nose if I have any, to kill the smell, until I get used to it—although, she says, you never get used to it. This is my penance for dropping the tall man. Now I have to help embalm him.

I don't have my own scrubs so she issues me a purple set that belonged to an embalmer who used to work here but left after an incident involving his wristwatch. Nat says she accidentally knocked the watch off a shelf in the dressing room. In response he tore off his clothes and ran through the parking lot in his boxers, took her to small-claims court for the cost of repairs, and quit his job. I think he had bigger problems than the watch, she says.

The prep room is smaller than in my workplace nightmares. The walls are white tile, and most of the space is taken up by a steel table, underneath which is a toilet, a lidless American Standard toilet. I know a toilet when I see one. I just didn't expect to see one here. The shelves are stacked with colourful liquids, oranges and reds and purples and milky pinks, just like the bottle in the *Canadian Funeral News* ad. Below the shelves, next to a sink, are the tools, tweezers bent and straight, probes and hooks and pokers and scissors, a cardful of bobby pins, Gillette disposable razors and a pump bottle of Helene Curtis ThermaSilk shampoo. Charts on the wall show the circulatory system in red and blue rivers, mapping a human-shaped continent. Nat and I slide the body from the stretcher onto the table and she sprays it down with blue Dis-Spray, which smells of rubbing alcohol. Both of us are dressed head to feet in splatter gear: scrubs, a paper bonnet, a plastic face-guard, a surgical mask to keep from inhaling chemical fumes.

You never know what you're going to get when you open the shroud, she says. Could be a bloody accident victim, or an old lady with no teeth, her mouth wide open. Nat's enjoying this. She loves the prep room and she wants others to love it too. With a snap she reveals a handsome bald gentleman, half smiling. His eyes are open, one more than the other, but they're dry and foggy. This is the unembalmed, undecorated, raw look of death. I take a close look. If he could be said to have an expression, it would be one of dopey curiosity, upper lip curled, as if he were trying to remember where he left his car keys. Maybe this is how it happens. You make a sand-wich, you scratch your ear with a butter knife, you try to remember where the keys are and then *whack*: lights out, forever. In any case, our job is to massage and prod and infuse the man back to a more palatable appearance. We start with a thorough washing.

Nat hoses him down, then soaps his head and encourages me to clean his fingernails with a file and a J Cloth. The radio on the wall plays the Foo Fighters and she sings along.

"That's just the way life is . . ." goes the chorus.

His skin is yellow and cold. To prepare him for infusion we have to "break rigor," which means bending his arms and legs at the joints to rid them of their natural post-mortem stiffness. Natalie cranks his arm over his head as if it were a rusty pump handle. I lift a leg, foot to ceiling, yoga-style. It's hard, heavy, physical work. The joints are seized, even his fingers, which we massage until they're no longer clenched. The man maintains the dim smile as if he's enjoying this, and issues a dribble of brown drool the colour of weak coffee, which Nat refers to as "purge": the stomach contents leaking out. Next she "fixes the features," setting them into a more dignified expression of repose before the chemicals go in and harden them into place. Make a face and someday it'll stay that way, your mother said: same principle at work here. To fix his jaw she threads a needle with twine, pops it through his upper palate and feeds the needle out through his nose and back again. Then, with some deft wrestling, it appears through a spot under his chin, and she pulls both ends taut until his head rises from the table. She saws the twine back and forth and ties it off over his teeth, and now his mouth is firmly shut. She tucks the ends of the twine under his lips, then plumps them lightly with one of her gloved fingers, and turns his head slightly to the right. In fact the textbook calls for exactly fifteen degrees of tilt, the proper "viewing position."

Then, the eyes. She uses plastic "eye-caps," little pink half-shell contacts, one side of which are pocked and nubby to keep the eyelids in place, so they don't open up at an inopportune time, say, in the middle of an open-casket funeral. The corners of the eyes and mouth are droopy, so she applies some Dodge feature builder with a syringe, under the skin. Botox of death, she calls it. All the while she tells me about the renovations she and Robbie are doing at the house. They're painting the walls dark burgundy, and employing an African motif: monkeys and zebras and whatnot.

Just as I'm thinking we must be running out of things to do to the poor man, she cuts a hole above his right collarbone and uses forceps to fish out the common carotid artery and a heavy vein, snips them, and inserts a cannula attached to a rubber hose. The hose leads to a machine on the wall the size of an air conditioner. Into it she empties bottles of Permaglo, a tinting formaldehyde-based preservative, and Metaflow, red like cherry syrup, to break up clots and condition the blood vessels, and a water softener to take the hard edge off the mix. Machine on, she steps back, and the rubber hose hops on the man's chest.

Formaldehyde changes the structure of the body's protein, cooks it the way lime juice cooks seafood in a *ceviche*, making it inhospitable to the bacteria of decomposition. The man turns from yellow to patchy pink, as the blood runs free from the hole in his neck along a channel in the steel table, where it soaks my J Cloth and the sleeve of my scrubs, then empties into the toilet, where it'll be flushed into the Winnipeg sewage system and, as sometimes happens when the pumps at the North End Treatment Plant fail, into the Red River where, at Lockport, sport fishermen catch catfish for supper.

Nat claps her hands.

"Clots!" she says, watching the stream of blood. "I love clots! It means he's getting good distribution."

We massage his limbs and rub his feet and the palms of his hands with our knuckles, to encourage circulation, aware of the time on the clock over the door. In thirty minutes his family will be in the Committal Space for the viewing. Natalie works with the speed and confidence of a professional athlete. She reads the body for colour and tumescence as if she were reading an opposing team's defence.

She deems the distribution of chemical "not bad," except for his legs and feet, so she calls an audible: we'll open the two femoral arteries in the groin and pump in more chemical ("we"?). She feels for a spot on the fleshy inside of the man's right thigh and cuts a neat hole, tears back and forth at the tissue with her probe and forceps, then isolates the artery and ties it off with twine. She then passes me the knife and invites me to do the same on my side. I figure it's worth stopping here to consider my options. I'm all for learning by doing, but as a beginner I feel it's appropriate to plea-bargain my way down to a lesser duty: perhaps I can comb his eyebrows or rewash the hair on his chest until it's pillowy soft. Cutting a man open, even a dead one, strikes me as an act, like hang-gliding, that I'd rather read about than do. Behind her hazmat chador, I can see Nat blink, waiting me out.

"Only if you're comfortable," she says.

I do as I'm told.

I cut the skin, dig through muscle with my thumb. The hole is cold and wet and meaty. I find what might pass as a blood vessel and hook it with my forefinger.

"That's a nerve," Nat says.

I try again. In my peripheral vision I see the man wince, but of course it's just a trick of the air or my mind. I can feel my own groin tighten and I suspect I'll sit funny for a week. My thumb hooks another wet wormy thing.

"That's a muscle."

Third trip in, I come up with the plum, if only by the sheer process of elimination: the femoral artery, as thick as a penne noodle.

"Good," she says, and after snipping a hole in the vessel and pumping it with fluid from the cannula until his knees turn pink, she shows me how to close the incision with heavy twine in a baseball stitch, which is even harder than finding the artery because I can barely sew a shirt button, much less a hole in a human leg.

As I sew there's a knock at the door. It's Neil. This is less a spot check than a moment with the corpse, since as it happens he knows the man: they took Icelandic language lessons together. The dead man, Neil says, had a sense of humour, a cottage at a nearby lake and grandsons who play hockey. Except for the hum of the ventilation, the room is silent.

"Well," Nat says finally, "he has amazing drainage!"

Everyone smiles, because in the prep room good drainage is a valued quality, like good manners and good diction.

The last step calls for stabbing the man in the belly with a long steel harpoon called a trocar. Attached to a vacuum hose, the trocar sucks the fluids from the abdomen and heart and lungs, which will be replaced by more preservative. Nat has to stand on a kitchen stool to work the trocar, spearing it in and out, in a kind of ballet-fencing move, until the man's belly drops and he's dry, then she pours two bottles of purple Spectrum cavity fluid down the hose. When he's done chugging the Spectrum, she caps the hole in his abdomen with a plastic screw, paints his face and hands with Kalon cream, wraps him in a flannel sheet, and ships him to the dressing room, where he'll be suited and casketed and smudged with purple lipstick. I follow.

After dressing the bald man and winching him into a Prairie Beacon casket, we roll him on the "church truck," a casket dolly, into the Committal Space, where the light feels too dim after the fluorescents of the prep room, and my ears pop from the quiet. Nat leans in close enough to kiss the man, and blows gently on his face to clear away any errant powder. Then, as she lines up the casket under the pot lights, the gum falls out of her mouth and lands on the lid of the casket. She flicks it into the wastebasket and wipes the wood with her sleeve. As I follow her back stage again, I can see the family in the parking lot, two boys with wet hair and hockey jackets and a woman stamping her feet against the cold.

During the visitation, I stay in the back and study the Dodge chemical manual. If I'm to understand the odd amalgam of clinical science and spa treatment that makes up the prep room routine, I have to figure out my Permaglos from my Introfiants:

Permaglo: "Where it is important to create an illusion of vitality, the embalmer can rely on this classic arterial chemical to impart a stable, natural-looking glow to lifeless tissue."

Chromatech Pink: "Here are some of the comments of our testers: Doesn't fade, even after a week; very natural, I like it better than any other dye I've tried; excellent, a true pink; it didn't have any of the red tones, just the pink I wanted; more lifelike than other pinks."

Chromatech Tan: ". . . is especially well suited to people with somewhat darker complexions due to exposure to sun, ethnicity, etc."

Introfiant: "Treats low-protein, low-albumen, aged and 'institutional' cases with excellent response. . . . May be safely used on normal cases without risk of 'burning' or 'leatherizing.'"

The illusion of vitality—I know squat about Freud, I can't read him without getting dizzy, but somewhere he's described the uncanny, that powerful notion of fear in the face of the in-between: not real, not unreal, not human, but still kind of sort of. It's a paradox that Japanese robot makers have been trying to solve. They keep building human replicas that look more and more lifelike (usually, for some reason, like hot Japanese women), but as a result of a Promethean behavioural twist, they find that the closer they get to perfection the more frightening the end product appears. A mannequin is creepy, but in the right context (say, in a store window, not in your bedroom at night) it's not a source of fear. A cartoon character with human features is downright cute. But as you approach the point at which real and unreal are confused, the natural response is revulsion: roboticist Masahiro Mori called this the "uncanny valley." Wax figures and zombies and automata live in the valley. Embalmed corpses, too. Natalie says embalming delivers to mourners the opportunity to face up to death, to see it for real, and to know the person won't be coming back: the body is its own therapeutic tool for the balming of grief, a tool for transcendence. But explain that to my cognitive wiring. The embalmed corpse is an in-between: both a person and an object to fear.

Still, ours looked pretty good, now, I'll grant her that: all sleepy and peach-coloured, his various holes and puckered stitchings well hidden under clothes. My hands, meanwhile, are ice cold. It occurs to me I've been through a rite of passage, like a Bantu boy who kills his first antelope. The experience was thrilling, in a primitive way. I should probably bay at the moon tonight. In any case, having literally got my hands wet and my garment soaked in blood, there's not much doubt that I've been baptized as a make-believe undertaker.

Six

FUNERAL FAMILY VALUES

*S*hifting into this new life calls for a few months of wrapping up the old, normal one. When I quit my job at CBC, my co-workers, smart young pop-culture journalists, take me for a ritual bye-bye lunch at the Paddlewheel on the top floor of the Bay, an accidentally hip place to get fish and chips and Jell-O squares with the afternoon crowd of mostly seniors who eat there every day. Quitting CBC, in its current climate of siege and underfunding, to work at a funeral home, we decide, is no weirder than quitting CBC to finish, say, a master's in French poetry at McGill, except for the business of tying people's mouths shut with twine and burning them to cinders, which might be weirder than deconstructing Baudelaire. Of course the Paddlewheel has a paddlewheel, like the back end of a riverboat, and if you chuck a penny into the waterless pool underneath it'll bring luck. I throw a quarter. The place is sparser and sadder than I remember it from the last time someone quit CBC and we took her for lunch. The few seniors on hand today I can't help studying for traits known to undertakers: light jaundice here, pale knotty hands there, which would call for a Metaflow pre-injection to bump up chemical receptiveness in the vascular system, maybe a restricted cervical too to avoid over-injecting the head, which leads to "eye pop." The woman gumming her rice pudding is a candidate for the mouth former, a clear plastic bite-guard, like boxers wear, to give toothless corpses a more natural look. A gentleman with pruned cheeks and pouched eyes stabs a cherry tomato. Natalie says to study the lines of the face for expression, and to resist the urge to smooth them away in the prep room: they represent personality. I'm already seeing the world through a different, disturbing lens. It's not unlikely that I'll see one of these Paddlewheel customers again, on the embalming table. Winnipeg is a small enough town, and the demographic is right for Neil: elderly, white, budget-conscious. How would it feel to know that the man at the table next to yours at lunch will someday be your undertaker?

"Do you have to touch them?" one of my workmates asks.

"Who?"

"Dead people."

"Sure," I say. "I mean, not all the time. Just in the prep room. And loading them into the retort, you have to check for pacemakers. And dressing them. So yeah, a lot, I guess."

"What do they feel like?"

I have to think about this. I look around the restaurant.

"Chicken breasts."

———

My wardrobe needs work so I buy three stiff white dress shirts at the Bay, not a natural fibre among them, and new black shoes. Richard says that at funerals I will meet men of the generation that look at your shoes before they shake your hand. I order books online: a 1951 hardback copy of *Successful Funeral Service Management* by Wilber M. Krieger, he of the Beautiful Memory Picture, and one of Jessica Mitford's favourite whipping-boys. In the book Krieger says boldly: you cannot create demand. "A huge advertising program a few years ago created a demand among women for cigarettes. I have never yet seen any program of advertising or public relations that created demand for funeral service." Apparently, it needed to be said: we are at the mercy of nature and chaos and, save the odd good flu season, medical science is improving, and this impacts the bottom line. Alan Wolfelt's *Funeral Home Customer Service A–to–Z* is more contemporary, of this century. Under *B* for Burnout, he talks about "funeral director fatigue syndrome," the symptoms of which include the following:

- **Exhaustion and loss of energy**
- **Irritability and impatience**
- **Cynicism and detachment**
- **Feelings of omnipotence and indispensability**

Some of these I bring to the table already. Feelings of omnipotence and indispensability will come when they come, if I work at them, but *B* for Burnout makes me think of what Neil told me about his family.

"It works very much like the family farm," he said of the funeral trade, which is true enough if you consider both are in the business of planting things in the ground for money. Beyond that, it gets complicated. To say the Bardal family saga is a story of easy succession from one generation to the next is to say *King Lear* is a story of easy succession from one generation to the next.

Neil's story starts with his grandfather A.S. Bardal, who, when he was a child in Iceland, once found a human skull in a field, tied a piece of rope to it and dragged it home to show his mother, thereby launching a hundred-plus-year family death-care dynasty through accident or fate, depending on how you read it. Later he would immigrate to Canada, setting up a wood-framing and horse-drawn taxi and livery service from a storefront on Sherbrook Street in Winnipeg. From there it was just a leap of imagination: like the Reese who first brought chocolate and peanut butter together, A.S. Bardal figured he could combine his efforts, retool the wood shop to build caskets and refit the carriages into hearses, and that's how he became the first Bardal undertaker.

The funeral home was one of the city's Original Eight, which still are spoken of with reverence, like the Original Six of NHL hockey. At the time, the city was informally split by the eight families of undertakers on geographic or cultural lines: A.B. Gardiner had the white Anglo-Saxons, the French Catholics went to Desjardins, the rich merchant families used Leatherdale, and to this day, if a Shriner dies, chances are Thomson on Broadway has the arrangements—if the picture in the newspaper obit shows a man in a fez, you know where the service will be held. Bardal's had the northern Europeans, German Lutherans and "assorted gypsies," in Neil's words. With respect, the Original Eight might have been more like the five Sicilian families in *The Godfather*: they knew their territories and they settled their disputes at monthly luncheons. Gardiner was titular head of the eight families, a white-glove undertaker who served sherry at arrangements, spoke of the greatness of the dead man and made it clear it was a privilege for you to be there. The Winnipeg undertakers were unambiguously more powerful than priests. Neil remembers seeing, from his bedroom on the second floor of the funeral home on Sherbrook, his grandfather on the church steps across the street, in a fur coat, arms raised to signal the end of a service, the pastor huddling behind him, knowing his place.

But they weren't businessmen, least of all A.S. Bardal, who sank money into a scheme for a better internal-combustion carburetor (which flopped) and travelled the country and overseas on behalf of the International Order of Good Templars preaching against drink with a slide show and a clicker. His sons Karl and Njall (Neil's father) tried to talk him into incorporating the business, and he told them, "This is my baby. If you want a baby, go out and make your own." Instead they waited him out, and when the senior Bardal died in 1952, omnipotent and indispensable to the end, they took over the funeral home and spent years driving it back into the black, one hardwood casket at a time. Or Karl did. Njall Bardal had less enthusiasm for the game. After having served in the Second World War, he had less enthusiasm for everything.

Neil's father had been with the Winnipeg Grenadiers, shipped to Hong Kong in 1941 just in time for it to fall to the Japanese. He'd spent the war in a prison camp, where they called him The Undertaker. There he watched men being tortured and beheaded, but he also saw how the Japanese disposed of the dead: cremated without ceremony. It was clean and efficient and it saved his mates from further harm, desecration and the indignity of being buried in enemy turf. This, Neil thinks, is what turned his father into a closet cremationist (sacrilege for a Bardal at the time), and his dad kept these ideas to himself when he returned to the family business, thin, depressed, but with the Icelander's skill at repressing it.

"My father had swallowed all these psychic hand grenades," Neil says. "And for the rest of his life they went off one at a time." He showed me a photograph of himself as a child, with his dad, just after Njall got back to Canada. The boy is smiling, the father is not, and his hand is barely touching his son's shoulder, as if the photographer had told him to put it there to create interest.

"That's what he was like," Neil says. "And look—he's wearing spats. No one told him they'd gone out of style while he was away."

Later, with his father and his uncle Karl running the shop, it came time for Neil to decide if he'd take up the trocar, but the decision was made for him: his father scored him a place at the Chicago embalming school and arranged for him to apprentice at Trull Funeral Home on the Danforth in Toronto. Njall Sr. said he had met Trull on a train from Calgary. It was all set. When Neil showed up in Toronto, Trull had to admit he'd never met anyone named Bardal, on a train or otherwise. But there was plenty of work (Trull had a handsome piece of the action east of Yonge Street, nearly half the city), so they took Neil on. Senior undertakers wore tails, striped pants and bowlers; juniors like Neil wore morning suits and homburgs, and in the summer they dressed up in powder blue suits. No hazmat gear in the prep room, they just flipped their ties over their shoulders and got to work, usually with cigarettes in their mouths, the ash dangling over the open corpse. Here he learned to cut clothing, a no-no at the Chicago school: you cut the collar, possibly the whole shirt, in the back, with scissors, to get a looser, more relaxed fit on the corpse (which tended to puff up in the prep room). Chicago considered clothes-cutting an indignity, a shortcut. At Trull, they liked shortcuts. They were busy. Viewings were scheduled from 2 p.m. to 10 p.m. daily, like cinema screenings. Trull himself was an infrequent visitor to the funeral home. He had his own railroad coach for skiing trips, and a house in Jamaica. It was a lucrative business, and a good life.

One day Neil got a call from his mother. His father was ill in hospital, so Neil flew home to Winnipeg. He found Njall Sr. not at the hospital but at the Legion playing pool with the rest of the Hong Kong vets.

Why did you lie? Neil asked him.

His father said: Because I need you here, and you wouldn't have come home if all I did was ask.

Again, his course had been decided for him. Neil gave up Toronto and settled into the family business. He kept his homburg from Trull. He wore it once, for a service at Chapel Lawn cemetery. The next day he got a call from Sam Sander's father who ran the Shell station near Deer Lodge on Portage Avenue, who'd seen Neil driving the lead car to Chapel Lawn. Sander asked him where he'd got the ridiculous hat. So Neil put it away and never wore it again. He was, for better or worse, home.

Two forces shaped the industry in the '60s: first up, the Mitford book and the seeds of a social revolution that challenged tradition and ritual and forced the undertakers either to accept cremation as an alternative or to ignore it in the hope it would go away, like the hula hoop craze. In Winnipeg there was only one local retort, at Pineview cemetery. When it opened in 1965, the mayor was there to cut the ribbon. The permit to cremate human remains was still pending, so, for the sake of ceremony, they cremated a pig. The pig burned out of control and blew the door off the retort. From then on Pineview was known as Swineview, and in Winnipeg it was easy enough to continue to dismiss cremation as a fad. The second force came from Texas and Des Moines, Iowa: the funeral conglomerates. They were buying up family funeral homes in Canada and the United States, building empires. Here was something Njall Sr. and Karl Bardal couldn't ignore. By 1968 they were exhausted, ready to cash out. Des Moines was ready to buy. Neil, who had assumed he would one day inherit the family funeral home, found out through a third party that his birthright was to be sold to an American chain. All he could do was scare up enough cash and bank debt to make a counter-offer. The senior Bardals grudgingly accepted Neil's bid. But their message was clear enough: this is our baby.

The Original Eight franchise offered ready access to raw materials (the funeral home was across the street from a hospital) and Neil had no reason to tinker with the business plan: embalm, casket, bury, repeat. The traditional model served him well through the early '70s when, as Neil says, it was impossible to be an undertaker and not make money, as long as you worked long hours and shunned vacations, as he did. Neil's own confrontation with cremation came finally from an unlikely source: his own father. "My father said, if you were smart, you'll have me cremated when I die and show people there's another way to do this," a simple alternative to the fuss and flowers of the full-fig funeral. The closet cremators had come out. "But when he died," Neil told me, "I'm sorry to say I chickened out. He had a very traditional service. Because that's the kind of business we were in." Njall Sr. was buried in the family plot at Brookside cemetery in 1977.

Where does Neil's son Eirik fit in? He's next in line for a throne with a history of being yanked from under its heirs apparent. Of course, Eirik grew up in a funeral home. As children, he and his brother Jon and their cousins played hide-and-seek in the showroom, lying in closed caskets until they were found. (As he was one of the few living people I'd met who'd actually been inside a casket, I asked him what it was like. "Surprisingly comfortable," he said.) But when he was old enough to work, he became the first Bardal in four generations to reject the call of the embalming room. "I was basically raised by my mom," he says. "She was my hockey coach, my swimming coach, my Cub Scouts leader, my Beavers leader. I saw my dad four times in like six years, and I decided I couldn't work like that." So he took jobs in construction, laying paving stones, on the ski lifts at Whistler and as a commercial fisherman on Lake Winnipeg. One winter his boat got trapped in a blizzard. Unable to see land (this is pre-GPS), the skipper pointed in one direction while the first mate pointed in another, and this was when Eirik decided he'd live longer if he went to work for his dad. He got his undertaker's licence in 2000.

"I grew up with the changes in the business," he says. "Unlike Dad and my grandfather, I didn't have all the baggage of how things used to be done." Eirik was a child of the cremation era. Which is why I was surprised when he told me about his own wishes for when he dies. "It's against everything Dad would want," he admits, "but I would go traditional myself. I would be in the plot with the family in Brookside, with a viewing and a service and a reception, with music I like. Dean Martin, Rat Pack stuff."

In the meantime, having learned first-hand what it's like to grow up with an absentee father, he's spending time with his own kids, ages seven and eight, taking them fishing and swimming and to weekend games of laser tag, even if it means sacrificing time at the funeral home. He wants his kids to have a father.

And what about the other non-Bardals who, by definition, can go only so far in this business before hitting the glass, or oak, or 16-gauge stainless steel ceiling? Richard will never own this place, Shannon will never own this place. They have the wrong last name. This is why ambitious young undertakers join the conglomerates where blood doesn't matter. And maybe this is why, while I was gone settling up my old life, Natalie quit. Glenn says she went into Neil's office one day, voices were raised, a door was slammed, and within weeks she was working at Eddie Coutu's in St. Boniface as an arrangement director, selling Last Supper–themed caskets and urns to Italian Catholics. They don't even have a prep room at Coutu, so she's no longer embalming. What happened? As far as Glenn knows, it came down to a difference of opinion between Natalie and Neil on how to run a funeral home, with only one person in the room in a position to call the shots. "Focus on what you have to do and keep your mouth shut," Richard says. This is his advice for working in a family business. Natalie's mistake, he says, was that she was good at the first, but lousy at the second.

We're driving to Starbuck, a small farm town south of the city, for an afternoon funeral. The back of the van is loaded with gear: wood planks, AstroTurf and the Device for lowering the casket into the grave. Starbuck cemetery is too small to have its own staff, so we'll be "dressing" the grave ourselves. The planks are still covered with dried mud from the last interment, their ends propped on the dashboard, banging the windshield whenever we hit a bump.

Richard has been an undertaker since the late '80s. His father was a bus driver who knew Neil through Masonic circles, and his daily route that took him past the old family funeral home on Sherbrook Street. When he got sick with cancer, he sat down with Neil, "held my arm like this," Neil told me, gripping my forearm, and made Neil swear he'd see the boy through medical school. Neil said he would. After his father died, Richard worked at Fort Ignition selling spark plugs and auto parts, but he grew bored, and wound up at Cropo funeral home on Main Street looking for work. Instead, Neil hired him, figuring that if the boy was intent on the funeral trade it was better to have him close at hand. Richard's been with Neil ever since. The closest he got to medical school was the prep room. He and Eirik became friends. They'd drink together at the Palomino Club and then go back to the Aubrey Street funeral home to listen to AC/DC and Rush on the sound system, just the two of them and whoever was resting on the casket bier in the chapel. Richard knew he was suited for funeral service, he tells me, when he first had what he calls "the dream." In the dream he was in the prep room, working on a body, and just as he was about to cut into the neck to raise the carotid artery, the body sat upright. The man wasn't angry, just confused. He didn't know why he was on the steel table or why he was naked. He told Richard he wanted to go home. So Richard found him some clothes and opened the door, and he was gone.

"Neil says every undertaker has the dream at some point," he says. "If you don't, it means you're in the wrong business."

That would be enough to scare me back into a career at Fort Ignition, but for Richard it was a mystical moment.

"It was neat," he says. "I guess it would've been worse if he was already in the retort."

Curtains

At Starbuck cemetery (established in 1902, ancient for the Prairies), he parks the van on the grass next to the open grave. There are only a few dozen headstones. Around us are nothing but grain fields, and in the distance I can see both ends of a long freight train, too far away to hear. We set the planks along both sides of the grave and cover them with the AstroTurf mats, their green tongues hanging into the hole. We use a big mat to cover the mound of dirt, presumably to disguise its purpose. Putting together the Device is like constructing a playground swing set when the instructions are in Mandarin: pipes fit into gear-boxes that fit into other pipes and then canvas straps are stretched over the frame and wound tight around the side rails. It works on friction and gravity: no batteries required. As long as the gears are locked, the straps will hold the weight of the casket. Once the brake is released, the side rails turn, slowly, held back by the gears, and the straps grow more and more slack. The casket sinks into the hole. The effect is as if God's own hand is lowering the box. Richard says when he dresses a grave he usually turns his suit inside out. Then, when it comes time for the service, he can flip it around and no one will see the dirt. I decide I'm too superstitious to take my clothes off in a cemetery, and besides, all I've got is a ring of muck around my pant cuffs. I wipe them on the grass.

When we get to the church, Neil's already there with the hearse and the casket. On top of the casket, in place of the usual spray of flowers, is a bundle of dried wheat, in honour of the dead man, who was a farmer. Inside, the church is late-model Lutheran with exposed brick and skylights, blond-wood pews and a Henry Moore-esque stone baptismal font. A sign by the door says BLESS YOU FOR NOT SMOKING. Richard decides to stay, to corral pallbearers and work out the seating for the family, who've yet to arrive, freeing Neil and me to head into town for lunch.

The main street of Starbuck is deserted, save four men in hunting camo outside Archie's Meats and Groceries, loading brown-paper bundles of bloody meat into the back of a pickup truck. Only the store and the hotel restaurant appear to be open. At the hotel, the man behind the counter asks us if we want the bar or the coffee shop. If we want the bar, it's closed but he'll open it. If we want the coffee shop, he's it. He opens a fridge and studies our options. He can offer us ham and cheese sandwiches, but he has no bread because it's the end of the week. The best he can do is to thaw a couple of frozen hamburger buns in the microwave. We pour ourselves two cups of coffee and sit down. The place is painted bright pink and green, and hanging on a bare plywood wall is a picture of a chicken.

I ask Neil about the dream.

Some people, he says, are born into funeral service. They have the name. They have no choice. Others think they'll make a whack of money, and they get into the trade for the nice suits and expensive cars, but they don't know how hard they'll have to work, answering calls at 3 a.m. and doing removals on weekends. Then there are those with natural talent. Natalie, he says, has it. She could tell just by looking at a body what chemical index to use in the embalming room. She set features like a sculptor. It's too bad, he says: Natalie had this idea I favoured Shannon over her.

"Do you?"

"I'm grooming Shannon for bigger things. She has natural talent too. She understands families. She understands where this business is going. If Natalie had stayed I would've given her all the space she needed in the prep room. It was hers. But I guess you can't have two queen bees in the same hive."

Or two brothers: Jon, it turns out, has left the funeral home too, to put all his efforts into becoming an electrician.

The sandwiches are delicious. As we're leaving, the man behind the counter says it's a good day for a burial. In our black suits we're either funeral directors or mobsters, and he guessed right.

"I want it storming for mine," he says. "Same as when I came in. I come from a farm family. So I've been crying from day one."

Back at the church, Richard fills us in on recent developments. The brother and sister are at war, he says. The sister hasn't been home for thirty years and the brother thinks she's only come back so she can get her piece of the dad's estate. He's seated them on opposite sides of the chapel. The pastor raises her hands and says, "We've come to hear the good news for Jim and for us. Please be seated."

A few hymns later the guests are sent downstairs for sandwiches and raisin buns and coffee while we load the casket into the hearse. Neil and I hustle to the cemetery in the van, and Richard follows, leading a procession of cars. Pallbearers lift the casket onto the straps of the Device and I hold my breath. The pastor makes the sign of the cross on the lid with dirt from our Gerber jar, and Richard flips the hand brake with his foot. Unlike at city cemeteries, they're not shy here about seeing the box all the way into the hole. The casket lurches, and stops. Richard kicks the Device. Now the casket sinks slowly until it hits bottom, and I can breathe again. The brother produces an ice cream bucket filled with dirt he brought from the farm. He drops a handful into the grave and I can hear it scatter on the wood. Then he hands the bucket to his sister. She won't take it.

When they leave to join their friends for lunch at the church, Richard and I strike the set, folding up the greens and dismantling the miraculous, if temperamental, Device. I look into the open grave, at the dirt on the lid and the sheaf of dried wheat, and I think of what Neil said: The funeral home works very much like the family farm.

Seven

To Keep Things the Way They Are, We Have to Change

*S*ummer at the Factory means the smell of freshly turned earth from Brookside cemetery, and Zep bug spray, which Shannon uses to fog the dressing room to keep flies off the customers.

"The last thing you want is to open the casket and have a fly come out of someone's nose," she says. Shannon's full of helpful hints. When threading a needle in the prep room, she says, resist the urge to put it in your mouth. Moisten the end with water from the sink: "Never lick anything in a funeral home."

I remember when I first came in here, how gruesome those curved needles looked, what it felt like to poke one through leathery skin. Neil told me to be patient, that my natural fear would evolve into something deeper: respect and awe for the body. We live in a caste system, where the Brahmins subcontract their problems to the unclean, the Dalit caste, the corpse-handlers. That's us. In time I'd get used to my social role. And the people I worked with would get used to me, once they figured out I wasn't after their jobs. This is a cutthroat business, he said, the corporates are panicked over low death rates and new competition from low-end discount cremationists. They are laying off staff. Every new face in a funeral home is a threat to someone's groceries.

At first my co-workers were polite but guarded, explaining and demonstrating technique while I took reams of notes, and absorbed the mantra: *We do this for the families, we treat the dead like we'd treat our own fathers and aunts, each case is handled with respect and dignity*—all fuzzy noble notions made fuzzier by repetition. When Glenn showed me for the eighth time how to operate secondary and primary burners on the retort he must have wondered: when is this guy going to leave? But I didn't (or I did and came back), and soon enough they grew bored with my presence, a good sign that I was fitting in. I did my removals, and cleaned orifices and fingernails, and I wet-mopped and swept my way from suspicious novelty to the guy who could be trusted on scut jobs, like picking up Super Glue (for closing lips on difficult cases) and a curling iron at Costco. I'd joined their caste. But I still can't sew up dead skin without feeling my own skin prickle. I've tried imagining it as not unlike trussing a pork roast, but these pork roasts at Neil's have hands, and fingers, and suntan shadows where wedding rings used to be.

I still find the morning meetings brisk and confusing. Richard chairs them from Aubrey Street, while the rest of us crowd around the speakerphone in the dressing room at the crematorium. Neil's in his office eating bran flakes and hot water, the same breakfast his grandfather ate every day. He's on speakerphone too, even though if we punched a hole in the dressing room wall we could reach through to his office and touch him.

"Concrete liner's been ordered, cemetery's been ordered," says Janice, one of the undertakers, reporting on the case of a woman who'll be on view at Aubrey this afternoon at one o'clock, with a service and burial to follow. "Flowers are ordered, they'll go to the church except for a single rose to come here, and that's for the family to put in the casket. Family's providing the music on their own, pastor is handing out bulletins and they're going to Robin's Donuts after the burial."

"Is that open to everyone?" Richard says.

"Yes."

"Good, because they've got the Sip to Win going on, eh?"

"Oh. Yes, the contest."

"Sip to Win, yeah. Who's next?"

Eirik reports on the prep for a man due tomorrow at Gimli Lutheran for a service followed by cremation. His family sent an American flag to drape over the casket. He was in the U.S. Air Force, retired, and the flag is very old, an heirloom, forty-six stars. Next is the case of the woman in the casket that may or may not be too small for her, depending on whether you agree with Eirik, who thinks it is, or Shannon, who thinks it isn't. Shannon says the woman's only five feet tall, and Eirik says it's not her height that matters but her width, and whips out a tailor's tape measure and stretches it with some drama across the woman's shoulders. She's lying in her casket just behind us in the dressing room. She does look a bit cramped, but not uncomfortable, if that's any way to describe a dead body. Shannon says the woman's sister picked out the casket herself, and Eirik says we're all wider when we're lying down, that's physics, and Shannon no longer appreciates the implication that oversights were made, and I look at the woman in the middle of all this. She's holding a heart-shaped picture frame in her folded hands. Inside the frame is a photo of Elvis.

Richard calls for order, and Neil says, "Wait a sec."

We all stare at the speakerphone.

"What the hell kind of flag has forty-six stars?"

We all stare at Eirik.

"Forty-eight," he says. "Sorry."

The working day starts in the prep room, where I meet Adina, the new apprentice, a tall young woman with her hair pulled back in a ponytail so tight she looks permanently surprised, or terrified, or both. She's studying for her licence online, with Shannon as her sponsor, and so far she has nineteen embalmed bodies to her credit. To graduate she needs fifty. Ten years ago this would've been a snap, a month's work, but with cremation overtaking the full-fig funeral as the disposition of choice, she needs every prep she can get her hands into. Today, Number 20 is a thin man with a few days' growth of beard, a scrubby moustache, dry cloudy eyes and a breathing tube still stuck between his teeth, which Adina pulls out with a wet *pop*, then drops into the garbage bin as if it were a dead mouse.

While lathering his face I remember what Natalie told me about shaving the dead: long easy strokes, never choppy. Corpses get razor burn too. Before we go any further, Adina wants a ruling on the moustache. Shave it off or leave it on? Half-hearted as it is, that may be the way he wore it, or it may be the artifact of a long hospital stay. Either way it's not our place to infer intention when it comes to grooming, so she calls Richard, who agrees to call the family. Families get calls like this all the time, between the arrangements and the funeral: Collar up or down? Shirt tucked in or out? Eyeglasses on or off? If a man wore his hair like Stalin in life he should not look like Dee Dee Ramone in the casket.

Clothes cutting is another matter. Families aren't consulted, it comes down to undertaker taste, although there's been a minor power struggle here vis-à-vis the practice. Eirik posted a rule on the dry-erase board in the dressing room, in four-inch black letters: ALL CLOTHES MUST BE CUT FROM NOW ON, NO EXCEPTIONS. Shannon meanwhile has made it clear she won't do it. At best it's lazy undertaking, and at worst it's undignified. This puts Adina in a pickle. Shannon is her sponsor, but Eirik is the boss's son.

"What would you do?" she says.

I have to think about this. I've yet to develop a philosophy on dead people's clothes. Natalie never cut, she said all it took was a little extra tugging and tucking to get a decent fit, but Neil was a cutter at Trull and for all I know clothes cutting is a Bardal family tradition, like ham at Easter. At the same time, can you run a man through with a trocar and bleed him like a trout into a toilet, but refuse to cut his shirt collar on moral grounds? This has little to do with clothing and the corpse, and everything to do with Shannon and Eirik and politics, and who's on whose team.

Richard calls back. The family took a vote. The moustache stays.

Neil says he's not worried about a little dysfunction on the Factory floor: he won't micro-manage. Glenn's quit so many times, Neil has a thick file of his resignation letters in his desk, and if Shannon's showing some pluck and ambition, good for her, it might light a spark under Eirik. As long as everyone remembers the mission.

"Which is what?" I'm starting to lose track.

"Getting the body from the bed to the grave in the most creative way possible, with the most meaning for the family," Neil says, whether that involves a casket and grave, or cremation and scattering, or all four in some elaborate combination. And transparency too: opening the door between front stage and backstage, letting families see the machinery behind the curtain—deconstructed death-care. Unthinkable in his father's time. Unthinkable right now in any other funeral home in Winnipeg.

"Let them see the cremation?"

"Yes."

"Let them see the bones being sorted?"

"Yes, it's happened already."

"Let them into the prep room?"

He pauses. There's no law that bars families from watching an embalming, and if someone asked he'd consider it. It hasn't come up yet. There was one time, a boating accident. The family wanted to see the body, but the boat's propeller had made a mess of it. So they covered up the face but left the hands exposed, and the family was able to touch the hands. There are ways. And limits.

On a slow day, Neil takes me along on a special delivery: a man from Roblin, a small town five hours northwest of the city, on the Saskatchewan border, has lately been autopsied at the Health Sciences Centre and is now free to go home for his burial. Instead of sending him by courier (the usual route: not inexpensive) we'll drive him to the local funeral home ourselves. It's a large day, the sun is bleaching the asphalt, and on the highway past Portage la

Prairie there's little to distract us but wheat, more wheat, a grain elevator, and then more wheat. We pass a collapsed farmhouse and Neil says, Imagine the family that used to live there, they thought it would last forever.

When he bought the family business in 1968 Neil had hooked up with a business partner, but the partnership was doomed. Ten years later they couldn't stand to be in the same chapel together, so they agreed to a shotgun divorce: the first to come up with the money to buy the other's share could keep the place, while the other walked, albeit with a pocketful of money. This would have marked the second time Neil had to buy his own family funeral home. But this time, the partner beat him to it, and Neil lost the business, A.S. Bardal's one-time frame shop and livery service on Sherbrook Street. He lost the family name, too: it went with the funeral home. (There's still a Bardal Funeral Home on Sherbrook, but there has been no actual Bardal on staff since Neil was bought out in 1979. This is very confusing for local consumers.)

Now he was on his own, both liberated and terrified. He'd followed developments in California, where the Neptune Society had launched its deep-discount cremation-only service: no pricey caskets, no embalming, no cemeteries, just a simple burning and scattering of the ashes at sea. Like Allen Ginsberg on pilgrimage to the crematory ghats of Varanasi in India, Neil flew to San Francisco to discover his inner undertaker, remembering what his father had told him: If you're smart, you'll show people there's another way to do all this. Neil came back enlightened, a born-again bake-and-shaker.

In 1983 he spoke in Toronto, at a meeting of the Ontario Funeral Services Association. The message was simple: As undertakers, he said, we have to go back to our roots. We're trained to take care of the body, not sell product. The age of the casket is over. With cremation growing in popularity, we should replace it with a simple cardboard box.

"I got booed off the stage," he told me. Colleagues called him a heretic. At a meeting in Penticton the next year, where he pitched the same message, he was described as the gum disease of modern funeral service. As far as Neil was concerned, his audience missed the point: he wasn't preaching the end of the funeral but calling for a creative response to its evolution. His colleagues wouldn't hear of it. The fact was, cremation terrified them.

He made plans to adapt the Neptune model to Manitoba. He acquired the crematorium near Brookside, although scattering-at-sea was ruled out on account of logistics, the nearest ocean being the Pacific, or the Atlantic, depending on whether you turned left or right on the highway at Steinbach. What the Prairies had were oceans of grain and oceans of trees, however, so Neil studied a parcel of land near Kenora on the Ontario border as a site for a scattering forest. Families could scatter remains and enjoy a picnic: no graves, no markers, just acres of woods. He commissioned a pithy radio jingle:

> Not to change what was meant to be,
> But provide a means for it to happen naturally.

But he never bought the land.

Next, in consultation with a plant scientist at the university who said cremated remains made for a potent fertilizer, Neil thought of buying farmland to grow wheat—magically, disturbingly tall wheat—until it became clear consumers might be disinclined to buy, much less eat, bread made indirectly from dead human beings. In the end he dug a kidney-shaped rose garden in the front lawn of the crematorium and pitched it as a third way, between the cemetery and what the industry called "wildcat" scattering: private disposal in parks, the river, the lake at the cottage, golf courses, places with personal meaning but without the tangibility of a permanent memorial.

Now Neil wants to expand. He wants to build a reception hall and an indoor atrium for the garden, so families can scatter in winter, enjoy a little garden-side ceremony with coffee and dainties even as it's minus-35 Celsius outside with the wind-chill factor. Instead of roses there'd be rubber plants. He wants to call it the Garden of Memories. If it works, he'll franchise the idea.

In the meantime, he wants to change the structure of his business, design it like a law firm. The family would hold the business in a central trust, but the undertakers, Richard and Janice and Shannon, would all work as associates, earning their way on billable hours, developing their own clients, until they achieved full partnerships. They'd have incentive to stay, invest in the place. In fact they'd be working for themselves, under the umbrella of the Bardal trust.

The corporates, he said, were stuck with their fusty, Kafkaesque infrastructure dictated from Toronto or Houston by the bier barons. "Me? I'm not stuck with anything," he says. "I'm not even stuck with family."

Roblin is little more than a main street with angle parking, a railroad station that hasn't seen a train since the route was cut (the station is now a restaurant) and a lot full of rusted school buses that says most people under sixty have already moved to Winnipeg or Regina. The funeral home is faux church with a gabled roof and heavy wood doors. This is a mom-and-pop shop, what Neil calls a typical rural funeral-a-week (if that) operation. Pop meets us in the parking lot. He's Neil's age, wearing suspenders, work pants and a plaid shirt. They exchange greetings and ask after each other's children and grandchildren. We unload the body and wheel it through the garage, past rolls of pink insulation and open boxes of brass cemetery vases, some crowded onto a kitchen counter like empty beer bottles after a party.

The prep room has two tables, one already occupied by a man in a blue suit and blue fuzzy slippers. In the corner is a red auto-mechanic's Snap-on tool chest, where pop keeps his embalming gear, and on top of the chest a few pink eye-caps are scattered like potato chips. A half-empty bottle of Plasdopake sits in the sink. He and Neil lift the body, still wrapped in hospital plastic, to the empty table (old-school, no latex gloves), then pop shows us around. He apologizes for his distracted state, but he has the flu, so does mom, and Canada Revenue Agency is on his back, again. The casket showroom is tiny and cramped (mostly hardwoods) but the chapel is huge, with wooden pews, baby-blue walls and dusty-rose curtains, a giant Jesus-ready cross on the wall over the pulpit. Where does one buy such a thing? The chapel is also where pop stores extra caskets that won't fit in the showroom. It's cold here. He keeps the heat off between services to save money.

"It's not like it used to be," he says.

"Things have changed," Neil replies.

"When the girls were young they used to play here. We had to tell them not to bounce their balls upstairs during services."

"With us, it was don't flush the toilet."

We follow him out to the parking lot, where he opens the door of his removal van. The tax people have told him he can no longer claim it as a business expense, that it's a personal vehicle.

"Look at it," he says. "Casket rollers in the back. You think I drive my friends around in this thing?"

Back on the highway, Neil says the visit was like stepping into a time capsule. Fifty calls a year, and the only reason pop survives is he hasn't lost the casket sale, not yet. He goes to church, the curling rink, and all the service club meetings; he knows his families and life and death follow a steady, reliable course. The word *cremation* never comes up. Someday it will. Funeral service has always been a panicky dialogue between past and present, and the past is no place to run a business. That's why the corporate chains only buy urban funeral homes. Out here it's less of a business, more of a hobby.

Are Neil and pop really that different? I think of the novel *The Leopard*, about a family of Sicilian aristocrats riding out the last days of a class system that's about to evaporate in the forces of modernity and Garibaldi's revolution. Same premise as the 1982 TV sitcom *Silver Spoons* with Ricky Schroder, only in the book, Prince Fabrizio, resigned to his fate, is told by his nephew, who's joined the rebels: "If we want things to stay as they are, they will have to change." Neil is an innovator, but at the heart of the Garden of Memories and the Wheat Field of the Dead are the same steady, reliable undertaker values his grandfather brought to Sherbrook—the body, the viewing, the ceremony.

What matters is the physical fact of death. We need to see it to know it, touch its hair or hands, feel how cold it is. Neil hates the word *closure* but it's apt. If you don't see the body, it's as if it was lost at sea and you can harbour dreams that your loved one is still alive on some desert island with a coconut tree sending messages in bottles like in a *New Yorker* cartoon. What makes an undertaker different from a casket salesman or event planner is that he understands the central role of the dead man in his own drama.

When his uncle died, Neil took care of the arrangements. When it was done, his aunt studied the bill and challenged him on one of the items: the removal of the body. It doesn't make sense for you to charge for this, she told him. After all, I would think it's in your interest to pick up the body. I shouldn't have to pay for it. Her children, Neil's cousins, rolled their eyes. Years later she attended a funeral at the Aubrey chapel. When the pianist played "The Lost Chord," she laid her head on her sister's shoulder, said, "That's nice," and quietly died. Again Neil handled the logistics, and when he presented his cousins with the bill, they pointed to the removal charge. She died in your funeral home, they said.

We pass grain fields, more grain fields, then cattle country. A billboard tells us Life is Sacred from Conception to Natural Death.

"This law-firm idea," I say. "What does Eirik think of it?"

Neil looks ahead. "He doesn't know yet."

His cell phone rings. It's pop. The man we just delivered is missing his wedding ring. The viewing is tonight. Neil tells me to check his briefcase, and there I find the valuables envelope from the Health Sciences Centre, the one we were supposed to have left at pop's. I can feel the ring. We turn around on the empty highway and head back to Roblin.

Eight

RESPECT, DIGNITY AND BLACK UNDERPANTS

In Winnipeg there are two types of obituaries, the "shorts" and the "longs." "Shorts" run in the weekday *Free Press* and are little more than service announcements, written by undertakers according to a template: who died, who's got the body, relevant times and dates for the viewing and funeral. "Longs" are written by families and each one can cover six column inches, with photographs, packed with trivia and detail, the best of them wandering cryptically, begging you to read between the lines. Sometimes it's clear they were written in advance, by the soon-to-be-deceased. The man who "didn't ask for much in life" but loved his cats Chester and Tickles and his wife Joanne left it to the reader to figure out why they were billed in that order. The "longs" are a local folk art. If you die in Winnipeg it is with some consolation that no matter how haphazard and coincidental your life is or seems to you while you are living it, it will all make narrative sense when they publish your "long." At last, you become the hero in your own story.

Annie and I had a ritual. On Saturdays, if I wasn't working, I'd make coffee and she'd spread out the weekend obits and have at them with a yellow marker, reading out the highlights.

"This one's days consisted of walking his dog Oreo, washing his car and bargain hunting," she tells me. "This one was a bookkeeper for the airport chaplain. She enjoyed her dinner and had a last loving phone conversation with her sister, when she became very tired and slipped quietly away."

"During the phone conversation?"

"They don't say."

A "fiercely loyal" mom who loved romance novels, soft loving touches, red lipstick kisses on birthday cards and lottery tickets shares a page with a man who preferred farm implements: "The first combine he used was a pull-type Case combine with the first day of combining taking place on August 24, 1945. He continued to operate combines for the next 63 years ending with operating a Case 2388 combine this fall for a good portion of the 2007 harvest." The "longs" were like condensed Russian novels.

Of course I recognized names. There were people here I'd met, in my own peculiar context, at the crematorium or the Silver Doors. Their backstories humanized them, gave them families and hobbies and obsessions with heavy agricultural machinery, and the more I read the more the details gnawed at me. These are people, but at work they are also logistical puzzles to solve. Each case in the prep room is assessed by age and weight and muscle mass and obvious infirmities (bedsores, knife wounds). The goal, always, is to demonstrate, through the application of Permaglo and Rectifiant, that something as chaotic as death can be displayed. My days go more smoothly if I don't think so much about what, or rather whom, I'm doing. The work is emotionally lighter when the dead remain anonymous, former someones wrapped in white plastic who've already lost their someone-ness by the time they get to me. To embalm a man is one thing. To embalm a man who had a dog named Oreo is another.

"Here's one," Annie says. "'The family wishes to thank those management and staff of the Charleswood Care Centre, Health Sciences Centre, Victoria General Hospital, Grace Hospital and Winnipeg Regional Health Authority that treated Donna with respect and dignity, and wishes God's mercy on those that didn't.'"

Monday, the Factory: Respect and dignity for Mrs. H., stored until now in the cooler, means honouring her wish not to be embalmed. Before she died she made arrangements with Neil, and she told him she wanted to go out like her late husband, in what's called a Bodyguard. The Bodyguard is a human-sized Ziploc bag. We keep a roll of them in the prep room, bracketed to the wall like giant paper towels: the body goes in, the air is sucked out with a Shop-Vac and the free end is wound up and secured with a heavy plastic tie. The bagged body goes into the casket, and the casket goes to the funeral without any worry that the corpse will raise a gassy fuss during the service. There's no viewing. Neil discourages open-casket services with the Bodyguard, on the same principle as with the boat accident victim: Grandma in a Baggie is not a Beautiful Memory Picture. But we'll dress her anyway, "in case the family wants a peek," Adina says.

"You go right ahead," says Glenn. "I'm not touching a body that hasn't been embalmed."

No offence to Mrs. H., it's not her fault she's dead, but Glenn won't lay hands on her unless she's washed and Dis-Spray'd, and that's his choice. But as far as science goes he's on loose gravel. The idea that dead bodies, unless they're embalmed or shrink-wrapped, pose a health risk is undertaker propaganda. Mitford debunked this forty-plus years ago, citing, among others, a pathologist from San Francisco General Hospital who put it this way: if dead bodies sneezed, we'd have something to worry about, airborne pathogens and all, but they don't, making them less of a communicable disease risk than the living. You'd be more likely to catch something from the widow at the funeral than the body. Embalming is an aesthetic tool, and the Bodyguard keeps the corpse from ripening during the pastor's homily, but neither should be framed, nor sold, as public-health necessities. Yet they are sold that way. Not as a ruse, but because Glenn and Shannon and Eirik were taught that the dead are health hazards and that the undertaker's role is to protect the public. Remember the mantra. Treat every body as if it were your own father or aunt, but add the qualifier: wear rubber gloves, and keep a sensible distance until it's embalmed or burned.

The woman's belly and sides are deep green and her arms and legs are limp. The rigor mortis has already faded, and she's starting to bloat, so Adina opts for a quick one-two with the trocar to vent the gases, handing me the wand so I can try. Mostly I'm an orifice and nail boy in the prep room, but I take a stab at it, literally, trying to remember what Natalie told me: long easy thrusts in a radial pattern (it didn't sound so pornographic when she said it). I mark the spot above and to the left of the navel, and punch the tip of the trocar through the skin. The rubber vacuum hose does its frothy work, emptying the cavity of gas and fluid, in and out, in and out: her belly drops. I get the tip stuck once in her spine, but I pull hard and it comes out. I rinse and wipe the trocar, hang it on its hook, and try not to replay in my head the violent act I've just performed. What I still lack of course is the undertaker's skill at deconstructing death into smaller, manageable Cartesian problems, getting hung up instead on some nebulous big picture that says it's wrong, somehow, to run people through with a spear until you hit bone, even if they're already dead. The woman wants a funeral but she doesn't want to be embalmed; therefore, the remains must be secured in some other way, by venting and then packaging them in a plastic bag (no one mentioned putting her on ice, but at this point I'm not going to back-seat undertake). It's a rational response to a physical problem. I need to remember that. Gentle, caring violence is just part of the job.

We dress her in pink panties and nylons, a blue skirt and white blouse.

"It's come to this for you," Adina says. "Putting pantyhose on dead ladies."

That and impaling them. Once the woman is bagged and the air is drawn out with the Shop-Vac, Glenn picks her up and sets her in the casket. She's tiny and light. The family sent a teddy bear with her and Adina lays it at the lady's feet. She now looks like a freezer-wrapped salmon, her nose squashed against the plastic, her mouth open as if struggling for breath. As transgressive as it looks and feels, packaging this birdlike little lady, we've arguably performed a cultural duty here, like shamans of any other tribe. According to the anthropologist Nigel Barley, the Toraja of Sulawesi wrap their dead tightly in absorbent cloth to preserve them until the next stage of the ritual, which may not come for years. He met a man who kept his dead grandmother in his house as a storage shelf for his collection of alphabetically organized cassette tapes.

All I can do is watch and learn from the undertakers. In the prep room, Shannon carefully cradles a man's head, rubbing his earlobe, before punching a needle through his palate to secure the mouth. During a cremation, Glenn shows me how to open up the skull with an iron hook to expose the soft tissue to the open flame, thereby getting a cleaner burn. The bone is fragile from the heat, and the hook is heavy, so all it takes is a light tap. Reg, the trade client from the LeClaire Brothers (the one who likes extra-purple lips on his corpses) is a master at arranging the body for viewing, with a knack for problem cases. Last week, we loaded a body into his rental casket only to discover the man was too tall for the box. Adina tried bending his legs at the knees but the embalming had stiffened the joints, and they wouldn't stay bent. Pushing him up in the other direction just forced his head deep into the tufted fabric: no good for viewing. When Reg showed up he studied the problem as if he were building a bridge.

"Have you got a piece of wood about yay big?" he said. "A broomstick or a piece off a pallet."

Adina disappeared to the tool shed and came back with a length of two-by-two. Reg bent the man's legs again and used the wood to wedge the knees against the sides of the casket, then pushed the lower lid closed until it locked.

"Now he's stargazing," he said, referring to the position of the head: tilted back, not forward in the viewing position. "I need something under the pillow."

"Do you want a phone book?" Adina said. We keep a stack of old phone books in the dressing room closet for these occasions.

"No, that's too much. Do you have a couple of empty Dodge bottles?"

Adina rushed out and returned with two spent bottles of Permaglo, which Reg tucked under the casket pillow to prop up the man's head. By now Reg was on his knees, eyeing the lines of casket and corpse. "Let's pull him down juuuust a rabbit hair. That's it."

Reg stood back, arms out as if the whole thing might collapse like a tower of toothpicks if any of us breathed. The man in the casket looked puzzled but peaceful, and no one but us would know about the wood brace, unless the family opened the bottom lid, but they never do. Reg called for more colour on the lips and a dusting of powder. Women's lips are shiny, but men's lips are not. By now he and the body were haloed in makeup powder, and before closing the top lid, Reg laid a sheet of paper towel over the face, so it wouldn't smudge the fabric on the underside of the lid if Reg hit a bump on the way to the church. Shroud of Turin, he called it.

After he left, I swept the powder dunes off the floor.

"Cast a cold eye / On life, on death." Yeats wrote that, and then he died and they put it on his tombstone.

This morning the retorts are quiet. There are two removals pending on the board, and Glenn's on the phone with the Grace Hospital trying to shake a recent decedent out of a bureaucratic leg-hold trap. A man, eighty-eight, died in the emergency room at the Grace last night. The family wants a service in two days. The hospital is holding the body, awaiting the medical examiner's review, not sure yet whether they'll perform an autopsy, so we're stuck. The whole health-care–death-care complex is a jurisdictional chain, each link dependent on the idiosyncratic rules of the last. The hospital's position is simple: what's the rush? He won't be any less dead tomorrow. Our position is: there's gravedigging to order, people flying in from out of town for the service, catering to be booked, and the pastor has two funerals and a wedding Tuesday and Friday. While Glenn sits on musical hold with the Grace, Adina and I head out for the second removal at Deer Lodge, the chronic care hospital for "adults with complex needs" in St. James.

Adina used to work as an aide at the Lion's Club seniors home on Portage Avenue. She dressed people, put on their makeup and nail polish, sound training for a career in funeral service. She held hands with them as they died. The worst part of losing someone, she says, isn't always the grief: sometimes it's dealing with the funeral home, with the bureaucracy and the tyranny of choices. She heard this more than once from families of her old charges. People need as much care when they're dead as they do when they're alive, she says, maybe more so, and that's why she quit, to be of use on the other side. She likes that Neil doesn't push product, the caskets and urns and vaults. Her family is German Mennonite, "not the crazy religious kind, more the good-works missionary kind," and when we drive together on removals, she announces traffic patterns as if I might be blind.

"There's a car parked in the right lane," she says, and indeed there is.

We leave the van at the loading dock at Deer Lodge. In the lobby, strings of paper butterflies hang low from the ceiling. We pass a harpist playing a soapy Irish tune for an audience of one, a man in a wheelchair, his head strapped to a neck-rest, a long straw in his mouth, one hand tapping his tray. It's not clear if he's enjoying himself or signalling for help. A security guard leads us downstairs into the mechanical heart of the hospital, past orange boilers, green and red overhead pipes, the corpse of a busted front-load washing machine. We snake the stretcher through a hall of old recliner chairs to the main elevator, which takes us to the fourth floor. This is a ward removal. Ward removals are unlike Silver Doors removals in that you're getting the body right out of the bed in which it died. You're mixing with other patients and visitors and maybe even the family of the deceased. The goal is to act smartly and efficiently without traumatizing civilians by waving the dead body under their noses: get in, get out.

The nurse points out the room. Inside, two tiny ladies sit at the ends of their beds eating their lunches, each watching her own television set. The bed with the body is in the corner, behind closed drapes. To get there we have to negotiate the narrow space between the TVs.

"Good morning, ladies," Adina says, but they go on watching their pingy game shows.

The dead woman is younger than I had expected, maybe in her late fifties, pale and heavy with a look of calm repose, as if her features had already been set. She's wearing a nightie. Our options for getting her from a bed that's too low to a stretcher that's too high are limited. We whisper so as not to disturb the two ladies, but in fact we could holler and they'd never hear us over *The Price Is Right*, and besides, they don't seem interested in what we're doing.

The woman is two hundred pounds, maybe more. We decide to lower the stretcher to the floor and let gravity work with us, but the space is cramped, and if she falls, the three of us will be wedged between the bed and the wall, and they'll need the Jaws of Life to get us out. I put on the latex gloves and hug the woman under her arms. Our cheeks are touching. She's still warm and smells of baby powder. One–two–three, we hoist her from bed to stretcher and then one–two–three we ratchet the stretcher back up to its cruising height, lock it in position and cover the body with the fitted cloth sham.

"Have a nice day, ladies," Adina says as we squeeze the stretcher between the two television sets, careful not to knock them over.

One of the women, without taking her eyes off her show, waves her hand as if she were shooing a fly. In the hallway we pass a nurse and three visitors who look at us blankly, then carry on with some conversation about cooking a turkey.

There's something spooky about Deer Lodge. In a weird way I'm getting a sense of what it must be like to be dead: ignored and invisible. The elevator closes behind us and Adina says, this is just how people are: they act cool and imperturbable, not because they're bored with death but because they hardly ever see it. If they push it away it loses its potency. What makes this ring true is that she's describing my own evolving attitude at work: cool, distant, pretending it's normal to bash a human skull before lunch. But what I felt from the two little old ladies in the room was different, more hostile, as if they might've pelted us with their remote controls and Salisbury steaks if we'd stayed any longer. It felt like a rescue mission. We need to get the woman to the funeral home, where at least she'll be more welcome.

But when we arrive at the Factory we discover there's been a mix-up: the family had made arrangements with the other Bardal's on Sherbrook Street, then called us to pick up the body by mistake. Neil admits it's an uphill marketing challenge, competing with his own name and the funeral home in which he grew up; sometimes we get theirs and they get ours and it all needs sorting out. All we can do is let the lady chill in the cooler until Glenn drives her to Sherbrook, her second road trip of the day. When she leaves I can't help imagining her on some endless journey, from one funeral home to the next, from Bardal's on Sherbrook to Cropo's to Glen Lawn to Thomson In the Park, like the dead man in Kafka's "The Hunter Gracchus," who sails from port to port looking for shelter and rest but never finds it. I used to think death was the end of everything but it turns out it's just the start of a whole new set of troubles.

Sundays I work with Sherman, semi-retired and a friend of Neil's. Weekdays he teaches waste management to engineering students at Red River College and on weekends he covers removals and cremations at the Factory (for Sherman, semi-retired means working seven days a week). His philosophy of funeral service is twofold: First, manage the details, and this includes ensuring the tools that hang over the sort table match their painted silhouettes on the pegboard. One day I will need needle-nose pliers to close a fussy casket hinge, and if they're not on the pegboard, if there's only the empty painted-on needle-nose plier doppelgänger, a funeral may well be delayed. Second, never lose your awe of the dead human body. It is neither an object nor a widget to be processed and packaged, but a highly charged and haunted thing. He knows this because he's had run-ins with spirits at the crematorium, brought on, he says, by his own hubris.

"Spirits?"

"Yes."

"What did you see?"

"I didn't see anything," he says, "but you know how it is with these Icelanders, they believe the spirit stays with the body for a time. We had this one case, a man who'd hung himself, and I was alone with the body in the dressing room."

My neck tingles. I don't like to be alone in the dressing room with the embalmed dead, for my own mixed-up superstitious reasons. I once thought I heard a corpse clear its throat, as if it had something to announce, but it turned out to be the lawn mower outside.

"I said something about how selfish it is to put your family through such a thing, and then I felt it, like I'm being pushed from behind by a pair of strong hands. But of course no one's there."

"Then what happened?"

"That was it. After that I keep my mouth shut."

The point was that he'd spoken out of turn, acted superior. You should respect death and respect the dead, not out of fear, but because it's the proper human thing to do. He says hospitals have made us ashamed of death. When we die we should all be allowed to leave through the front door, same way we went in, "not [be] shit out the back through the so-called Silver Doors."

I think about this, the difference between respect driven by fear and respect driven by compassion, next time I'm in the dressing room with Shannon. The body to be dressed is male, tall and pudgy, with a thick neck and earlobes like dollar pancakes. His suit is hanging on a hook in the dressing room, still in its dry-cleaning bag, so I unwrap it, lay out his shirt and tie, and discover a problem: no underwear. And we have no spares. Shannon makes the judgement call: we'll dress him anyway. Time is burning and there are two more in the on-deck circle.

The pants are snug and the shirt's a size too small, maybe from an earlier, skinnier time in his life. Families often make this mistake. They pick the clothes they like, even if the dead man hasn't worn them in years. I struggle with the top button while Shannon ties the tie, Natalie-style, standing at the head end of the gurney, making a neat knuckle of a knot. But now the man looks choked and unhappy. One of his arms flops off the table as if in protest. Judgement call: Shannon finds a pair of scissors in the cupboard and cuts the collar. Sometimes you have no choice, she says.

"I told Eirik, when the Rapture comes and all these people get out of their caskets to meet their God, then what? Their clothes will fall off because we've cut them. And he said, God will come up with something for them to wear. I told him we'd take it case by case."

Once the man is dressed, she steps back to review. He's barefoot. The family forgot to send shoes and socks too. It's hard to peg, but there is something unwholesome about a man in a suit and tie and bare feet. Then, just as we're about to move on to the next case, Shannon spots a Safeway shopping bag on another hook, which I should've noticed, and inside of course are the missing shoes and socks, dentures in a blue plastic case (now moot: his mouth is already tied shut) and the underwear. Porn-star brief and black.

What to do? No one would ever know, same as with the man wedged in his casket with a two-by-two. Plus we'd be saving him from an eternity in ridiculous underpants. But Shannon doesn't blink. We undress him and start again. It's not our call, she says, it's the family's. This is the proper human thing to do.

Friday, at home: I've been making notes in my Big Book of Mortuary Tips (never lick anything in a funeral home, et cetera) and lurking on Facebook groups for funeral professionals, including the "I Embalm Dead People And I Enjoy It" group where students and apprentices trade tips on tough cases ("What's your cauterant of choice for skin slip?" "Why settle for a bulgy stomach?"), but when it comes to the intangibles, respect and dignity and the rookie undertaker's relationship with his dead, there's not much chatter, just a note from an embalmer in Florida, an open letter to his clients:

> We do not grieve for your dead, but we understand that this is difficult. We promise to work with your family, your clergy, and all the other disinterested bureaucratic bodies because of two reasons:
>   1. **You're paying us.**
>   2. **Because we care.**

Annie and I rent a DVD, a French film I've read about called *They Came Back*, which can best be described as a quiet, existential zombie movie. For reasons that are never explained, the dead of a modern French village simply wake up and leave their graves (in the same clothes and over-coiffed hairdos, presumably, they had going in), not to wreak brain-eating zombie havoc but to return home to their former lives. Only they've changed. Emotionally flat and unreachable, as if in some dopey half-dream state, they have difficulty reintegrating into society. They're just not as bright as they were before they died. After the shock of their return wears away, their presence evolves into a collective social issue (this is a very European film). Town meetings are held. Where will the dead sleep? Should they be eligible for health and social benefits? Should they get their old jobs back if they've lost the skills to perform them? Arenas are turned into shelters, make-work programs are devised. No doubt the movie is a parable about discrimination and the treatment of refugees, or a meditation on loss and the impossibility of connecting with those who have passed, but I can't help but read it literally: death is a logistical problem, and the dead, like kittens, God bless them, are both helpless and at times a bloody nuisance.

"It's like being at work," I say.

Poor Annie: this is what counts as Friday entertainment with a trainee undertaker. As a labour lawyer she has a different take.

"They need to organize," she says. "The dead need a union."

Nine

Grief Sneaks Past

'm sitting in the back seat of the Dodge 300, the black sedan we call the lead car. Adina's at the wheel. We're parked behind a low-rise apartment block off Pembina Highway where a road crew is laying down fresh pavement in a hissing cloud of blue exhaust and asphalt steam. It's noon, cloudless and hot. The air conditioner's on full blow. At the back door of the building, through the haze and the heat thermals, I can see a small, elderly woman in a pink tracksuit and flip-flops, hugging her purse and looking our way.

"That must be her," I say.

Mrs. G., recently widowed, contracted Neil to bury her husband for $3,500, which in the end, after taxes and what Richard calls "wiggle room," came to $3,800.15, less the thousand-dollar down payment received at the time of the arrangements. We're here to collect the rest of the money. This was Janice's idea. Like any business we deal with accounts receivable, and part of Janice's job is to chase down outstanding accounts. At the funeral home she's known as The Banker: before she became an undertaker she was a financial analyst at the Royal Bank of Canada. In this case she figured we'd be doing the widow G. a favour by driving her to her bank ourselves so she could cash her husband's death-benefit cheque and pay her bill without having to shell out for a taxi. The woman is frail and has no relations in Winnipeg. In the funeral trade they call this "after-care": maintaining a relationship with families after the funeral, helping them with the finicky administrative details that pile up when someone has died, not just so that they'll remember us the next time there's a death, but if that happens, so be it: good karma comes around. So there's no reason I should feel like a hired thug today, or that there's something sinister about two people in matching chinos and polo shirts hustling an old woman into an idling black sedan, even if it might look that way to the road workers who are watching us as we do just that.

"I hope I don't get confused," the woman says, once she's settled into the passenger seat.

Her head barely clears the neck-rest, and when she speaks her dentures clack. Before Adina can put the car into drive, Mrs. G. reaches into her purse and pulls out a government cheque for $2,500 and asks if it would be all right if she just signed it over to Adina, here in the car, so she can go back to her apartment. I catch Adina's eye in the rear-view mirror. She calls Annette, Neil's wife, and explains the development. Annette tells her to stick with plan A: take the woman to the bank. Besides, not to put too fine a point on it, she owes $2,800.15, not $2,500. When Adina explains this to

Mrs. G., the woman goes back to her purse, where she finds another $2,500 cheque and offers to endorse that one as well. Adina tells her again that she can't accept the cheques, and we drive off.

There's a lineup at the bank. Adina delivers the widow to the customer service desk, where a manager is called to manage, while I stand at the door, arms crossed, unsure of my role except as witness to a very awkward and uncomfortable transaction. Adina joins me.

"She keeps pulling out more cheques," she whispers. "She says she's confused since her husband died."

Soon the manager leads Mrs. G. to where we're waiting.

"Are you the daughter?" she says to Adina.

"No," Adina says, looking down. "We're the funeral home."

The manager blinks, looks at me, then counts out a short stack of cash into the widow's hands, who then passes it to Adina. We're just short the fifteen cents, the manager says, and Adina tells her we're not going to worry about the fifteen cents, which comes as a relief to me, since I thought I'd have to pick the woman up by her ankles and shake her upside down until the nickels fell out of her tracksuit pockets and her dentures skittered across the floor.

On the drive back to the apartment, the widow is silent. Adina offers to take her to Safeway for groceries, but the woman shakes her head no. She has a friend coming in from the country later in the week, she says. We drop her at the door and carry on, after-care accomplished, and all I can think is that I should've said something proper, that I'm sorry for her loss or I'm sorry we dragged her out of her apartment to ride with the Angels of Death, or whatever it is you say to strangers when they're so clearly lost in grief, or just lost. It occurs to me I've got used to the silent and unreachable dead, but that I don't have a clue what to do, or what to say, or how to act with the silent and unreachable living. At funerals I stand at the back handing out memorial cards, positioned as far from the families as I can get away with. Why? Grief scares me more than death; it may be as simple, and as complicated, as that.

Pointy-heads like Zygmunt Bauman say that previous generations, for whom death was natural and inevitable, had experience with grief but that we've lost it: we're insulated. Without a religious script or community to tell us how to act, families are left on their own. They come from a foreign country. Mourners speak a different language. All we can do is shrug, send a card, go to the funeral and talk about the weather, make some human gesture based on guesswork. Even worse, Bauman goes on, we've replaced the comforts of religion and tribe with a near-hysteric faith in technology and medical science, to the point where we've deconstructed death into a series of solvable puzzles: cancer can be beaten with drugs, heart disease can be avoided through yoga and diet, and aging is a problem of biochemistry and grumpiness. So if someone dies, it means something's gone wrong. It may not be the dead man's fault, but he's implicated, and so are his wife and children. Who messed up? It's not normal, and the family wears the stigma. Add a third factor: the fetishization of happiness. Sad people just don't fit the social bell curve. We worship entertainment as much as technology, and there's nothing less entertaining than grief. That's why God invented lorazepam, and selective serotonin reuptake inhibitors, and vodka and television—which in my experience work best in combination, with a pizza. Three strikes against the modern widow: she is exotic, suspect, and she brings us down. So she keeps her grief to herself. Geoffrey Gorer says we treat mourning as a weakness, a self-indulgence, and that a modern widow would no more throw herself on the casket than she would take off her clothes or pee in public.

So what does she do? At the funeral she plays hostess. I've seen this at services. I've seen widows and widowers, children and siblings working the room, making sure their guests are watered and fed, thanking them for taking the time to come to the funeral. During the eulogy, or when Shirley and Ed, our musicians-for-hire, sing "Wind Beneath My Wings," a funeral standard, the Kleenex is passed around, but these are moments of sanctioned, performative grief. Only a monster wouldn't cry. Otherwise the family leads by example: they're brave, selfless, the hardest-working people at the service. The widow is often the last to leave. She gathers the flowers and packs the photo boards and helps clear dishes, which is my job, but what a relief—and this is my guilty admission—that she's not a mess. I wouldn't know what to do. Thankfully she knows her role in the drama. Joan Didion calls the funeral an anodyne, a brief bit of theatre after which well-wishers go back to work and their normal lives. Later of course the widow is left on her own to go through her husband's clothes, cancel his credit cards, and stare at the door waiting for him magically to reappear.

But that's none of our business.

I worked a service for a woman who died young, of cancer. After Richard and I had stacked the chapel chairs and rolled the comfy couches and coffee tables in for the reception, to create the usual atmosphere of post-funeral fellowship, the widower held court. Men shook his hand and discussed fishing. One of them asked, "So what are you going to do now?" The widower thought about this, and with his wife a few feet away in a La Precia urn flanked by two lit candles, he said: "I think I'll find myself a pretty squaw and go live in the bush for a while." His friend smiled stiffly, and another laughed too loudly. If the man was joking, he was bombing. But it seemed to me he was doing what the script told him to do: put people at ease by lightening the mood. That was his role.

But sometimes, rarely, real grief sneaks past. Funeral service and the rituals we choreograph are meant to tamp down the wild, animal fact of death, but I've seen gaps open up, brief flashes of reality, and it's like watching a glass vase fall and hit the floor.

When Neil renovated his crematorium in the '80s he put in the Committal Space because he wanted to bring ritual to an otherwise technical event, the cremation of the body. For him, cremation and burial were the same act, the final disposition: in time all that's left are bones and a few teeth, it's just that cremation gets there faster. People gather at the graveside for a committal ceremony. Why not do the same at the mouth of the retort? It's how they do it in England. A pastor does his thing, makes the sign of the cross on the lid of the box with dirt, and the family watches the casket go into the oven the same way they might watch it lowered into the hole at the cemetery. But taboos are hard to shake. The so-called Committal to the Flames is a hard sell in Winnipeg. More often families will have a short service in the Committal Space and then leave. We watch the last car disappear down Notre Dame Avenue, and only then do we roll the box back stage for the final event. I call this Committal Lite.

A family of three arrives at the Factory. They've brought their pastor, a major from the Salvation Army, in uniform, and while Adina leads them to the Space, Glenn and I set up the body in the casket nook, behind closed drapes. The body's in a cardboard cremation container. There'll be no viewing. Instead we lay a quilted pall overtop, and then Adina joins us.

"I don't know what I'm doing," she says. "Where's Neil?"

Glenn tells her to bring them water. Mourners are always thirsty. She fills four cups from the cooler, and I follow, to hold the door, and we run into one of the family members, a woman, possibly the widow.

"Are we supposed to pray in here or what?" she says.

"Yes," Adina says. "Neil will be here shortly."

With little else to do until the boss arrives, Glenn and I wait in the dressing room. He reads *Esquire* and I wet-mop a floor I wet-mopped yesterday. Then Adina rushes in, this time waving a pocket copy of the New Testament.

"It's a Committal to the Flames!" she hisses. "They want a Committal to the Flames!"

We snap into action, or rather Glenn does and I follow. First we roll the body from the nook into the tight workspace near Retort Two, hoist the box onto the scissor-lift, whip off the pall and open the retort door. The overhead fluorescents are shut off in favour of more flattering pot lights, and Glenn unfolds a pair of accordion screens on either side of the retort to block the view to the rest of the backstage, with the tools and the sort table and the vacuum-hood that looks like a fat evil snake. But there's no way to dress up this room, with its concrete floor and all the overhead ductwork and the big black mouth of the open retort. The fake dusty ficus plant in the corner just makes it worse. We can hear Neil's voice, and Adina runs out to brief him.

"He doesn't look happy," she says on her return.

"When does he ever look happy?" says Glenn.

I brush the dust off my shirt.

Adina's stomach growls. "I'm starving," she says.

Glenn briefs us: on Neil's cue we'll roll the box from the scissor-lift into the retort, being mindful not to jam it against the stone wall, or we'll have to pull it out and try again, which will disturb the gravity of the event. Now my stomach growls: performance anxiety. I've humped dozens of boxes into the retort without incident, but now, with an audience, I can picture the box sliding the wrong way off the lift and onto some mourner's foot. The backstage door opens. First Neil then the pastor enter, the pastor holding a bible and patting his thin hair with a shaky hand, then the family. The woman is twisting a Kleenex. One of the men is wearing a black eagle T-shirt and red suspenders. He holds the woman at her elbows. Then, as the pastor reads from Scripture, how the Lord is our shepherd and we shall not want, and Neil makes the sign of the cross on the head-end of the box, the woman reaches out and lays her head on the lid and says, simply, "No." The man in suspenders helps her up. She looks at the open retort, then at us, and she gasps, a short sharp yelp, like the sound a dog makes if you step on its paw just hard enough to surprise it. My hands are shaking like the pastor's. I shouldn't be here; this is too private. I feel like a voyeur.

Neil nods and we push, one–two–three. The cardboard whines on the steel rollers of the lift. The box goes in smoothly, the door to the retort slides down and the rollers on the lift keep spinning. Glenn engages the fan and the machine roars to life, its walls rattling. As if they've seen and heard enough to get the point, the woman and the two men depart, followed by Neil and the preacher, leaving us to finish the job.

"That's nothing," Glenn says. "We had a guy, a drug dealer, he did a header off the Maryland Hotel. His girlfriend was in here, she threw herself on the casket and all these other drug dealers had to haul her off."

But it wasn't nothing. That animal noise, quick as it happened, was no performance. That was the real thing. Unfiltered fear or grief or a stormy mix of both. It seemed to me she looked into the open retort and knew: he's going in and he's not coming out. And for a beat, she forgot the rules about keeping her pain to herself.

Tuesday: Richard is juggling a tight schedule at Aubrey. He's booked an ash interment, otherwise known as an urn burial, for Chapel Lawn at 12:45, and another family is due at noon for arrangements. We need to be done with the arranging family and out the door by 12:30 to make it to the cemetery on time. I pack the 12:45 urn in a blue velvet bag, the standard travelling kit, but next to the urn I find a wristwatch. Richard tells me to put it in the bag, it belonged to the deceased, and he'll give it back to the family when we get there.

"Remind me," he says.

The noon family arrives, two women and their husbands. The women are sisters: their mother has died. She was Catholic and they've already booked Father Sam at Holy Rosary for a visitation and graveside service, followed by a catered gathering.

"My mother wanted a viewing," the first sister says. "She was very definite about that. But the four of us are very uncomfortable with it. Is a half-hour enough?"

"An hour," Richard says.

"The point is I really don't care," she says. "We need to do it and then close the casket for the service. We'll have a photo on the casket."

And flowers: azaleas, hibiscus, calla lilies, carnations, and something blue to make it all "pop."

"Okay. Father Sam will have a blessing, bless the cross and hand it to you, then we're off to the cemetery. Send your flowers straight to Holy Rosary, we'll go half an hour before to set up. How many people are speaking at the memorial?"

"I'm speaking," the other sister says. "It's terrifying, but it's closure for me."

"Coordinate your efforts," says Richard. "Keep it to four or five minutes. Once you start it's hard to stop. But that part you sort out. Our part finishes at the grave. Now, the removal's been done, the embalming's done—we need clothing."

"Can you take her glasses?" the first sister says, sliding them across the table to Richard. "She'd want her glasses." Her voice catches.

The four of them stare at the wire-rimmed glasses, smudged with fingerprints. Richard puts down his pen and folds his hands.

The first sister looks up. "Can we get some Kleenex, please?"

Again I'm caught, waiting for an intimate moment to pass. Kleenex is distributed, cups of water too. At 12:30, Richard rises to signal the end of the conference. Hands are shaken. I scoot to the back room to get the blue velvet pouch and we follow the family out the door. They go their way, and we head off for Chapel Lawn for the 12:45 ash interment.

When we turn in to the cemetery, I can see a small group of people trekking across the grass. We pull up near the grave, which has already been dug, just a post-hole for the urn; it's dressed with AstroTurf even though it's summer and the real grass is lush. Two women and two children, a boy in a fedora and a tot in blue rubber boots swinging a Hot Wheels umbrella, gather around the hole. There's no preacher today: Richard is clergy-by-proxy. He reads a passage from the Anglican short book, then, holding the blue velvet pouch by the strings, kneels and lowers it into the grave. The watch. I forgot to remind him about the watch. I whisper in his ear, and he reaches into the bag and pulls it out.

"Do you want me to bury it or would you like to keep it?" he says, passing it to one of the women.

"Oh," she says with a sharp gasp. "It's her watch."

She turns it over in her palm.

"It's still ticking," she says. She hands it to Richard, who drops it back in the pouch.

If we're supposed to build a protective wall between our customers and the nasty fact of death, it's a fragile wall. All it takes to punch through it is a wristwatch, or a pair of eyeglasses, some real object made suddenly unreal by its new, unwelcome context. To Richard and me the glasses are a prop. Same with the watch. To the families, they're the women who wore them.

As if to signal the end of the ceremony, the little boy stamps in a puddle and chases a goose. The family leaves, and Richard and I head for the car, where I tell him I'm sorry that I dropped the ball and turned a simple graveside ritual into a cheap magic trick: ta-da! He might as well have pulled out a rabbit. He says it's no big deal, what you do is stay loose and act like it's normal. Never draw attention to mistakes. For all they know, pulling jewellery out of the grave at the last minute is part of the Anglican rite.

According to Adina's textbook on interpersonal skills training, the most vital characteristic of the successful undertaker is "the ability to convey accurate empathy." This I find wildly unhelpful, but let's pick it apart. For a stranger: I get your pain, but not overly so, let's be honest here. We just met. But I do feel accurate empathy. Not sincere empathy, which would mean I feel it like I feel love or a cold coming on, but accurate, which means within the reasonable pluses and minuses of bona fide empathy. And did I say "feel"? I meant "convey." It's a performance, a kind of method acting, but why not cut the textbook some slack and say it's a benign, well-intentioned faux emotion-ette intended to put the grieving at ease. The corporate funeral homes use fake empathy as a lever, Neil says. They understand your pain, and they understand how pain can be relieved through the act of shopping. Neil picks on the corporates: they're a broad barn of a target. But he's right, people do throw money at grief, and he would know. It happens at his funeral home too.

Monday, the Factory is buzzing. Shannon and Adina are wrestling with a problem case in the dressing room, a man who was dead a week in his apartment before he was found by the usual route: a peculiar smell. *What is that smell?* These are ominous words to hear in an apartment building. And the smell is what hits me when I walk into the dressing room. It's more of a taste than a smell. It reaches past your throat and squeezes your liver. There's a strong oily base of fish rot, with hints of black licorice and cooked turnip and burning rubber. This is the decomposing human body. Shannon and Adina were both in on the weekend trying to prep the poor man, poking for collapsed arteries and trying to bring moisture back to his dried lips and fingertips and ears, which are now black. The top of his head is red and blotchy. He looks like one of the mummified bodies from the Franklin expedition chipped out of the ice. The man deserves to be buried and have done with it, but instead we're dressing him in a suit, because his sister wishes to view him.

"She says she needs to get a few things off her chest," says Shannon.

Adina holds up his shirt, still in the store package.

"Is this periwinkle?" she says.

I put on the full prep-room gear, mask and rubber gloves, and together we wrestle the man into what Shannon calls the space-suit, a full-body form-fitting white plastic garment, with arms and legs like a union suit. This will keep down the smell during the visitation. Adina scoops San Veino powder into the spacesuit ("for use on: cancers, bedsores, floaters, burned bodies, incisions, autopsied bodies, mutations"). It smells of pine air-freshener, but it's fighting a losing battle. We wrap the plastic suit at the wrists and ankles with packing tape, then wrap more tape around his torso, and the San Veino powder puffs out in clouds. I feel it sting my eyes. There's no debate over whether to cut the clothes: the shirt and jacket are sliced clean through the back and tucked around him.

"Holy moly," Shannon says, checking her watch.

The sister is due in twenty-five minutes. I winch the body into the casket, a Champagne sealer, the most expensive piece of furniture in Neil's showroom. Shannon paints his face with a thick layer of Dodge foundation, but the black shows through, so she lays on more until he appears plastered. We roll the casket into the Committal Space, and Shannon sets a chair at the head end, then changes her mind and moves it to face the centre of the casket, so the sister won't be staring down at his red blotchy scalp. He's a carnival attraction, a rough rubbery fright of a former man, but we've given the woman what she asked for, and paid for: the most one-sided conversation she'll ever have in her life.

The sister is with him half an hour, then forty-five minutes, and by five o'clock when it's time to go home she's still there.

The next day, to the man's relief, I'm sure, he's buried at Brookside. Twenty people gather at the graveside with no volunteers to bear pall, so Glenn and Neil and Adina and I corral two Brookside gravediggers in Carhartt overalls and the six of us carry the casket from the hearse to the hole, where, after a long week of cooking in his apartment, being prepped and jacked into plastic long-johns, painted and then left with a sister he hasn't seen in five years, he'll finally get his rest.

Neil says you'll go mad trying to parse the motivations of families. Grief is mixed up with guilt and shame and the dynamics of family politics. Sons and daughters will compete for the role of Most Crushed by the Loss, they'll fight over the menu for the reception as if it's the dead man's estate, and Neil's seen families break apart over the issue of where to emboss a fish or a tree on the urn. The best we can do is tell people there are no rules. Conventional wisdom has mashed Elisabeth Kübler-Ross's five stages of dying into the five stages of grief, which was never her intention when she wrote *On Death and Dying*. There are no stages. But families still do what's expected of them. They follow a social script. The script does not leave room for a heavy sigh of relief, though Neil says it's sometimes the case that when someone dies your life will get better, not worse—especially if the dead man suffered a long illness or was simply an irredeemable prick. Pricks die too. Part of the funeral director's job is to give people room *not* to be sad.

"I had this lady," he says, "she told me she wanted her husband's ashes to bury in her garden. I told her that sounded like a nice idea. She said, you don't get it. I want to *cement* the sonofabitch into it."

Ten

Two Hundred Cubic Inches of You

I need to spend more time at the sort table. The trade clients are complaining about the quality of the cremated remains. They say they're used to nice, clean, ivory bread flour, and what they've been getting is dingy and grey—not what they expect from Neil. Neil is not the cheapest crematorium in town, but his brand depends on attention to detail, which includes the colour of the cremated remains (in the industry they're called "cremains," but we don't stoop to euphemisms here, except that we call embalming the "preparation," and the hearse the "coach," and the funeral the "service." In any case, "cremains" sounds too much like a name-brand coffee whitener). There are two reasons why Neil insists on a hand sort. First of all, he wants to be sure that when families scatter remains in the rose garden out front there are no impurities that'll choke the flowers. Second, it's an aesthetic issue.

Some crematoria dump everything into the processor and have at it. Neil thinks it matters to people that the bag they get back is as close to pure former-human as us Factory monkeys can make it. That's why he charges more than the local deep-discount bake-and-shakers. It's the difference between a silk tie and a clip-on.

So what am I doing wrong? I dump the pan of bones onto the steel table and crunch through it with the heavy magnet, which brings up a few staples and a black pants zipper. These go into the slag box, which will be emptied later into the Dumpster. The magnet is covered in red powder, which I take to be iron, from the blood, but Glenn says it's just red powder that sticks to the magnet. Now I'm facing a pile of shattered bones, including one intact humerus and a snapped femur that I toss into the processing machine with a clang. The long bones feel like unglazed pottery. The skull is already broken into ladle-shaped pieces (Glenn would've smacked it with the iron hook during the cremation to expose the brain to the fire), and I use a rib to poke through the pile for the medium-sized chunks, the sponge-candy vertebrae and the crumbly ball joints. Most of it's too shattered to identify, although a skilled sorter can usually spot the hyoid bone, one of the smallest bones in the body (after the bones of the inner ear), which sits at the base of your tongue, not much bigger than a clipped thumbnail. To me it all looks like broken seashells, and as I sweep through with my hands, looking for more foreign objects, pieces get under my fingernails. They're sharp. They hurt. I should wear gloves, but the heavy suede work gloves don't give me the fine motor control I need to pick out the disposables.

The heartbreakers are the black bits of coral, and there's local dispute over their source: so much of this stuff sticks to the inside of the skull, it could be cerebral tissue, or cartilage, or possibly embers from caskets. I've seen wood embers that still glow on the sort table. Blow on them and they glow brighter. If these coral bits wind up in the processor, that's how you get your unappetizing grey powder. They're the source of my problem. So I flick them aside with a screwdriver, into a separate pile for the slag bin, and sweep the white bits into the processor with a horsehair brush. This goes on for half an hour. It's hypnotic, Zen-like. I imagine how long it might take me, with tweezers and a tube of Testors airplane glue, to rebuild an entire skeleton: weeks, months, years. I would like to do this one day and shoot a movie about it, and then sell it to a studio that makes movies about meaningless, obsessive and doomed projects and the obsessive and doomed people behind them, like the fellow who built a castle out of pop bottles.

Once the remains are sorted, the processor grinds them into powder with its heavy blender-blades. Six minutes on Purée. Then the powder is poured into a thick plastic bag, using an old, dented desk-lamp shade as a funnel, and the bag is heat-sealed three times. It's important to put the ID sticker on the bag before you fill it, otherwise you could end up with three identical blank bags full of powder at the end of the day and no way to tell who's who. We're all roughly equal at this stage, 200 cubic inches, or 5 pounds, of mineral powder, mostly calcium phosphate, and the DNA's gone up the chimney, so there's no room for mistakes. Families want to scatter or bury *their* loved one's calcium phosphate, not someone else's.

Today's bagful is the colour of driveway gravel. Close, but not gleaming. I need a keener eye or a better screwdriver. Packing the bag into the urn, a square wooden "starter model," as Shannon calls it, I discover it won't fit. There's at least a cup too much of him. I try to put the lid on the urn and it topples off. I bring the urn to the front desk to show Janice, and Jean, the receptionist.

"Oh my," says Jean. "There's a whole extra little old lady there."

Janice suggests splitting the remains into two separate bags, but then checks herself: the family will think we're trying to sell them a second urn. It takes Glenn to come up with the solution. He finds a flimsier plastic bag in a box on a shelf I didn't even know existed, uses it to line the container and then decants the remains from the original, heavier bag directly into the urn. With the flat side of a hammer he tamps down the powder. It's tight but now the lid fits, and he screws it in place.

"He was a meat packer," Jean says, holding up the man's tick-sheet. "That explains it."

And it does. A lifetime of manual labour bred a man who, in the end, yielded more than the industry standard of 200 cubic inches of cremated remains. This is the problem with standards in an industry where the raw materials are annoyingly non-standard. An off-the-shelf casket measures 24 inches across but the fact is that a growing number of corn-fed North Americans do not. They have a hard enough time finding belts, or fitting into airplane seats, and when they die, they represent an under-addressed market. In answer, Batesville, one of the big casket manufacturers, has already retooled its plants, launching a line of plus-sized caskets called Dimensions ("New Caskets to Offer a Little Extra Room for Life's Final Journey"), and the Goliath Casket, Inc., of Lynn, Indiana, which covets the big-and-tall niche, manufactures a 52-inch-wide casket (almost four and a half feet) nicknamed, among the likes of us, the B-52. That's for burial. For cremation, the problem is more complicated.

"Have you heard?" Adina whispers to me. She's come over to watch Glenn work on the overstuffed urn, as if he were a cardiac surgeon performing a pig-heart transplant.

"Heard what?"

"We're getting a body from MacKenzie's tonight. Five hundred pounds. The fire department had to carry him out of his house. We're cremating him."

"What do you mean tonight?" We never cremate at night.

"Are you kidding?" she says. "He's 500 pounds! He's going to smoke like crazy. Neil wants us to do it after dark so no one can see."

I'm used to 98-pound grandmothers; it's work enough getting them into the retort, since that's 98 pounds of literal dead weight. A 500-pound man is more than five grandmothers in one pair of pants. And how much of that is raw fuel? He'll blow the door off the retort, if he fits. The oven's not exactly an airplane hangar: even with a normal casket it's a tight squeeze. I have to see this. Adina and Glenn are booked for the cremation and I volunteer to help.

The Factory at night is a menacing sight. Locking up my bike, the only lights I can see are those of the airport to the west, and the open garage door of the crematorium, where Adina and Glenn are waiting for the delivery. Behind me, Brookside cemetery is black. Adina seems giddy. She brought her ten-year-old son along. He's in the arrangement room doing his homework. Glenn's nervous. He's seen big bodies in the retort before: the fat melts and pools and then burns out of control, and sometimes it'll weep through the gap under the retort door and you have to use kitty litter to soak it up. The biggest body he's cremated was 300 pounds and this man's twice that size.

I can see headlights now on Notre Dame Avenue. A grey hearse pulls into the lot, riding low. It backs up to the open garage door. The driver is Ken, one of the undertakers from MacKenzie's, our trade client from Stonewall. MacKenzie's is run by two young sisters who took over the business when their father died of a heart attack while driving home from an interment. Most of their business is traditional burial for a rural clientele, but they also control a valuable piece of turf, the highway between Winnipeg and cottage country to the north, where, if there's a fatal car accident, they usually get the first call. They use us for cremations.

Ken opens the back door of the hearse. Inside is a plywood box as wide as it is tall, with yellow rope handles. The top of the box touches the roof of the vehicle. Ken made it himself. First he prepped the body so the family could view it (it took him an hour, standing on a stool, just to close the autopsy Y-incision), then he built the box, from scratch, around the body, to save the family from having to order some oversized custom casket that would just wind up in the retort. It takes all four of us to drag it from the hearse onto the groaning scissor-lift. The trip between garage door and retort is twenty feet and it takes us ten minutes. The wheels catch in the gaps between the tiles on the floor, and halfway there, we get stuck in a drain-cover, and have to rock the lift back and forth to free it. If it tips, and I'm under it, they'll have to peel me off the floor like a cartoon cat, take me home, ring the doorbell and slide me through the mailbox for Annie to find, but it doesn't tip. We reach the retort and I pump the jack-handle, leaning all my weight into it, until the box is level with the mouth of the oven.

Glenn releases the lock on the rollers and we push, the wood grinding on the stone retort floor, until the box clears the door. Then he stacks a line of bricks at the lip of the oven to act as a dyke, to keep the excess fat from pouring out.

The door closes, secondary burners are lit, and we watch the temperature rise. At 500 degrees, Glenn hits the primaries to ignite the box. Through the peephole I can see the jets, then the sides of the container catch and collapse and fly-ash from the man's burning clothes scatters in the turbulence.

The machine is factory-tested to top out at 2,400 degrees Fahrenheit. "But I've never seen it get there," says Glenn.

"I say it won't go higher than 2,000," Adina says.

I can see where this is going.

"Want to make it interesting?" I say.

We agree on the parameters of the bet. Whoever gets closest to the maximum temperature without going over, *Price Is Right*–style, wins, and the other two will buy Tim Hortons coffee and muffins. I opt for a conservative 1,800 degrees. Ken declines a piece of the action.

The gauge hops, 20, 60 degrees at a time. It passes 1,000 degrees without looking back and steadies at 1,500. Come on, 1,800. Then 1,800 flies by without a blink, and 1,900 and 2,000. The cover on the porthole rattles. Glenn taps it open, and all we can see is a white wall of flame. Tongues of fire lick out from under the retort door, and we stand back. Glenn picks up the fire extinguisher and aims the nozzle, ready to pull the trigger. I'm no veteran cremationist, but fire *outside* the retort doesn't seem right. The floor shakes.

Adina calls me to the side door and I follow her outside, to the parking lot.

"Look," she says.

Orange sparks fly up from the chimney, swarms of them, and every few seconds a blue flame shoots out with an audible *whoosh*. On the one hand this is all physics, the second law of thermodynamics, which says a closed system, if given a nudge, will seek to increase its entropy. The more stored energy there is, the more heat and light and sparks and blue jets and chaos you get, and this man is a load of stored energy. But physics can't explain this amazing light show. In Hindu cultures the body is burned on an open-air ghat using fire brought from the dead man's house by the oldest son (or, in the case of the mother, the youngest son), and once the fire takes, the son will break open the skull with a bamboo pole to release the spirit, just as we do with the iron hook. Japanese Buddhists will only cremate on certain days of the week, never on *tomobiki*, or "friend-pulling days," when the spirit, once it's freed by the heat, might grab the closest mortal and take him along to the afterlife. With burial what you get is a slow release of potential energy, the second law dragged out over twenty years, but with cremation it happens in a flash, and if you watch, at night, from the crematorium parking lot, you can see something spectacular, either billions of chemical bonds breaking or the spirit being freed, depending on whether you've put your faith in Isaac Newton or some god. I can't help but think I'm witnessing a kind of second life.

The temperature never goes past 2,000 degrees. There's no more fire under the retort door, no conflagration. Glenn's theory is that because the body was prepped, the chemicals rendered the fat less flammable. In fact, as I take another look through the peephole, the white blaze has cleared now and the body is glowing under the primary burners, not so much flaming as roasting.

"This is going to take a while," Glenn says, "but at least the building isn't going to burn down."

He'll stay and wait for the cremation to run its course and then process the remains so Ken can pick them up in the morning. The rest of us go home.

In the morning, Adina brings us Tim's coffee and cranberry muffins. She seems to have missed the point of winning the bet. The ashes of the 500-pound man are already bagged and sitting on the shelf for pickup. There's not much left: an average batch, less even than the big-boned meat packer.

It's hard to overstate the impact these benign bags of ashes have had on the industry in the last twenty years or so. Every bag represents a potential loss of cemetery revenue, the mothballing of a fleet of funeral director's vehicles, hard times for the florist, the clergyman, the tombstone maker, and the casket and vault manufacturers. Twenty years ago that body would've been buried with fanfare, but now, anything goes. The cremationist's boast is that the remains, after two hours at 1,600 degrees (or more), are inert and sterile. Now there's no charmed and haunted and perishable body on your hands: you can take the ashes home and display them on the mantelpiece like a Hummel figurine or scatter them to the wind or mulch them into Neil's rose garden, wall them into a columbarium niche or, if your mood is old-school, bury them in a grave.

But whatever you do, an option exists that never existed before: you can handle the ritual yourself, or skip it entirely. All you need from the undertaker is his removal van and his retort and one of his heat-sealed bags, and even then there's no law in Manitoba that says you can't pick up the body from the hospital yourself in an SUV. Cremation is liberating. And cheaper, of course. The average direct cremation in the United States in 2007 cost $1,500, while the National Funeral Directors Association pegged the average full-fig funeral at $7,000, before cemetery fees. I've seen the increasing number of weekday shorts in the *Free Press* announcing that "cremation has already taken place, and at the request of family there will be no service." People are taking death into their own hands, clawing it back from the undertaker.

When Kurt Cobain died, his widow, Courtney Love, had him cremated. Some of his ashes were buried in the garden, and some she spooned into a Buddhist shrine she and Kurt kept at their Seattle home. She approached two local cemeteries about interring a third bit of Kurt in a permanent spot. One declined, and the other asked for $100,000 a year to cover upkeep and security, knowing that Kurt's grave would become a shrine, a mecca for overripe plaid shirt–wearing Grunge pilgrims and romantic kids who weren't even born when Nirvana released *Nevermind*, but who would presumably make a mess of the place. That was the end of Courtney's relationship with the mainstream funeral industry. She packed the rest of Kurt, along with her wedding dress, into a teddy-bear knapsack and travelled the country. At hotels she'd empty the sack for private communion, warning the cleaning staff not to be overzealous about any ashes they found on the furniture: she'd sweep them up herself.

Her travels brought her to Ithaca, New York, to a Buddhist monastery. The monks welcomed her and agreed to consecrate the remains by mixing them with clay to make votive tablets or *tsatsas*, and to pray Kurt into his next bardo. Courtney poured out the contents of the teddy bear: the wedding dress, now covered in ashes, and the rest of her late husband. "We inhaled a little bit of Kurt that day," someone who was there told *Esquire* magazine. There were enough remains for twelve *tsatsas*, which, as of February 1996, when *Esquire* printed their story, Courtney had yet to pick up. The head monk explained he was happy to help, but the fact was, "We're not the final stop. We're no Graceland."

I knew there'd been problems with what the industry called "wildcat scatterings" at Disney rides. Cast Members (i.e., the kids who worked the rides, some of whom spoke to the insiders' Web site MiceAge.com) reported that people had been smuggling ashes into the Pirates of the Caribbean ride and the Haunted Mansion, tossing them from DoomBuggies and gumming up the works— making long days longer for the custodial staff, who had to use special HEPAfilter vacuums to clean up the mess. In Disney-speak, a "HEPA Cleanup" was code for an unauthorized death ritual on park property. Disney's official position is that it never happens. But ashes are scattered at ballparks and golf courses, and in the United Kingdom, the Manchester City football club had so many wild-catters that it built a separate memorial garden, to keep cremated remains off the pitch. Management at Jane Austen's house in Hampshire had to ban scattering. So many people were using the garden, the gardener was worried about the health of the flowers.

In Neil's father's time, the undertaker owned the ritual. In his grandfather's time, even the clergy deferred to the funeral direc-tor. Now Neil faces a paradox: his stiffest competition, after the corporate chains and the deep-discount cremationists who adver-tise their low-low prices in full-page ads and on the sides of Winnipeg Transit buses, comes from his own customers, who can do what they want with their bag of remains. They don't need his hoary old customs. Neil decided a long time ago he wouldn't take the deep-discount route, since he'd need insane volume to survive, and besides, it wasn't funeral service so much as a kind of assembly line: retorts blazing all day, no time for hand sorting or ceremony. He believes in the ceremony. I think he's right, to a point: there's some value in marking the event, even with a quiet prayer or a drink at the pub. Still, why, in a tough economy, would I pay to mourn in his Committal Space with coffee and dainties and a quick scattering in the rose garden when I've got my own rose garden at home? I'm no longer bound by tradition and religious strictures, or the physical fact of the body. And while we're at it, if the local deep-discounter charges $695 for a direct cremation, why would I pay three times as much to Neil to get the same result? If there's one thing I now know intimately, it's that there's not much to distinguish one set of ashes from another: cremated remains are cremated remains, even after hand sorting.

But Neil insists that when you're dealing with a man who's operating solely on an economic imperative, you're not dealing with an undertaker. You're putting the body in the hands of a canny businessman, where the intangibles like care and respect and dignity don't necessarily come into play. But does that matter? It might, if the body's your mother or father or wife. Can you trust the businessman? He picks up the body and days later you get the ashes. What happened in the time in between? Are you sure of what's in the bag? With Neil, you can come and watch the cremation. Or, you don't even have to watch: as long as you know you can, he's played his trump card—transparency, and the peace of mind that comes with it. What an amazing mind game.

Mention Tri-State to any death-care worker and she'll bow her head. The Tri-State Crematory, Inc., in Walker County, Georgia, first came under suspicion in 2002 when, on an anonymous tip, the Environmental Protection Agency found a skull and human bones on the property. Within weeks they'd turned up more than three hundred decomposed corpses, some half buried in a swamp, some stored in a shed, "like cordwood" (most reports of the time couldn't resist the image). The owner, Ray Brent Marsh, was arrested and charged with desecrating the dead and theft by deception: instead of cremating the bodies, he'd dumped them and then given the families bags of concrete dust. As Stephen Prothero, author of *Purified By Fire*, an amazing history of cremation in North America, wrote at the time, it's not like Marsh was mad. The judge in the case pressed to keep it all in perspective: the man hadn't murdered anyone. He was a father and a local basketball coach and a respected businessman, yet in the course of his business somehow he thought it was Okay to leave a baby's corpse to rot in a rusting hearse. Why? It was cheaper for him to dispose of the bodies than burn them, given the cost of fossil fuels. In a way it was a rational act. But of course the community was horrified, and that, Prothero writes, is because they were haunted: the dead deserve rest, and these dead had been abandoned. They feared them, but wanted to protect them at the same time. What made Ray Brent Marsh different from his neighbours was not that he was insane, but that he'd lost all reverence for and fear of the dead. The charge was theft but the crime was moral. He pleaded guilty and got twelve years.

In Princeton, British Columbia, a funeral director was charged with thirty-four counts of fraud and negligence for allegedly giving the wrong cremated remains to families, or in some cases filling the urns with kitty litter. A woman who'd buried her husband's ashes in his favourite hockey skates, or thought she had, later learned the ashes were somebody else. The skates were dug up, cleaned out and reburied once the right husband was restored. A couple who'd kept their son on the mantelpiece, and who lit a candle for him every day, sometimes taking the urn with them when they shopped, found out it wasn't their son at all. When a reporter asked police what recourse there'd be for the affected families, the police said, "It depends on how you define 'affected.'" This is the key. How *do* you define *affected*?

Words like *horror* and *desecration* are easy enough to get your teeth around. Bodies in the swamp: this is bad. Where things get fuzzier is in the day-to-day mundane business of death-care, where one man's transgression is just another man's fair business practice. Customers who feel duped or who sniff hanky-panky have, in Manitoba, a provincial funeral board to which they can complain, but as the chair of the board told me, "We're not here to stifle innovation."

"Funeral directors," she said, "even some of my bad apples, are very sympathetic to people. That doesn't mean some of my boys and girls don't, how shall I say, oversell and up-sell, but an individual entering any transaction has to enter it with a certain level of knowledge." In other words, buyer beware.

I'd gone to see her about a local story that ran on CBC Television about a widow who'd contracted with one of the deep-discount cremators. There are three in Winnipeg, and I've come to refer to them as Curly, Larry and Moe. Moe was a bit player, but Larry and Curly accounted for the highest volume of calls in Winnipeg, higher than Chapel Lawn, the big funeral–cemetery combo owned by the Arbor Group, and more than Neil: they were burying him.

Curly had come up through the corporates, and Larry was a former wedding deejay; now they were in bitter competition over the so-called "shoppers" market, the customers for whom price meant everything. When the widow, Mrs. D., lost her husband to a heart attack, which he suffered while riding the Number 12 bus, she went to Curly because of his advertised price: $695 for direct cremation, $1,500 for cremation and a "service of remembrance." She agreed to the latter. By the end of the arrangement, after totalling costs for the casket (a simple cardboard model with a faux velour covering), cremation and a "priority rush" feel, the estimate came to $2,977.83—not including disbursements for the church rental, the pastor's honorarium, the catering, a mixing-board operator for the sound system, and flowers, all of which added up to an additional $1,040.

She asked what happened to the $1,500, and was told that was the "sit-down price." Not knowing what else to do, she signed. The insurance would cover it. Only later, when she discovered there was no insurance, did she call Larry, who cut her a better deal. In the business they call this "unplugging": switching from one funeral home to another. It's a common if annoying practice. Curly would be paid for his time and the removal fee, and Larry would get the body. Only there was no body: Curly had already cremated it. And he told the widow D. she could have her husband's ashes back when she paid the bill in full: just over $4,000. The family didn't have the money, so Mrs. D. held her own memorial at home in the backyard, without the dead man present, with food she bought at Safeway. The remains stayed on a shelf at Curly's funeral home for three months, as collateral. Then Curly took the widow and her family to court.

He held up the estimate signed by Mrs. D. With some sympathy for the confused widow the court played Solomon and awarded Curly a compromise: $2,100. The family paid, and only then did they get the ashes back, in a plastic shopping bag with Curly's logo on the front.

"The biggest set of complaints we get," the board chair told me (speaking in general: she wouldn't comment on Mrs. D.'s complaint specifically because it was before the board), "are people who see an advertised price and they're very unhappy when they get there and the price escalates."

So what do you do about that? I asked.

"Well," she said, "there's not much we can do."

In the end, a simple cremation, advertised at $695, wound up costing the family $2,100 with the province of Manitoba's blessing.

No one but the widow challenged Curly's right as a businessman to hold the remains until the bill was paid. "There's no such thing as debtor's prison," she told CBC. "My husband wasn't a dog. He was a human being."

But no laws were broken. Curly had a contract. The death of Mr. D., an immigrant from Yorkshire, the former lunchtime maître-d' at Old Bailey's on Lombard and retired beverage manager at the Marlborough Hotel, was a heartbreak for the family, but for Curly and the provincial small-claims court, it was a transaction. This is a business. Neil says if you want to run a funeral home based on low price and volume, you need a strong stomach. The modern widow, Jessica Mitford wrote, has to be a cool customer indeed. And in Winnipeg she has to be prepared to stand up alone, without representation or support from a governing watchdog, and say: All I wanted was to do the right thing for my husband. How did we end up here?

———

I'm standing at the front door of the Factory, looking out at Brookside cemetery, watching a misty rain darken the tombstones. "Come on," Neil says, handing me my jacket. "Let's go see our lady friend at the Norwood Hotel."

The friend is a soon-to-be widow: her husband is in palliative care at St. Boniface hospital, close to the end. We meet her at the Jolly Friar coffee shop at the Norwood. She's young, fifty-ish, with two children. Her nails are bitten to stubs, and she orders coffee but doesn't drink it, just folds and unfolds a sugar packet.

"What do you want to do?" Neil says.

"Whatever he wants."

"Well, it's got to be what you want too."

She's thought about a service at Holy Trinity, something for the boys, nothing big. What she needs is someone to handle the cremation.

"What about the ashes?" Neil says.

"What do you mean?"

"What do you want to do with them?"

She looks down at her sugar packet. We're talking about a man who isn't dead yet.

"I can't get out of him what he wants," she says. "I guess I'll keep them with me."

"I want you to think about that part. Because it's like waiting for the other shoe to drop. Think about cremation, then burying them or scattering them before the service, and then when the service is over, it's all done. What about an urn?"

"Do I have to buy that from you?"

"We've got one for $6,000," he says, and she looks up.

He's smiling, and she sees that he's joking. She laughs. "I think I'll use the money for the kids' education."

"You can use anything you want. Do you have something at home?" Neil has buried people in coffee tins and fishing tackle boxes.

"How much?" she says, cutting to the chase.

"Twelve hundred." He's offering her a deal. And he'll throw in four hundred memorial cards, otherwise a buck apiece.

"The guy in the newspaper says $700."

"With administration and all the extras, the memorial cards and the guest book, it won't be $700. Does it matter how the cremation is done?"

She folds her legs under her chair and looks out the window at the traffic on Marion Street.

"Do you want to know the process?" he says.

"No."

"Are you going to want to see him before the cremation?"

"No."

"What about the boys?"

"No."

"You've had a difficult year," Neil says. "We'll get you through this."

Neil pays the bill, and we leave. He tells me on the drive back to Aubrey Street that we'll never see her again, that she'll end up at Larry's or Curly's or Moe's. As long as cremation is seen as a commodity like gasoline or wheat or carrots, people will price-shop, and for all the right reasons. For the kids. That's what her husband would've told her: Instead of blowing money on a funeral, do it yourself, save the money for the kids, for God's sake. I don't want anything fancy. But will she be in any condition to take care of all the finicky details of a service? What if the priest is late, or takes a day off? What if the printer forgets the memorial cards? All the things that Richard takes care of. You can pull your own teeth if you want to, he says, but most people use a dentist.

Eleven

TURN THAT FROWN UPSIDE DOWN:
THE "CELEBRATION OF LIFE"

It can become a habit of many of our funeral colleagues to close their arrangement books when a family requests direct cremation. . . . Without a body—poof—all opportunity is lost!

—*American Funeral Director*, **January 2008**

*H*ave a heart for the mainstream funeral director. Consider his overhead, his infrastructure. What does he do with a $100,000 hearse when there's no casket to drive to the cemetery, and what does he do with the two-hundred-seat chapel when there's no service for the body that isn't in the casket that isn't being driven to the cemetery in the hearse? You might say the only logical response is to do what we did for the banks and automakers: bail him out. It's not his fault that the burial bubble has burst, that the U.S. cremation rate, 14.9 percent in 1985, is expected to rise to 59 percent by 2025. It's another case of Japanese innovation (cremation rate 98 percent) clobbering a North American heritage industry. But corpses don't vote, and the funeral lobby in Washington and Ottawa is weak compared to, say, all the others, so what does he do? He refits, innovates—lemonade from lemons and all that.

He has to accept that aside from certain pro-burial ethnic and geographical groups (Asian Catholics, Filipinos, Latin Americans, southern Baptist African Americans, Atlantic Canadians, especially Prince Edward Islanders) he's lost the casket sale. For most cremation families, buying an oak casket just to see it burned in the retort is considered a waste (although, as undertaker-poet Thomas Lynch points out, the same mental calculus doesn't apply to the body inside). Instead he focuses on what the trade calls "personalization and memorialization options": thematic urns to match the personality of the deceased, glass and porcelain keepsakes shaped like dolphins or angels blowing kisses that hold just a spoonful of remains, or memorial jewellery: heart-shaped pendants, lockets, rosaries, bracelets and rings that contain just a few grains. The *Wilbert Catalog* ("Expressing a Loved One's Essence") offers oak, cherry and mahogany urns etched in a variety of motifs: The Rose, The Eagle, The Golfer (male and female), The Covered Bridge, The Galloping Horse, Pheasant Heartland (a bird perked up and waiting to be shot), Fisherman's Paradise (a jumping bass), The Wheat, The Elk, The Skier, The Moose, Saguaro Sunset (cactus), Lariat and Cowboy, The Watering Can, Our Lady of Guadalupe, Sailing at Sunset and Ducks in Flight. Ashes can be mixed with oil paints to create an original abstract expressionist work of art, or portrait of the deceased, or bagged and zippered into a teddy bear. The

Huggable Urn (as seen on *Rachael Ray*) is a plush toy available in Snow Angel, Cocoa Angel or Military Teddy Bear designs, the latter with your choice of tiny, bear-sized T-shirts with the logos of all five branches of the U.S. armed forces including the Coast Guard. "Boy!" says the inventor of the Huggable Urn. "I have never talked to my dad so much in my whole life as I have since he passed. . . . It gives me such comfort to be able to pick up my Teddy Bear and give my dad a hug anytime I want."

And just because a family has chosen cremation doesn't mean they don't want some kind of ceremony. Maybe what they don't want is a funeral. According to Glenn Gould (not the dead pianist but the CEO of MKJ Marketing, a death-care consultancy in Florida), "For nearly two hundred years, funeral service has had a firm foundation in American culture based upon Judeo/Christian priorities. . . . The question is, what does the consumer really want, and how could operators achieve superior profits by breaking with the past?" Focus groups commissioned by four different product manufacturers came to the same conclusion: "There is far more profit in creating memories and keepsakes than in caskets."

All it takes is a semantic shift: gather a few dozen people in a room to mark the passing of one of their own, with or without the ashes present, and it's no longer a funeral but a "Celebration of Life." Margins realized on room rental, catering, PowerPoint presentations and service fees (based on whatever the market will bear: is $2,000 too much for a catered event? $4,000? $8,000? What do people spend on weddings?) offset the lost casket sale and the mothballing of the hearse. And speaking of the hearse, why not keep it on the list of options for cremation families? Accubuilt makes an elaborate bracket, called a Hidden Gems urn-holder, that fits into the back floor of the coach and allows for a traditional, if a bit over-roomy, procession to the cemetery. Whatever the customer's taste, cremation and the Celebration of Life open up—rather than narrow—the undertaker's options. When 75 million North American baby boomers are ready for their last transactions, the industry is betting this is what they'll want: a cocktail party, then into the retort. They've controlled everything else in their lives. When it comes to their deaths, they'll want to control that too.

For today's service Neil's booked the Pan Am Room at the Winnipeg Convention Centre. He's excited, pacing a hall lined with posters for next week's professional mixed martial arts Ultimate Cage Wars. The guests are mostly captains of middle industry, Rotarians in knit vests, hair either blow-dried or wet-combed for those that have any, plenty of lapel pins that are too small for me to decipher but that I assume represent some Winnipeg social pecking order. The crowd is small, maybe fifty people, well behaved, not overly formal. One woman wears rubber gardening clogs. At the door, I invite newcomers to sign the guest book. A matron in a fur-trimmed suede coat hisses at her husband, "Make it readable for a change, please." Neil and Eirik have set up rows of chairs in front of a podium, but no one's biting. Mostly they hang back at the food table where there's coffee, tubs of fruit juice on ice and diabetic cookies.

Shirley Burton, wiry and electric, with shaggy black hair and wearing heels, sits down at her keyboard and plays "Misty." The volume of chatter in the room rises to match the music.

"I work with seven funeral homes," Shirley whispers to me. "This is 75 percent of my business, I always talk to the family first, to help them 'create.' We need this, we need the service. We have a lot of unhealthy people walking around with a lot of unresolved issues. You should see the smiles on their faces, that's why I do this. It's the send-off, the healing, I'm passionate about it." She segues to "Stardust" and the guests take their seats.

Speeches are short. A man tells us that we've all been called to live right, and that we must not only remember but also affirm what we remember, but it's not entirely clear what he's talking about. He mentions God's will, and then stacks up his memo cards, ceding the podium to a family friend who reports on the dead man's happy retirement (the dead man has already been tilled into Neil's rose garden). Four years ago he bought an RV; he had big plans to travel, but then he died. Neil thanks everyone for coming and then Shirley launches into a bossa nova rendition of "Night and Day."

"This was great," Neil says afterwards. "They threw in more religion than I wanted but that's the risk you take. I really think this is exactly what the boomers will want."

I help Shirley pack up her gear.

"Families love what I do," she says. "I sing to them on the phone. It's like design. Do you like warm colours, vivacious colours? Like the right throw cushion or a rug that completes the room, the music completes the service. Let's say they love Broadway, I can do Broadway tunes, or lounge it up. I can do jazzy or traditional. I don't just use the piano sound, I got string guitar sounds, trumpet and saxophone. I can do a country ballad."

I follow her down the escalator, carrying her amp. She's parked on the street.

"People should take control of how you celebrate that life," she says, opening the trunk. "I did a lady, thirty-five years old. She had a six-year-old and a six-month-old, didn't feel good, went to the doctor: boom, full of cancer. She was on chemo and died a week before Christmas. The husband had money, he bought twenty-five floral arrangements with pink bows and we did Blue Rodeo songs. For him, he could move on in his grief journey."

She drives me back to Aubrey Street, stopping her monologue just long enough to answer her cell phone.

"Faith is a huge part of my life," she says as I get out.

True believers like Shirley exhaust me. Maybe it's because I have so little in my own life that I'm as sure of as she is about her work. She has faith in the power of soft jazz to sooth grief. Neil adores her. She gives him a commercial edge. He's heard "Rock of Ages" so many times in his career he could play it himself on spoons without sheet music. What Shirley brings to the funeral, or the memorial, or the Celebration of Life, or whatever it was I just witnessed at the Winnipeg Convention Centre, is what the modern ritual not only needs, according to Neil, but what it will perish without: a taste of showbiz.

Other funeral homes find their own ways to stand out. I've had a tepid but otherwise tasty cappuccino at Salon B, the Euro-chic glass-and-halogen espresso bar and art gallery upstairs from the Alfred Dallaire funeral home on trendy Saint-Laurent Boulevard in Montreal. Students and locals too cool to be creeped out by the Gothic vibe hang out, play chess, read books on art and mortality in the Library of Death, eavesdrop on funerals (although the day I was there, the funeral space was being dressed for a CD release party). The Michigan Memorial Park in Flat Rock has an on-site grief therapy dog, a golden retriever named Zoey, for guests to pet during visitations and memorial services. According to Zoey's "business card," his best friend is Clare the cat, and his favourite toys are socks and slippers.

On the ceremonial side, plenty of funeral homes offer the services of "celebrants," or humanist motivational speakers, to meet the needs of non-religious families who prefer not to use priests or other clergy. Kate Smith of Seattle is both a Certified Funeral Celebrant and a professional clown. "Clowning is, among other things, ultimately an intensely spiritual experience," she says. "I believe this spirit is natural to death, meaning that in good clowning, you have some of the same elements that you might like to have in a death ritual: genuine human connection, truth, sadness, and, yes, humour."

And there I think she's nailed it. The big, fat-sucking spiritual void that a death creates used to be filled by the redemptive magic of religion, through ritual: pray over the body, sing the body into the ground, mark the casket with the sign of the cross or place a stone on the grave marker, light candles, burn the body on a riverside ghat and scatter the ashes to the water. All the sacred customs were ways to signal to one another that we're not alone, that there's some continuity even in death, a consensus that we could beat back the senseless, arbitrary fact of it by holding hands and chanting. Death was rendered powerless. God had a plan, even if His blueprints were impossible to read.

Take God out of the picture. What's left? The sucking void is still there. How do we fill it? With new sacred customs, or by picking and choosing the best from the lot and adapting them for the occasion: a bit of Zen, a touch of Zoroastrianism, yes to candles, no to

Psalm 23, a clown, a puppy, show tunes, trained doves released at the graveside to symbolize the flight of the soul, or whatever else reflects the unique life lost. We're no longer part of a community of believers, but a marginally organized tribe of individuals, where each life story is as important as the next. Each funeral or Celebration of Life is different from the last, a variation on a ritual that used to matter back when we believed in something bigger. For the modern undertaker in the arrangement room, a man is defined not by his faith but by his hobbies and quirks. Did he golf? Was she an avid gardener? Everyone is an avid something: an avid bowler, an avid water drinker, an avid sailor or avid snake charmer. Avidity is the key to unlocking the story that can be told in the chapel, through readings and eulogies and props.

Deirdre Blair, an event planner in Florida, markets theme kits for funeral homes, Tupperware bins full of ready-made decorative items with which to dress the chapel, for added value. The avid gardener's kit includes a watering can, gardening tools, gloves, artificial flowers, garden-themed picture frames and a plaster snail. The undertaker arranges them around the urn, and when the service is done, he packs it all up for the next time: $250 a box (her fee, the undertaker can charge what he wants). Men and women are defined by separate, gender-specific "passion lists." Men might be artists, Audubon Society members, avid readers, car collectors, cigar connoisseurs, motorcycle/RV enthusiasts, movie buffs, musicians, outdoorsmen, pet lovers, ranchers, war veterans; women might be bridge players, cooks, antique collectors, interior designers, needleworkers, grandmothers or travellers. "I believe in 'take-aways,'" she says. "I did an avid basketball player. Everyone signed a ball with a Sharpie. Now the family can leave the funeral home with something more than the death certificate. They're blown away that someone's created this environment." Look at the wedding, she says. "We try so hard to personalize it. We talk about the bride's lifestyle, her colours. She despises green, she loves pink. Is it going to be casual or formal? Will it be all organic food? Are you holding it outside?" These are all questions that can apply to the death ritual too.

So, what's your legacy? What will be your theme in death? You've been liberated from the one-size-fits-all casket with two nights of viewing and a church service, we all have, and herein lies my existential angst. Who am I? What's in my Tupperware box? I'm a member of nothing, I can dribble but not with a basketball, and cigars make my tongue itch. At most I consider myself an avid procrastinator. When I die, they can dress up the chapel however they want, then tear it all down and do it again two days later when I finally show up.

Mark Krause, who runs three funeral homes in Milwaukee, told me, "Absolutely, a funeral is all about the show. When I see a family walk in the door, I tell the staff, 'It's *Riverdance* time.'" He ditched the selection room in favour of banquet tables, got beer and wine licences, and served food and drinks at visitations. Not after, but during. "Like at any other family holiday," he said. "We are not in the funeral business, we are in the hospitality business." A funeral is an experience that should touch all five senses.

Krause's role models are the Ritz-Carlton and Disney ("Look at their attention to detail. They know how many steps between each wastebasket at Disneyland. Twenty-six!"). At his wife's and daughter's urging he bought a therapy dog (different breed but same concept as Zoey in Michigan). "I said he can't be a little foo-foo dog," he said. "I need to be able to walk around the neighbourhood with dignity." The dog's name is Oliver and he's trained not to jump up or eat off the floor. In the arrangement room, every family gets the same pitch: directors are drilled on presentation, they have lines to memorize. They talk food, they talk music. Their "Signature Service" includes a produced DVD of family photos, a video of the service itself, a memorial candle with the person's picture on it, use of the therapy dog, and for $195 extra they stream it all live on the Web ("We put up a sign in the chapel: this service will be broadcast"). The payoff? Eighty percent of his cremation families have funerals, with the body present, an amazing number. Neil is lucky to hit 20 percent. And Mark never mentioned the word *casket*, but even I could figure it out: if they were buying wine-and-quiche services with live webcasting, they weren't putting the body in a hockey bag.

Richard says that this is Winnipeg—we don't hang tiki lanterns at funerals. But if a family wants to "personalize," we'll work with them. We have top-end urns in the showroom: an autumn-yellow blown-glass inverted bell-shaped sculpture-thingy that weighs as much as a ten-pin bowling ball, $725. A picture of an empty canoe at sunset is in fact a keepsake urn: in the back is a clear plastic ant-farm chamber for the remains. "It's supposed to sell for $400, which is nuts. But there are desk clocks that are really nice." Jewellery too—he carries a C-shaped bracelet with two small channels at the ends for cremated remains, capped with your choice of birthstones. "Wickedly expensive," says Richard.

"There're some really neat keepsakes from Quebec that hold hair. You cut off a lock before the cremation. We might sell one every four years," he says. "Video collages, memorial pamphlets, silkscreen posters, stained glass pictures that double as keepsake urns, these ideas keep flying around. You don't want to take up people's time with all this crap. You don't want to be cynical, but, balloons at the cemetery, dove releases: you look like a pot and pan salesman. Doves. I mean every funeral director, if he's honest, says, dear God, what are the doves supposed to mean?"

An elderly woman and her two middle-aged sons are seated in the arrangement room. The woman's husband, father of the two men, died just this morning. They want him buried. The man bought a plot in Brookside in 1954 for $50, so now all they'll need is $750 to open and close the grave, plus a casket and some kind of service, maybe a small gathering at the graveside. There are grandkids in Europe. Richard suggests they bury right away, then hold a memorial service later in the summer so the grandkids will have time to get home.

"You don't want to deny the grandchildren," he says.

"That's very true," says the widow.

"The death certificate," says the first son. "Do we get that now?"

"No, there's a backlog, two and a half months."

"Too many people dying?"

"Passports."

"Oh for heaven's sake," says the widow.

"Our role in all this," says Richard, "is going to be the permit for the cemetery, the paperwork, removal from the Health Sciences Centre, and we'll do the embalming."

"He loved his shoes," says the widow. "Put them in with him. He said just the other day, God, I love these shoes."

The second son reaches out to hold his mother's hand, and she lets him, but then pulls it away.

"We can talk about flowers for the cemetery," says Richard.

"Oh, and Pringles chips. He loved Pringles. He ate them all the time with root beer."

"So the clothing," says the first son. "Can we bring it tomorrow?"

"And his shoes," says the widow, "'cause he loved them."

He loved wood too, and was very particular about finish and grain, which becomes an issue in the casket showroom. The ash "hybrid" cremation casket, suitable for earth burial too, matches the trees on their property. There's an oak with a deeper grain but it's a lady's casket. They like the ash, but if they could get a men's oak, they might like the oak better. They can't decide. The son wants a bell to ring at the graveside service. His father loved trains, they had a recording of whistles and train sounds that he and his father would listen to, at top volume, when the mother was out of the house. Mother looks at her son. She's hearing about this for the first time.

"I can get you a bell," says Richard.

They settle on the ash with an eggshell interior, based on its grain, which the dead father would've admired. The sons want to decorate the casket with racing stripes, like dad did all his cars.

"Can we do that?" the first son asks.

"It's your casket," says Richard. "You can do whatever you like."

The next morning, minutes after Richard unlocks the door, the widow arrives with a bag of clothes, shoes and a can of Pringles chips. Her husband will be buried like a pharaoh, with his most valued earthly possessions.

For families who want a secular service without a preacher, Neil uses Lee Barringer, a celebrant and freelance undertaker from nearby Stonewall. By "freelance undertaker" I mean that he has no bricks-and-mortar funeral home, just a cell phone and a Toyota and a listing in the Yellow Pages. He subcontracts all the technical work: for removals, he calls Winnipeg Funeral Transfer Services (two men with a grey van and a stretcher), and for preparation or cremation, he has the body sent to Neil's. He rents space for services, including the chapel at Aubrey Street, and does arrangements at the family's home or a coffee shop. This way (and it took me a while to get my head around this), he can offer a direct cremation for less money than Neil charges, even though it's the same cremation, in the same retort, with the same hand-sort. Without overhead, he can afford a lower markup. Once Neil's friends figured out that they could get a cremation at Neil's for a cheaper price than a cremation at Neil's (still with me?) they took their business to Barringer. Neil had to drop his price to compete with himself through a third party. But there are no hard feelings: Lee did his apprenticeship here years ago, and Neil likes him. And he'd like to see Lee as part of his law-firm model of associates, to bring some fresh, as it were, blood to the business. So when families want a celebrant, he calls Lee.

A small crowd, mostly women, is gathered in the chapel at Aubrey. Shirley opens with a stringy "My Heart Will Go On" and moves to a jaunty barrelhouse "Spirit in the Sky" before Lee brings the event to order. "This is a chance to come together," he says, "and we want this to be a celebration of life." Again, no body, no ashes are present, but next to Lee is a picture of the deceased, named M., a smiling woman with white hair and glasses.

"Khalil Gibran said, what is it to die but to stand naked in the wind and melt into the ground? When you have reached the mountaintop, then it is time to climb. Pictures of heaven come from whatever your faith is, but perhaps death is nothing but a doorway, an exit as well as an entrance. Sir Edward Arnold said death may give more than birth, colours we don't now see, sounds we don't now hear . . ."

Aphorism after aphorism, Lee is lobbing them into the air and smacking them out of the ballpark.

"Edward Arnold," I whisper to Richard. "Wasn't he the husband on *Green Acres*?"

"I think so."

"We celebrate life," Lee continues. The crowd is attentive. "One day we too shall have to die. It's important to live each day as if it's your last because one day you will be right. Death brings down our walls and our comfort zones, but perhaps, like M., we need to go on more walks or visit Hawaii."

Then the daughter takes the podium.

"I'm going to try to do this," she says.

She read in a magazine that there are three details on every headstone: the name, and two moments in time, the date of birth and the date of death. But between those moments in time is a dash, and that, she tells us, is the most important part of the headstone.

"It represents the moment my mother first smiled, or her first step, or her first time on a horse, or when she stepped off the train in Winnipeg, the moment she retired from Eaton's, the terrible moment she got the call that Dad was gone, the moment when her friends came to the hospice, that dash is Mom, an energetic, sweet, loving person. Now think what that dash means to you."

Shirley plays "Circle of Life," and the guests rise and gather in the reception room for coffee. My own default setting, the cynical hard-shelled bastard I've nurtured since college, knows that this business about the tombstone dash is at the heart of another sub-industry, based on a poem by Linda Ellis, of hardcover gift books, a DVD movie, a music CD, and "Dash" daily-planners that funeral directors can sell as add-ons or as part of some casket-urn-celebration-of-"Dash" package.

And there's an uneasy imperative in that little granite notch: the opportunity it provides to be as competitive in death as you were in life. Fill up that dash! What you achieve from now on will be fodder for your eulogy. Why are you wasting your time watching *Everybody Loves Raymond* or raising a family when you could be getting a tattoo or dining at La Chevre d'Or or skydiving or seeing Stonehenge or driving a Shelby Mustang, all items on the bucket list from the movie of the same name, starring Jack Nicholson and Morgan Freeman as two terminally ill men whipping through a list of last-minute goals before they kick the bucket. Taj Mahal, check. Serengeti, check. Great Wall of China, check. Why leave your life up to chance? Choreograph it, script it, as if it were the film you always felt like you were starring in anyway. Lives don't just happen. They are projects. This is what gives them meaning, in lieu of some modest, mundane story about love, community and family. It's old-fashioned boot-strapism: you are responsible for the contents of your own celebration of life, and if you don't have the tools to build your own project, there are books: *1,000 Places To See Before You Die, 1,001 Movies You Must See Before You Die, 1,001 Foods You Must Taste Before You Die.* Get cracking.

"Now think what that dash means to you," the daughter had said, which to chronic underachievers like me could mean: acquire, conquer, move on, time's galloping. In the end they may not embalm your body, but if you've hammered away at your bucket list, filled your dash to the limit, they'll embalm your life story, make it look even better than it was when you lived it.

Still, I'm either tired or I'm entering a post-ironic stage in my life, because I am actually choked up by a stranger's eulogy for her mother, and I didn't see it coming. It's hard to admit to unearned emotions. They're not quite real, are they? I don't have to bear the impossible weight of actual grief here, just a featherlight spinoff. Same effect as being moved by a cheese-ball pop song that you would never, even under threat of water-boarding, admit you liked. I know that there's more truth about the human condition in Verdi, but "I Want It That Way," by the Backstreet Boys, I'll confess, makes me soft and mopey. It's just less work than unpacking *Il Trovatore*.

Maybe this is what the celebration of life has to offer, a kind of pop ritual. The heavens don't open up, you can't touch the face of God, but with the right minor-key music and aphorism you can be moved to something approaching an actual human emotion. Yet there's something else here too, something deeper. Even framed by a popular feel-good Oprah-ready ditty, I feel like I've encountered something rare: a life that mattered not despite of but because of its simplicity.

Twelve

Contributing to Shareholder Value,
One Corpse at a Time

*S*unday, and I'm booked to work. There's no traffic biking in, just the bottle-collectors pushing grocery carts, working weekends like me. When I pass Brookside I see a couple laying a bouquet in the cremation section, a treeless stretch of densely packed bronze markers, each with its own vase for fake flowers: purple, yellow, red, blue. In winter the colours poke through the snow. Last time I walked through there I saw the other offerings people leave: plastic racing cars, Mylar balloons, a full cup of Tim Hortons coffee. The cemetery prefers its visitors to stick to the fake flowers.

At the Factory, two new arrivals are posted on the cooler door's dry-erase board, an M-1 and an F-2, which means a skinny male and a not-so-skinny female. These are codes for the cremationist: they're both candidates for Retort Two, svelte enough not to smoke. The big boys and girls, the M-3s and F-4s, are saved for

Retort One. A Moore's suit bag hangs on the hook in the dressing room, marked for *The Late Mr. H.*

Neil's in the arrangement room, flipping through the latest call sheets. As usual he knows some of the dead.

"Is that Peter B.'s brother?" he says to Shannon. "I did a service at Riverview, we asked Peter to provide music and he did all Scottish songs. The minister said, those aren't hymns, and Peter said, they are to the Scots."

"They wanted scattering in the rose garden in late fall," says Shannon. "What's great is I got storage fees out of them as well."

Neil has big hopes for Shannon, as he once had for Natalie. One time, on a drive through Brookside, he told me they were both ambitious young women who scared him pantless, but on the other hand, they fit the future of funeral service, which was no longer a business for old men. The problem with Shannon, he said, is that when she opens her mouth, she sounds like she's trying to sell you something. The corporate chains would love her. In fact, Chapel Lawn's called twice, offering her a job.

"How was your Friday?" says Shannon.

"I did the L. ash interment," says Neil. "They had a shaman. They held hands, people told stories. What I thought would be ten minutes went forty-five. It was neat."

They wrap the Sunday morning briefing and Neil says he's going to church, "To prove I'm a hypocrite." But in fact he goes every week, has for decades, to St. Stephen's–St. Bede's, an Anglican-Lutheran hybrid where he likes the music and the community of old ladies who've helped him through his tough times. I walk him to his car, and he tells me how the "old dears" rallied around him when he first got his cancer diagnosis.

We stop by the side of the rose garden, where he confides that he's been through dozens of treatments for prostate cancer already, the radioactive pellets, the works, but the bad numbers keep going in the wrong direction. He's lost weight. People are starting to notice. He tells them it's because he's been power-walking through Brookside cemetery every morning before work, which is true, and that he's never felt better, which is also true. But as long as the numbers refuse to co-operate, he's been left to wonder if all his plans to build a new crematorium will still be only plans when he dies. Men die young in this business, he says, at least compared to the clientele. His dad and his uncle Karl were both seventy-two when they died: Neil is five years away from the magic Bardal number. Tommy Cropo, the modern godfather of Winnipeg undertakers, who always wore a red rose in his lapel, never made it to seventy. Neil's doctor says that in men Neil's age, prostate cancer tends to creep slowly, and that he may well die of some other ailment before the cancer has a chance to spread. Still, Neil's told his wife that when the time comes, he wants a three-part funeral: a service at the Pantages Playhouse Theatre with the Manitoba Symphony Orchestra playing Scott Joplin, a reception but no dinner, and then cremation followed by a scattering in the Garden of Memories, his rose garden. You have to believe the religion you preach, he says. Neil's religion is redemption through the burning of the body. Church is more like a club, like Rotary. I'm struck by his matter-of-factness, and how mortality, for him, calls less for some panicky peace-making with your God than for attention to practical details. But again, that's what he expects of families in the arrangement room.

Neil's middle name is Ofeigur, same as his father. *Feigur* in Icelandic means "fated to die," but by adding an O, he says, the curse is mitigated. "I knew a man in Gimli," Neil says, "who had a boat called the *Ofeigur II*. I asked him what happened to the *Ofeigur I* and of course it sank."

Next to the rose garden I see something I've never noticed before, a bronze grave marker under a stubby evergreen bush. That, Neil says, is Mr. L., the first man into the rose garden. He heard what Neil was doing and said, that's for me, and when he died, Mrs. L. asked if she could plant a tree and put in the marker. The tree never really grew. Now Mrs. L. is dying. Neil told her that once the place is renovated they'll have to take out the tree and the bronze plaque, but that maybe there'll be a wall of memories too, with names of the people in the garden, or an electronic kiosk. He just needs the bank to hand him a million dollars for the work, and as yet, they haven't been inclined to do so. They don't like current market trends vis-à-vis death-care.

"So," I say, "what if I want to be scattered in the garden but I want a statue too, like a Venus de Milo with water squirting out of her mouth?"

"Okay," Neil says, hopping over the stones in front of the walkway. "Lookit here," and he sweeps a hand, directing my gaze to a wide swath of newly mown grass next to his building. "If this guy would sell," he says, pointing to the tombstone carver next door, "all this could be living space."

"Living space?"

"Space for the living. To sit down and have a picnic."

Cemeteries are big on living space, out of economic necessity. The burial business is tanking, and to justify their existence and to raise money for their perpetual care funds they're promoting themselves as tourist destinations. Hollywood Forever, the cemetery of the stars in Los Angeles, shows movies at night on the wall of the mausoleum where Rudolph Valentino is interred. People bring blankets and food. *Rock 'n' Roll High School* is on heavy rotation: Dee Dee Ramone is buried just a few dozen yards away from where they show the film. Other cemeteries hold dog parades, jazz concerts, mausoleum brunches and Halloween parties. Oakwood cemetery in Troy, New York, has plans for a Renaissance fair with knights in armour and jousting matches. The industry calls it rebranding, making graveyards into "destination necropolises." Neil wants something more modest, a few benches, a path and a gazebo. Families can bring a lunch, then visit their loved one in the Garden of Memories. There might be room for monuments of the kind I've described.

"What if I want a statue of an angel riding an elephant?" That one just came to me.

"Then Chapel Lawn would be happy to help you," he says, gets into his car and drives off to church.

Neil calls Chapel Lawn a waste of good farmland. One of the oldest commercial cemeteries in the city, west of the Perimeter Highway and across from Assiniboia Downs racetrack and the drive-in, it's modelled after Forest Lawn in Glendale, California, the original lawn-style cemetery that Evelyn Waugh lampooned in his 1948 novel *The Loved One: An Anglo-American Tragedy*. It's an eye-catching splash of green and trees and ponds with firehose fountains in the middle of the dry prairie. There are no headstones, only flat bronze markers that you can't see until you're standing on one of them, and a few towering white stone statues of Christ and the apostles and the Old Testament prophets. The intended aesthetic appeal of a lawn cemetery is the open vista: no upright stones to get in the way of the view. The economic spinoff of a lawn cemetery is that it's cheaper to mow the grass: no upright stones to get in the way of the equipment. It looks like a golf course if that golf course had been designed by Presbyterians. And it's divided into themed "gardens": the Garden of Everlasting Life, the Garden of the Old Rugged Cross, the Garden of the Last Supper, and the accidentally ironic (if you say it out loud) Garden of Four Prophets. Chapel Lawn is owned by the Arbor Memorial Corporate, a minor conglomerate compared to, say, Service Corporation International, the big guns from Houston, but they own a number of funeral–cemetery combos in Canada, and do well in Winnipeg, which is where they started.

The reason Neil spits when he hears the name is that Chapel Lawn has taken him to court over the rose garden. Their position is that it's a cemetery by another name, and should be licensed as such. Neil should have to pay the perpetual care fees for its long-term upkeep the way any cemetery does, by law. In other words, he's running a bootleg graveyard.

Neil's argument is that he's a private landowner who is giving people permission to scatter on his land. A cemetery is for the interment of human remains. Cremated remains, he says, are not human, not the way a flesh-and-Plasdopake body in a casket is human. This is a tough call for the courts. They'll have to decide on an itchy existential question: what are ashes? Are they people? I can say when I poke through a pile of broken bone pieces on the sort table and come up with a tooth, it looks human. When it's whisked into a powder in the processor, it doesn't. Did it lose its human-ness in the blender, or in the retort, or when the man in question stopped using it to chew his food? What an arbitrary mess of a semantic argument, and as long as the court case hangs over

Neil's head, the bank won't give him a loan to build his dream: the reception centre, the indoor scattering garden.

The best place to go at Chapel Lawn if it's rainy or cold is the Lasting Tribute indoor columbarium. It's heated in winter, bright in the summer, a labyrinth of marble and glass-front niches where the dead repose in their urns, surrounded by intimate thingums from their previous lives. Toy trains, Hot Wheels cars, Shriners' fezzes, golf balls and airline bottles of VO whiskey are laid out in diorama. In one niche, a laminated ticket stub from a Supertramp concert is propped against a square wooden urn. Most have family-album photographs: men playing with dogs, women in canoes. Anything you might keep on your office desk or corkboard can follow you into your Lasting Tribute niche. The most expensive are the ones you can touch, at what industry types call the "head and heart level." If you have to stand on a chair or kneel on the floor to see in, they're cheaper. The place smells of wet flowers and baby powder, and through the looped Muzak system I hear what might be the Stones' "Satisfaction" played on harp and zither. There are no other people here but I feel as if hundreds of eyes are watching me, so I find my way out through the maze and follow the path to the funeral home.

The lobby has homespun charm: rose and gold wingback chairs, a faux fireplace, fake trees with twisted trunks, lit votive candles in hexagonal glass lanterns and prints on the walls of Mediterranean scenes that, like every painting I've ever seen in a funeral home, have no people in them. Just boats and empty bodegas. Maybe they represent some kind of earthly heaven into which we can project the recently departed, or maybe they just match the wingback chairs. Down the hall is the jewel of the Arbor brand:

a reception hall with a full-service kitchen and a covered patio facing the parking lot, with a barbecue and propane heaters for chilly post-funeral gatherings. It's Arbor's position that if funeral homes don't get into the hospitality game, then cremation customers will take their business to golf-and-country clubs and hotels and mall restaurants.

Annie and I are here to meet with a pre-need counsellor. As if by divine hand, a card appeared in our mailbox last week inviting us to answer questions about our future memorial plans. I checked off every available box on the questionnaire. Yes, I was interested in cremation. Yes, I was interested in burial options, and memorialization and personalization and pre-planning, yes yes. I sent the card back and within forty-eight hours got a call from Chapel Lawn. I had made their hot-lead list. They invited Annie and me to come down, so we did.

The counsellor is pleasant, if a bit tightly wound, red-faced with a thick neck and a hedgehog haircut. The three of us sit down at a conference table in a small basement room, the walls of which are lined with bronze grave markers and urns. Thick binders are opened. He's been with Arbor Group for eighteen years, and before that he worked for Snap-on Tools. You're young, he says, we just did a service, two parents of a nine-year-old girl, both killed in a car crash. The airbags worked fine. It was the fire that got them. Now imagine that poor girl in the back seat. What's she going to do? They didn't plan ahead. You can never plan too early, and by buying now, we can lock in the cost of a funeral, a burial, a cremation, whatever we want, at today's prices, without burdening our children and families with difficult choices. Matthews, the company that manufactures bronze markers, can cut one this week with our names and birthdates and store it in their warehouse until we need it, if we don't want to store it ourselves in the garage or basement.

"I'm not sure what I want," I say. "I think I'd like to be cremated and have my ashes scattered somewhere nice."

He turns to Annie. Okay, he says, let's pretend your husband here is dead. Think of the details: even if you don't want a casket, there's the newspaper obituaries, and maybe his family wants a service—so where do you go? He's left you nothing but questions.

I tell him I don't want a service, but he hushes me. Remember, he says, you're dead. "You're not sick or anything, are you?" he says, touching my arm. "Good, so I can make jokes."

The thing about scattering, he tells us, is that it's illegal. Once he was in White Rock, British Columbia, sitting on the beach, when he felt something sharp. "I've got this bone fragment sticking into my butt cheek. I dig around and come up with this little coin, the size of a loonie or toonie, and I'm in the business so I know what it is. It's the identification marker from a crematorium." With this coin he was able to trace, through the funeral home, the social insurance number, driver's licence and address of the woman who'd paid for the cremation.

"I showed up at her house with an RCMP officer," he says. "She was fined $2,000 for littering." He looks at me, and I sink in my chair. "On the coast you can go twelve miles out to sea and scatter, no problem, but punting them off the pier at White Rock? Sorry, no, that's not okay.

"You think you're scattering to the wind," he says, "and then— plop—you've got Dad in your pants cuff. Nobody wants that. My own father said he wanted to be scattered in Lake Huron, and I told him, number one, you're from Saskatchewan, and number two, you can't swim. So why would I do that?

"Indians go home, they scatter their ashes in the Ganges, then people swim in it. I don't want to know about it. I like pickerel—I don't want you putting human remains in the lake where I catch them. What if you had cancer and they put in those radioactive seeds? Then you're scattering remains that are radioactive."

By now I'm not only dead, but implicated in crimes against humanity and nature and obliquely responsible for the scar on his butt. We could debate the facts, but I won't. I'm supposed to be an average consumer here, a role to which I'm naturally suited. I tend to believe the last thing I read or heard. I don't want to put him off his game, hang him up on a technicality, but the truth is there's no explicit law in Manitoba against scattering cremated remains. It's perfectly legal to scatter on private property as long as you have the owner's permission and do it "discreetly," according to the province's online FAQs. Ontario is even more explicit. You're free to scatter on Crown lands, provincial parks, conservation reserves and the Great Lakes. In fact Ontario officials are more hung up on the flowers people leave behind, which might hurt the wildlife. They ask that you don't. Cremated remains are pure mineral. After two hours at 1,600 degrees they're as sterile as dental tools. Glenn says radioactive pellets have short half-lives on purpose. By the time a body's cremated these can barely raise a Geiger tick. But I don't get into it now, and besides, he's after bigger quarry here: shame, and the "ick factor." We either live in a civil collaborative society or we live in anarchy. My choices affect others. People should be free to walk in the park without fear of getting bits of me on their hiking boots. Scattering is romantic but selfish, and it robs future generations of a permanent place to visit to honour my memory. He's plucking all the right emotional strings.

I nod to Annie that it's time to go, but before we can he stands, looks up at the ceiling and ends his pitch with a poem he recites by heart:

> *Scatter me not to the restless winds*
> *Nor toss my ashes to the sea*
> *Remember now these years gone by*
> *When loving gifts I gave to thee.*

We leave with a handful of brochures.

No wonder Chapel Lawn is taking Neil to court. Neil has four hundred people in his rose garden. Do the math. When I spoke to Andrew Earle, the manager at Chapel Lawn, he put it this way: cemeteries are protected by legislation, they put 25 percent of every sale into a perpetual care fund so the taxpayer won't bear the burden of upkeep when the cemetery is full.

"Neil Bardal is a private for-profit enterprise," he says. "Ten years from now, he falls on hard times. Then the airport or Red River College expands. Grandma pulls down the road to visit her husband in the rose garden, turns the corner and now it's an Old Navy store. Look, Neil is old. What if Eirik decides to pave it over?"

What the corporate chains sell, besides caskets and vaults and urns and a place to bury them, is something more nebulous: the illusion of permanence. In Europe, where land is scarce, cemeteries lease graves for fifteen years. After that the family has the option of extending the lease, but if they don't, the bones are removed and put in a "charnel house" (a community vault for skeletal remains) or buried in a garden. In North America, where property is a right and we value products that last, this would never wash: a grave is forever. It's paid for. The rules of commerce mean we're entitled to a kind of secular immortality. But it's become harder to deliver. In 1997, the Cremation Association of North America found that 23 percent of families who cremated went on to bury the remains in a grave, and 10.5 percent bought space in columbaria. Meanwhile, 36 percent took them home and 18 percent scattered on land or on water, while 6 percent never bothered to pick them up from the crematorium at all. We live in a transient society; our families are global. We're born in Toronto but move to Winnipeg and St. John's, and wind up at a seniors villa in Victoria gumming root vegetables. When we die, there's no obvious place to put the remainder. And if we believe that death means a physiological lights-out, that we won't be called at the Rapture, then it's even less relevant what happens to the body. Scatter, flush, pack me in a teddy bear— whatever. The culture of whatever is what's killing the corporate funeral industry. That and the boom–bust cycle of the market.

Ten years ago they were flush, buying up family funeral homes like candy. Funeral directors, tired of doing more for less, were motivated to sell. The model was simple: by establishing economies of scale, such as buying caskets in bulk and clustering services like embalming in central locations and sharing hearses and other infra-structure, the corporates could cut costs and boost shareholder value. In 1996, Service Corporation International (SCI) owned 2,882 funeral homes, 345 cemeteries and 150 crematoria in North America, with an eye to expanding in Europe and the Pacific Rim. Revenues topped $2.3 billion (US), and by the end of 1998, the company had $3.7 billion worth of pre-arranged sales on the books. It was publicly traded, with share prices in the high $40s. The problem, says Neil, is that in their swift expansion they paid more than market value for properties and piled up huge debt; when the bubble burst, the corporates were stuck. The Loewen Group was the first to go. Run by Ray Loewen, a buddy of Neil's from Steinbach, Manitoba, the company was second only to SCI in volume and sales, and a hungry consolidator. Ray Loewen would fly funeral directors by helicopter to his yacht in Burnaby, British Columbia, serve them brandy and steaks and cigars, and then announce he was buying them out. But in 1999, the Loewen Group applied for Chapter 11 bankruptcy protection. It turned out not enough people were dying. In fact they were living longer than the number-crunchers had predicted. Thanks to flu vaccines, the annual cull of the elderly herd had levelled off. Those who did die were increasingly opting for cheaper cremation. Death rates weren't expected to rise again until 2020, when the boomers would hit their stride, and shareholders who studied these trends the way they studied other commodity futures dumped stock. In 2000, SCI's share value was $7. To tackle the debt, the corporation unloaded properties acquired during the feeding frenzy at a loss, sometimes to the same families that sold them in the first place. Caught in the middle were the big casket manufacturers, Batesville and Matthews. Sales had fallen and the Chinese were flooding the North American market with cheap knock-offs. Matthews closed its factory in Marshfield, Missouri, and moved it to Mexico to compete with global labour costs.

According to Ed Horton, with the accounting firm Citrin Cooperman & Company, it was time for the funeral trade to shift priorities and develop new revenue streams, charge for that which they used to do for free: estate planning, investment advice. Shift from a body-centric industry to a knowledge-based service. SCI launched Dignity Memorial, "the first transcontinental funeral service brand in North America," which offers tiered packages of goods and services including casket, embalming, hearse and prayer cards, but also Web-based memorials, a twenty-four-hour grief counselling hotline, discount airline tickets for the bereaved, assistance in booking hotels and rental cars, a phone card (one hour) and a child/grandchild protection program. With this, a parent or grandparent who buys a Dignity package gets an additional free funeral for their unmarried child or grandchild, provided that child or grandchild dies before turning twenty-one. To help promote the brand, SCI established the Dignity Memorial Escape School, which teaches kids how to recognize threatening situations, get out of car trunks and such, through seminars led by "trained Dignity Memorial® funeral care professionals." In 2007 SCI joined the American Diabetes Association in a three-year campaign to promote awareness of the disease. In the same way Starbucks wants us to feel like we're saving a Guatemalan child every time we buy a coffee, the Dignity Memorial brand reflects a set of values: Are you against child abduction and diabetes? So are we. Unlike the local family funeral home, which is only after your body.

As well as going after new revenues through fee-for-service, they're gambling on the North American consumer's fondness for brand names. Is it working? In 2009, SCI's profits dropped 64 percent from the previous year, and by the time the global economy tanked, its share price sat at $4.25, or a tenth of its worth in the booming late '90s. They're down to 1,300 funeral homes (and 365 cemeteries) in forty-three states, eight provinces, and Puerto Rico. European expansion plans have been shelved. They're focused on the Sun Belt states: 30 percent of their properties are in California, Florida and Texas, where people go to retire and often never come home, except in urns. In 2009 SCI sold the Swackhamer, Blachford & Wray funeral home in Hamilton, Ontario. It will be turned into student housing.

Maybe, like me, you're just a hard-wired anti-corporate curmudgeon, and when it comes to conglomerates in death-care the bad taste gets worse. There's something unsavoury about dealing with funeral directors who have sales targets and a head office in Houston. In 2002, CBC News's *Marketplace* investigated five independents and five SCI funeral homes in Vancouver. For a traditional service, excluding casket and extras such as flowers, the prices ranged from $1,935 at one of the indies to almost $3,400 at an SCI home, 75 percent more for the same basic package. But indies have sales targets too. Look at the widow D. who shopped for a deal and wound up with an estimate of $4,000.

The chains sell pre-need packages like mad, to people on tight budgets. The shame-game is a powerful motivator: do you want to burden your family with the cost of a funeral? Why not take care of it ahead of time in two hundred easy monthly payments. But then, plenty of indie funeral directors have skipped town after draining their own pre-need trust accounts. The big guys are easy targets but there's plenty of commercial foul play to go around.

My best window on the conglomerate philosophy came from Darin Hoffman, a former big fish in the corporate tank. He'd been a general manager at the Alderwoods Group, working his way up to vice-president and director of sales, based at Thomson "In the Park" in Winnipeg, the funeral–cemetery combo everyone around here called the Taj Mahal. When SCI bought Alderwoods, he got his pink slip, but now he runs an independent home called Mosaic, which focuses on pre-need sales in the local Filipino community.

"The corporation is a product of society," he said. "It's the face of society. The investment world and public greed drives it. The challenge is to balance that with what the community wants. The family's need is a noble cause, but we have to have a paycheque too." The indie directors burned time at the Rotary and other service clubs, scratching for leads, but the corporates know the power of direct marketing, working the phones, and they have the resources. "We can be fairly aggressive too," he says, "because it's what people want. They're dealing with wills and estate planning. We have products and services they need. Fine. Why not do it all ahead of time? People plan weddings a year in advance."

I told him my walnut-sized brain had a hard time with insurance. I understood that if I bought my funeral now, the Taj Mahal or Chapel Lawn would lock in the price, then earn their end off the commissions. Still, Neil has pre-need contracts in his drawer from the 1980s guaranteeing a price of hundreds of dollars for funerals that will cost thousands when it comes time to cash them in. What was the point in giving up revenue in the future just to get the sale today?

"If I sold a policy ten years ago for a traditional funeral," Darin explained, "and the person died today, in the cremation era, then I've delivered a traditional funeral into the cremation age." He was beaming about this. In a way, it seemed to me, the pre-need was a hedge against trends towards cheaper disposition. In the future, when we all drive flying cars, maybe the dead will be processed at home, in the microwave or through some iPhone app, reduced to cuboctahedral blocks of salt and mineral like on *Star Trek*. By selling even a direct-cremation contract now, Darin would guarantee his own survival. Locking in today's prices sounds like a bargain for the shopper, but what if death-care just gets cheaper and cheaper? For Darin, pre-need insurance was a form of economic time travel. I liked that. It put me in mind of parallel universes.

One of the problems with pre-needs, as I see it, is that you're giving money to a funeral director or a corporate chain for them to play with in the meantime. There are regulations, but every trust fund holder is allowed to invest a certain amount of the money (12 percent in Manitoba) and earn interest. It's no longer yours, it's theirs. You could put the same amount in a savings account or a trust account that pays out to a named beneficiary when you die. If you change your mind, it's still your cash. You can take it out. Buy something frilly. Plus in Canada, if you've paid enough years into the Canada Pension Plan, you get a $2,500 death benefit. Spend spend spend while you're alive, and let the feds cover the brunt of the funeral, provided your survivor's tastes are modest. The other problem is that when you buy a pre-need, it might amount to little more than a down payment. Neil says he knew a man who made pre-need arrangements with one of the chains. He wanted to be cremated. He spent $5,000 on a grave with a marker, an urn, and an outer box for the urn to be buried in: the works. When he died, his wife figured it was all covered. But the funeral home told her she'd still have to cover the cost of the actual cremation, plus the opening and closing of the grave, and if she wanted a service, that would be extra, plus disbursements for the minister and flowers and cards and the newspaper notice. "She pays another $5,000," Neil says, "and curses her dumb sonofabitch husband. You wind up with two people overpaying on two separate occasions. The funeral home gets two cracks at a sale instead of one. No wonder they're raking in the cash."

Richard and I meet with a woman, a forty-one-year-old pharmacist who wants to pre-pay for her funeral. She wants to be cremated but she doesn't want to leave the worries of arrangements to her family. She has no children, but there's a niece in her thirties.

"Do you want a memorial service?" says Richard.

"It's kind of funny to think of who would come to my memorial service," she says. "I guess I sort of want what my dad had, except without the alcohol."

"Let the family worry about the service and anything that goes with it. We'll keep it on the basis of doing the cremation. It's a year deal, 20 percent down if we do it today. In twelve months it comes to $1,995 plus GST."

"Nineteen ninety-five," she says. "You mean two thousand. I thought, wow, twenty bucks."

"I don't get out of bed for twenty bucks."

"That's what I thought. For a service, I guess I'll be dead, I won't care."

"Let's not set too much in stone. Ten years from now you'll probably have been to three or four other funerals and you'll have seen something you liked, a video display or something. You may want to revisit it, like if you get involved in a Church."

"Not that I don't believe in God," she says. "I guess I never imagined a funeral in a church. I'm not Catholic or Jewish where it's a big thing. I'm pretty . . . I don't know. I don't want a headstone.

People I know will carry me with them. I'd like donations made in lieu of flowers, probably something to do with the hearing impaired or the deaf."

Richard takes her vital stats, tells her he'll keep information on file for the obituary. He explains the cremation process in some detail. For the pre-need, there's a ten-day cooling-off period if she wants out. The contract won't cover disbursements: flowers, printing, clergy—all the costs that we don't control. If she plans on travelling, he says, there should be someone charged with calling Richard if anything happens while she's away. She tells him she probably won't leave Winnipeg. But she'll keep his card on her fridge. She pays the deposit and I witness her signature. Now all that's left to do is wait for forty or fifty years, while Richard's card grows yellow on her fridge door.

Thirteen

"SHALL WE GATHER AT THE RIVER?"

*I*n celebrating Mom's life," says the silver-haired man at the lectern, "there are three things. Her handwriting was superb. The other thing was her ability to solve puzzles. And the other thing was her ability to keep a secret in a big family, but anyways, in my opinion, she was basically a pillar of strength, however you consider a pillar of strength."

It is a big family, nearly 150 of them filling the Aubrey chapel: daughters and husbands, nieces and cousins, three wailing infants and at least two sets of identical twins, some of whom are playing hide-and-seek behind the chapel chairs. Two kids run past me in the office spraying it, and me, with Dixie cups full of water. The eulogist is one of the sons-in-law.

"Right now," he says (he really does sport an impressive hairstyle, shellacked like a helmet, like it would ping if I tossed a paper clip at it), "she's experiencing the hereafter. The most oldest and authentic document is the Bible, written between 1500 BC and 100 AD, which has also been a best-seller for sixty-five years, did you know this? And that in itself is a feat. Jesus Christ is the saviour of the whole world, and that includes Winnipeg, Manitoba."

The crowd is attentive but reserved, hands folded in laps, parents whispering at children to knock it off. No doubt they've heard his routine before, at summer suppers and Thanksgiving, or whenever there's enough of them in a room for uncle to take a crack at saving their souls.

"If our lives are but a puff of smoke, guess what? We have a million years in eternity and it will be with Christ. The Bible promises us seventy years, and to be born of the spirit is to be born again, born spiritually, so we trust in our saviour Jesus Christ, and we wish Mom a swift fulfilling life afterwards. She is blessed beyond anything we can think of."

Time for food. The family brought their own: carrots and dips and a Black Forest cake from Costco. Men gather at the door to decide if they'll have another cigarette, discussing the likelihood of an al-Qaeda attack on Manitoba. A legless nephew is lifted from his wheelchair onto a couch where he moans until someone brings him a coffee. The twins are now running in circles, grinding Black Forest cake into the carpet, until one of them smacks forehead first into a door jamb and hollers. A teenage cousin picks him up and carries him into the chapel where people have lined up to view the body. The funeral has all the frantic energy of a dysfunctional family reunion, with none of the grim, repressed bleakness of the standard, secular service. It's as if Mom's being sent on a cruise, "blessed beyond anything we can think of," instead of into the retort, which is where we'll be taking her in the morning. Can it be this easy?

I'm so caught up in my own community of lovable cynics and born-again pagans and Facebook friends who bark about alienation and a mechanized, globalized world where the old myths no longer hold up that I forget there are people who've got the whole puzzle solved: Believe, and even death is no biggie. When the family leaves, I scrape cake from the rug.

The main distinction between human beings and all other life forms, according to Sheldon Solomon, a psychologist in Sarasota Springs, New York, and a student of Ernest Becker, who wrote *The Denial of Death* (and who, as fate would have it, died just before they awarded him the Pulitzer Prize), is that we're smart enough to recognize that we exist. Unlike the houseplant, we experience the awe of being alive and knowing it. But once we know that we're here, it's a short step to knowing that one day, maybe tomorrow or in an hour, we won't be. Without some system of defence we'd be paralyzed with overwhelming terror over the fact that we're "breathing, defecating pieces of meat, no more important or durable than a lizard or a potato," he says. So what we did, cleverly and quite unconsciously, was to collaborate in the construction of a culture to give us a sense that we live in a world that has meaning, a world with art and industry and borders and trade rules and quality daytime talk-television, all earthly distractions from the nasty fact parked in our heads: we are doomed. Is it enough? Of course not. Anxiety gnaws, and we build our protective walls higher. We invent a God.

All religions, says Solomon, have one thing in common: some belief that is in violation of natural law. The Christian resurrection, the Hindu belief in reincarnation are "facts" for which the empirical evidence is still pending. So why do some of us accept them as true? Three possible reasons: (1) we're idiots (this would be Nietzsche's view, that we're children who haven't outgrown our fantasies); (2) it's an accidental by-product of some adaptive cognitive process (this would be Richard Dawkins's view, that religious belief is a wiring mix-up, a relic of some other, important evolutionary development, like the sensible human fear of bears and poison mushrooms); and (3) religious belief is an essential adaptation, and our lives would be unsustainable without it. If we think that we just disappear—*snap*, lights out—we'd never get any work done, either at the office or in benefit of the gene pool.

In the past, when faith wasn't an option but an expectation, in the pre-postmodern heyday of the Judeo-Christian tradition, the clergy got all the hot rituals: birth, coming of age, marriage, death. Except in pockets like Steinbach, deep in Mennonite country, and the Jewish chapel in Winnipeg, they've lost them to commerce. At most the clergy are hired as consultants. Don Johnston, the minister at Silver Heights United, told me that when it comes to funerals, he deals with two streams: his small congregation and the "street trade." For the street trade, the walk-ins and cold calls, he meets families at home or a coffee shop or what he calls the "spooky alternative," a hotel room. "People are so removed from Church tradition," he said, "we don't speak the same language. They've never heard of the hymns. They want 'In the Arms of an Angel' by Sarah McLachlan. This is a dangerous area. 'Jeremiah Was a Bullfrog'—does it belong at a Christian funeral? It's tricky."

One family had worked out the order of service. They wanted him to say, "God, put on a pot of coffee, Mother's coming," then blow out a candle. His response was, You don't need me. This is a theatrical presentation, and you don't need me. He wouldn't do it.

Walk-ins are less of an issue for Chesed Shel Emes, the Jewish chapel. They bury Jews, Orthodox Jews, that's it. Arrangements are made through the synagogue and the body is prepared without embalming, washed and dressed in a linen shroud by the volunteer Chevra Kadisha, the burial society. Everyone gets the same casket, a variation on the Mennonite Special, with rope handles and no metal parts. The family sits shiva for a week, and friends bring food. They cover the mirrors, men don't shave, and when the week is done, a son (or if there's no son, some other male member of the family) goes to synagogue every day to say Kaddish with the congregation. Kaddish is a prayer in praise of God but it's also a kind of intoned music, meant to reassure the mourner that he's not alone.

Annie's friend Nola said she found shiva a great comfort when her brother died. "I can't imagine how you goyim do without it," she said. She also didn't get why we keep our people on ice in the funeral home. "It seems barbaric to leave your loved ones in some no-man's land." Jews bury right away, and during preparations at the mortuary the body is never alone. There's always a volunteer who stays overnight, sleeping on the couch to keep the spirit company. The chapel on Main Street has been there since 1930, a flat-faced red-brick building with a round window over the door like a single eye peering at the Knysh brothers' Ukrainian funeral home across the street. I went there, and met Rena Boroditsky, the only paid staff member, new to the job. Her predecessor had been a Holocaust survivor who'd held the position for twenty-eight years.

The room where they wash the bodies has a morgue table and a shower head and a Tupperware bin full of broken terra cotta pottery to place on the eyes. A candle burns on a shelf by the door. A space heater keeps the place warm. Some Chevra Kadishas, she says, use a bathtub to cleanse the body, but she rigged the shower to shut itself off after the prescribed twenty-four quarts of water has passed over the corpse. They say prayers in the prep room, prayers about the beauty of the human body as the vessel of the soul. They never cover the face or pass tools over the body. For men, they sprinkle earth from Mount Olive in Israel on the eyes, heart and genitals. Until it feels the earth the soul won't stop wanting. Women don't need it. "There are times," she laughed, "when it starts to sound like a fairy tale." They get their earth from Rose Solomon's, a burial supply company in New York, in little plastic mustard packets. The terra cotta pots come from a gardening supply store.

Jewellery comes off. Not long before we met, Rena had her first belly-button ring: a teenager who'd died in a car crash. Blue nail polish too, which she removed. Catheters and IVs come out, but bandages, anything with blood, go with the body. They bury amputated limbs too, even if the amputee is still alive, as long as he's willing to buy a plot. "Usually legs go in an infant casket," she said. Caskets cost $340, there's no markup, but a $10,000 solid oak would still be kosher, although custom prohibits burying metal with the body, so the handles would have to come off. The linen burial clothes look like gauzy pyjamas with booty feet, meant to come apart in the grave. The faster the burial the better.

"Someone dies," she said, "I'm the nudnik who says, Why not have the funeral tomorrow? But people are spread out, there's travel, there's catering for the meal of consolation, they can't book the synagogue. It's like planning a party."

Chesed Shel Emes gets $1,265 per call including the cost of the casket, to cover heat and lights "and my extravagant salary." But the whole nut, including the plot, the hearse, the opening and closing of the grave, an annual Yahrzeit letter to the family on the anniversary of the death, can come close to $12,000, and that goes to the synagogue, which also sells pre-needs.

"I can't afford to get buried," Rena said.

Not everyone in the community is comfortable with the rules. Winnipeg is traditional, she said, but not observant—there's a difference. Some Jews go to Knysh, for cremation, which Rena finds abhorrent, "especially after the Holocaust. People phone me, they see it in the paper. Someone's been cremated, they're horrified. 'How can a Jew do that?' they're yelling at me, like I'm the Jewish answer lady." She's trying to reinvent a religious rite for a secular world, she says, "but the truth is, the non-Jews are more fascinated by this than the Jews. Maybe people are searching for something."

I am, and there's enough latent Catholic in me to feel guilty about not being Catholic enough to know what it is. But she's right, there's a lesson for goyim in the hard-core Jewish ritual and it has something to do with community. In my world it's possible to lose someone, spend two days in the embrace of family and friends and then wake up alone, staring at an empty crusted scalloped potato dish, with no clue what to do next. The Jews have a schedule you can pin to the fridge, and when you go to the synagogue, people you don't even know will sit with you and say Kaddish.

The Catholic Church has always owned cemeteries, but just recently, like the synagogues, they've got into the funeral trade. In

Hayward, across the bay from San Francisco, the Oakland Diocese bought an existing mortuary with a retort next to Holy Sepulchre cemetery, the first Church-owned funeral home in North America. They'd been approached by Stewart Enterprises, one of the consolidators, which ran five funeral homes for the Los Angeles Diocese under a combined brand. But Oakland wanted to strike out on its own. Stewart, they said, charged too much, and at every other funeral home the so-called "Catholic package" of a vigil and a funeral mass and a committal at the cemetery was invariably the most expensive item on the price list, $10,000 or more. So their idea was to find a way to preserve the ritual while keeping the price in reach of the flock, or more important, those who wanted to return to the flock before they died. So they set a single service charge: $2,400 for a mass at the family parish, a viewing at Holy Angels, their new funeral home, and a graveside ceremony. It didn't matter if the body was prepped or cremated, the price was the same. Casket, grave and marker were extra. The independent funeral homes that identified themselves as Catholic called foul. The owner of the Chapel of Angels in Freemont said he felt betrayed by his own Church: "My great-grandparents helped to buy the dirt for Holy Sepulchre," he said, accusing the diocese of using low-cost funerals as a loss leader to get people through the door to sell them high-priced cemetery property. Robert Seelig, who runs the funeral wing of the Oakland Diocese, told me it was unlikely that people would opt for burial in a cemetery they didn't like just to get a cheaper funeral. Meanwhile, the CFO of Carriage Services, another chain, said the Church had the advantage of a "somewhat captive audience."

Holy Angels, Chapel of Angels: it's not hard to see how the consumer could get confused, sorting out who ran what funeral home for which reason. And of course the whole secular industry uses churchiness as a carrot—you can buy a rosary or Our Lady of Guadalupe trinkets to decorate the corners of your casket at an Alderwoods showroom. Loewen used to run cemeteries in Arizona for the Church, and in 1998, SCI donated a "major gift" to the Pontifical North American College in Rome to build a new chapel and a suite for the bishop. The industry likes its Catholics. They buy caskets, and even though Vatican II declared cremation kosher in 1962, they tend to go into the ground or the mausoleum crypt whole. In the cremation era, they represent a breath of fresh capital.

"We're not about the 'Our Lady' stencil on the casket lid," Seelig said. "Our job is not to overdo the symbolism and become some kind of amusement park. The industry is coming out with new marketing ideas because they think families want something new, but I think it's the opposite." Tradition is on the lip of a comeback. The mainstream industry is the religion of self-invention, where every man is defined by his preferences, and every woman gets her personalized ritual of bagpipes and bunny releases. The Church, meanwhile, provides an alternative by not providing any alternatives. A pall is placed on the casket (this must drive Batesville bananas, like putting a tarp on a Maserati) to level the playing field. There's no eulogy. In Catholic death everyone's equal.

Seelig told me they're building an even bigger mortuary in San Pablo and hope to add a second retort to Holy Angels; they're pulling in new business from non-Catholics, including the local Sikhs. On three acres of property at the edge of Holy Sepulchre cemetery they're planting a vineyard: Pinot Noir, Zinfandel, Chardonnay. Three acres means three hundred cases of wine.

If it's any good, he said, they'll sell it at fundraisers, and if it isn't they'll use it for the sacrament.

It all starts to sound like a fairy tale, Rena said. At least religious faith, when it comes to death, is a fairy tale that soothes. It doesn't deny there's a monster in the closet or a wolf in the woods, but it tames them. A study at Yale, published in the *International Journal of Psychiatry in Medicine*, found that "bereaved individuals who relied on religion to cope generally used outpatient services less frequently," compared to non-believers. The authors said that a greater reliance on what they called "religious coping" could add up to huge savings for the U.S. health-care system, up to $180 million a year by their numbers. While the rest of us pile on the sleeping pills and antidepressants, widows of faith tend to visit the church instead of the doctor.

I find it oddly comforting when science ponies up evidence of the benefits of faith: if we're hard-wired to believe, if piety is a full-on evolutionary advantage, then maybe I shouldn't fight so hard to squelch it. If it brings comfort in the face of death, why not seek it? Neil's happy to leave religion to the Church. Music, he says, is what brings meaning to the ritual. But I think the believers have a leg-up on meaning. And even as I go back and forth on my own faith (Buddha? Christ? Shiva? Who's got the goods?), I feel better knowing the faithful are out there, as if the world is a better place as long as someone, if not me, lights candles in a church.

The Birchwood funeral co-op in Steinbach is decorated in standard mortuary chic. Green wingbacks, dusty rose carpeting and pictures of empty benches and misty waterfalls on the walls, which are also dusty rose. I'm here on a special assignment, to drive the coach for one of their funerals. Birchwood owns one hearse, so when they get busy and need a second, they rent Neil's, plus a driver, and today I'm it. I jumped at the chance to get out into the world, meet new corpses.

Bill Dyck is the funeral director on duty. He points me to a water cooler and invites me to sit while he tends to a family in the casket showroom. I pull a brochure out of the rack. Birchwood, it says, was formed as a response to the growth of corporate chains. By buying shares (a minimum of two hundred at a dollar apiece) members get discounts on services, voting rights at Board of Directors meetings and a stake in the company, like at co-op gas bars and lumberyards. It's odd that Steinbach, a Mennonite community, was ground zero for one of the biggest funeral chains in North America; down the street from Birchwood is the original Loewen family funeral home, now owned by Alderwoods since the Loewen Group went bankrupt.

Bill returns and invites me into the chapel. I peg him at Neil's age, maybe a few years younger. Sturdy and stiff-backed, he speaks with a clipped, hoarse voice due to what he describes as a partially paralyzed larynx. He says he asked his doctor if it mightn't have been caused by a mini-stroke, and his doctor told him that sounded like as good a reason as any other. He used to work for Ray Loewen, then Alderwoods, but quit when the prices got too high to defend.

"Have you ever seen a man with no septum in his nose?" he asks me.

I admit that I haven't. He shows me to the chapel. Up front is a simple grey-chintz cloth-covered casket (the Mennonite Special) surrounded by flowers, and sure enough, the man in the box has a single big nostril instead of the usual two. Not knowing what else to say, I commend Bill on the embalming. You can judge a community, I think, by the colour of its dead: the more traditional the clientele the brighter the corpse, and this man's been juiced to the eyeballs, as pink as a crayon. Bill smiles. This one's staying here, he says. Ours is in the back. I follow him down a bright corridor where we find another cloth casket, which he wheels into the garage where I've parked the hearse. He opens the box to reveal a gnomish man wearing glasses and a plain suit: no lapels on the jacket, no collar on the shirt, the uniform of the ultra-conservative Mennonite. I count nostrils. There are two. We're taking him to Reinland Mennonite Church, near Grunthal, southeast of the city. The crowd will be mostly "white caps," Bill says, women in bonnets and men in plain suits like the one worn by the body in the box. They work hard and pray hard, and when one of them dies, the routine is the same: they gather at the church, pray and sing, and then after a meal of cold cuts and raisin buns, they bury the body themselves. Not much for us to do but deliver the box. This will not be a Celebration of Life, but a celebration of death: for the hardcore Mennonites death is not tragic, but a deliverance. It's like being called up to the Majors.

We load the casket into the coach, and then Bill gives the vehicle a quick rinse with the hose, wiping the doors with a chamois to get rid of the road dust acquired on the drive from Winnipeg. I take off my coat to help. The breeze from the open garage door feels chilly, and I realize I'm not wearing my suit jacket. I look in the front seat of the hearse. It's not there. In my head I can see it, hanging on my dining room chair at home, where I put it so I wouldn't forget it. It would take me two hours, there and back, to get it. Maybe there's a spare in the prep room, some dead man's jacket I can borrow for the afternoon, but I'm likely to forget that too, and wind up wearing it home to Winnipeg. All that's left is to admit I'm a moron.

"Sorry," I say, holding up my arms in shirt sleeves. "I forgot my suit jacket."

"That's fine," he says, buffing the door handle on the back of the coach, and I think to myself: here's a species I've never encountered, the mellow funeral director.

On the road to Grunthal I stick close to Bill's Cadillac so I don't get lost, but in fact, this is the Prairies: it would take days for me to lose sight of him. We pass factory hog farms and chicken barracks and a few bored dairy cattle, and at every mile, according to the grid system that creates order out of acres and acres of nothing, another crossroad. I turn on the radio, browsing the pre-sets from classic rock to country to Winnipeg's BOB-FM ("Hits of the 80s, 90s, Whatever"), but then check myself. The man in the back is off to his eternal rest. He needs hymns and prayers to get him there, not "Mr. Roboto" by Styx. I shut off the tunes and drive in silence.

Reinland church is a white clapboard box that looks less like a house of God than a hockey rink or community centre. I back the hearse against the concrete apron at the front door, and Bill and I dolly the casket inside. According to custom, it will be left in the foyer, open, so that parishioners can see the dead man before they take their seats. The chapel is lit with fluorescents that buzz, and the walls are bare: no cross, no pictures. Up front is a bank of chairs with microphones, like in a courthouse or at a Senate hearing, and the pews are straight-backed and worn. The building smells of old, sour wood. Off to the side of the foyer is a "crying room" with an iron crib, painted white. Bill says it's where women bring their babies if they start wailing during the service. The place is stripped down to basics. Leave the art and architecture to the Roman Catholics: in Grunthal, Jesus is a minimalist.

Two shy men and a handful of big-eyed children approach the casket. The girls wear their hair in long double braids, and the boys are in white shirts buttoned to the top. They stare silently at the body. Bill briefs the men on how to bear pall, which way to turn the casket so it'll open to face the congregation when they're ready to start the ceremony. One of the girls plays with the dead man's hair. When the briefing is done, we leave. Protocol prevents us from staying for the service, but we're invited back for sandwiches and snacks before the burial, which will be at the churchyard in Roseau River, forty minutes south, near the Minnesota border.

"Come on," Bill says, "I'll show you my horses," and we head out in the Caddy to his farm west of town, passing a ranch for miniature ponies ("those things are tough as nails"), and Freebird Auto Body, the sign for which is a Confederate flag. Bill tells me his father and mother sold caskets in Rosthern, Saskatchewan, near Saskatoon, simple wood flat-tops that his dad made himself. He and his mother would dress and casket the bodies after they'd been embalmed at the local funeral home, then families would come to their house to pick up the finished package and take it to church themselves. He spent time in a lumber camp in British Columbia, and shows me the stub where his left index finger used to be. He also worked at Penner Dodge in Steinbach where he once sold a pickup truck to the man we left in the casket at Reinland church.

Birchwood has three thousand members, many in Winnipeg. There was talk of opening a satellite shop in the city, but then

Walter Klassen, an undertaker with deep Mennonite roots, opened Friends Funeral Home on Main Street across from the golf course, thereby scooping them on the demographic. Birchwood's business is mostly traditional burial. "Around here the orthodox do not tolerate cremation," he says. At the farm he lowers my window and calls out to a horse named Jazz, a spring foal, and two other colts on awkward legs come over for a look. They snort through the window. I wipe horse snot from my face with my tie.

By the time we get back to the church, the congregation is filing out, singing "Shall We Gather at the River?" Those who are going to the cemetery get first crack at the food, with a second sitting for the rest. I follow Bill into the lunch hall where teenage girls in white caps work the room, serving coffee and water from jugs. The tables are laid with raisin buns, orange cheddar, ham and lunch loaf, butter, brownies and lemon curd squares. The woman to my right asks where I'm from and if I speak Low German and why I'm still wearing my coat. I take it off. People stab at buns with their forks, and an elderly man scoops a cut-glass decanter of Coffee-mate with his knife to slide it closer. The children sit still and don't make a noise. Two old men giggle and whisper into each other's hearing aids. The mood is festive.

The second sitting is called and we move to the foyer, to ready the casket for transport. "See that woman?" Bill says, pointing to a lady with a tumbleweed pile of red hair. "She never misses a funeral."

"A Birchwood groupie," I say, and he nods.

A man in a western-cut rodeo shirt and a dinner-plate belt buckle looks down at the body as we shut the lid. "I worked with him the summer he cut off his fingers with the baler," he says. It occurs to me that I might be the only one here who still has all ten.

On the highway, Bill leads and I follow, with a few dozen cars in a long line of headlights behind me. At Roseau River I pull the coach into a dirt lot behind a white church, as plain as the last one but much smaller. I park nose-first against a pile of hay next to a wooden swing set. Behind me, in a bare spot that could be confused with additional parking, is the graveyard, with a half dozen or so flat stone markers. The hole's been dug, the Device installed (Bill was here earlier today), and next to the grave is a pile of sandy dirt with half a dozen shovels stuck into it. Six men carry the box from the hearse onto the straps of the Device, and as it's lowered, the crowd around the grave sings "Safe in the Arms of Jesus" from photocopied sheets. Children make faces at one another over the open grave. The men shovel dirt in by hand. It hits the box with a startling thump that I feel in my chest.

By now the sky is bruised blue and pink, with clouds like unstirred ink in water, and I hug my arms against the cold. A woman lays a crocheted caftan over an elderly man's shoulders, which she rubs to bring them both some warmth. Even with the cold and the growing dark, watching the pile get smaller I feel strangely uplifted. Unlike at the other burials I've seen, no one's in a rush to get it over with, and no one's checking their watches or their cell phones for text messages. They have a ritual to complete, a responsibility to stay until the grave is filled. *"How beau-ti-ful heaven must be, must be, / Sweet home of the happy and free,"* they sing, and they mean it. Bill shakes my hand. I'm released from duty.

On the drive back to Winnipeg, I play the scene again in my head: the singing, and the rhythm of the sand hitting the casket. It's the same ritual that sent their grandparents and great-grandparents to the sweet home of the happy and free, and when they die, and their kids die, someone will dig a hole and bury them too. There's a symmetry that's also oddly liberating in its lack of choice. The rest of us get to argue over casket and urn catalogues, flipping from the La Precia to the Fredericksburg Cherry, pricing keepsakes and ash pendants and white-knuckling through a stack of CDs for music for the Celebration of Life. Randy Travis or Travis Tritt? Which one did Dad like? We can't remember. Play "Wind Beneath My Wings." We pay thousands for an improvised ritual, a one-off, where only the family gets the inside jokes in the eulogy about Dad's ill-fitting dentures and the childhood dog he accidentally shot on a hunting trip, who went on to live a long three-legged life, while the rest of the mourners just scratch their heads, as if they're watching some cryptic home movie.

The Mennonites have it easier: same casket, same hymns, same prayers, and everyone knows the script. This is what it must be like to live in an ordered universe, where the roads meet at right angles at every mile and, if you're good and you pray and marry the girl God wants you to marry, His plan will be revealed when you die. You just have to get through the hard part: life, with its endless string of chicken-plucking and lousy weather. Forget self-expression or personal dreams and goals, especially if you're a woman or gay or have doubts, in which case you may be shunned and lose your place in the queue for paradise. You can't be sort-of orthodox. You're on the team or you're not. But the trade-off is clarity. You will go to heaven, and your neighbours will bury your body and send you on your way.

It's dark by the time I get to the Factory. The lot's empty, except for a van I don't recognize. A light's on in the building. I key-code the back door and find one of the trade clients inside with a late delivery. He's wearing a hunter's camo jacket and cap, and he's buttering the dead woman's face and hands with Kalon cream. "Don't want her to dry out," he chirps.

Tomorrow there'll be three more just like her, folks who are alive tonight but who won't be by morning. The next day there'll be three or four more, and so on. If God reveals Himself at a funeral home, it's through His regularity: they just keep coming. Some of them will be carried to the grave and sung at or psalm'd at, but most will be cremated, their ashes sent home to their families, who, with all good intentions, will store them away until they can come up with a good idea for the last, final step.

Fourteen

THE STORM

Monday morning, and we're heading for a ward removal at Tuxedo Villa, a seniors home on Corydon Avenue. Glenn parks the van in the back between two blue BFI recycling bins. The last time he was here, he parked in front and the staff barked at him about the optics. We roll the stretcher down a dim hallway, past residents in wheelchairs who ignore us. The drapes are drawn in the room with the body. The roommate is on the toilet, door open. In fact there is no door. The dead woman's slippers are already in the wastebasket, her clothes in a dry-cleaning bag on the dresser. On top of the bag is the death certificate, which Glenn attaches to his clipboard. She was ninety-one. Her head is tilted back in the usual pose, mouth agape, as if she were caught mid-snore. Glenn hands me gloves and we lift her onto the stretcher; she's very light. She spent her life as a nurse in England, one of the staffers tells us, and when she came to Tuxedo Villa "she thought she could run the place," but that was a long time ago. The last years have been hard. Back down the hallway, we turn at the loading dock where an alarmed Purolator deliveryman holds the door open. The service is the next day, ten people, cookies, with Shirley Burton on piano. The ashes are sent back to England in a DS008, a simple wood urn that costs $395 and is made by a local craftsman.

Thursday afternoon: arrangement conference at Aubrey with one family member, the son-in-law. His wife's mother died last night and he's the executor. She used to be hale, he says, a gardener. When she was eighty she shovelled a truckload of topsoil and tilled it into her garden bed herself. But in the last few years, she's been unreachable, "probably schizophrenic." She died at home.

"So," Richard says, checking the file, "cremation?"

"Yes, please."

Forms are signed. Afterwards, she'll be stored at Aubrey, and scattered in the rose garden in the spring.

"How about April?" says Richard.

"You decide," the man says. "In fact I don't care to be there, so whatever the weather permits." His wife, he says, has three siblings, but none of them are coming home, so there's no need for a service.

The bill is $2,282.80 with GST. The man takes out his credit card, then pauses. He says his bank has offered to settle estate matters and funeral costs at a lower interest rate than Visa.

"You sure you don't want the Air Miles?"

He pauses again. "No," he says, "I'll go with the bank."
We're done in twenty minutes.

We're deep in a period of what Neil calls the "big black hole," when the phone never rings, no matter how much he glares at it. Those who do call are looking for cheap and fast. For an industry that should be recession-proof (death and taxes, and all) the numbers are down, not just in Winnipeg but across North America. SCI's calls fell 11 percent in the first quarter of 2009, which company president Tom Ryan described to investors as a drop "that many of us have never seen in our business careers." Blame medical advancements against the big three (heart disease, cancer, stroke) and the fact that the current crop of those-most-likely-to-die come from a generation born in the 1920s and 1930s when birth rates were low. There are simply fewer old people and they're living longer. But here's the corker: modern death is preceded by an average ten years of chronic illness or dementia, according to the United Kingdom's Office for National Statistics. In effect people are dying years before they're technically dead, lost to Alzheimer's and such. Family members who processed their grief and loss early, when the disease first took hold, are exhausted and possibly relieved by the time grandfather finally stops breathing. As he has outlived his peers, there's no call for an elaborate funeral, so they call the crematorium. Is this the fate of the baby boomers? Will the most self-absorbed generation since the Habsburg Austrians peter out in their nineties, die at a hundred and then simply . . . disappear? Into Neil Bardal's rose garden?

The light in the tunnel, if you want to call it that, is that the boomers are getting a head start. *The New York Times* says middle-aged Americans represent "ballooning crises" of addiction and high-risk behaviour, including double the number of binge drinkers compared with teenagers and college students combined, and a 30-percent higher incidence of fatal accidents and suicides than people ages fifteen to nineteen, according to the National Center for Health Statistics. At the age at which their fathers retired and bought their first La-Z-Boy chairs, they're still skydiving and competing in triathlons and running the bulls in Pamplona. Yoga and colonic irrigation won't save them if they keep this up.

William "B.T." Hathaway, an independent funeral director in Fall River, Massachusetts, has been studying the numbers. The normal death rate up to age 29 is one in 10,000, but over age 60 it increases a hundredfold. If you define the boomers as those between ages 45 and 74, the number of what B.T. calls "prime of life" deaths will increase in the next five or ten years, up to 400,000 in the United States before the demographic hits peak mortality. These are people with jobs, living spouses, school-age children and social lives. "At the very least," he says, "baby boomers will offset the trend seen in recent years towards limited gatherings and non-facility memorial services," by dying early enough to warrant well-attended funerals. "Now is not the time to get out of limousines," he says.

Still, for the most part, the self-same boomers are engaged in a standoff with death-care. I brought this up with Neil, who's also on the board of Riverview, one of the chronic-care hospitals. At some point, he said, simple economics will kick in.

"Your generation has to make a decision," he said. "When I grew up, twelve people lived in the same self-contained house, the grandparents lived upstairs, and it didn't cost the state a cent. But a hospital is driven by tax dollars. By keeping mother alive for eight years at $300 a day we might ask: can we afford it?"

"What's the alternative?" I said, knowing that he always has one.

"We need to teach people my age who'll be in that situation fifteen years from now to be agreeable to things like a living will, but with more of a definition, giving the state some room to be proactive." The elderly should take on a new leadership role, he said, by spearheading a social revolution and taking themselves voluntarily out of the economic loop.

"You mean . . ."

"Overdose," he said, and his eyes brightened up for the first time that day. "You can't put a family member in that position, you have to do it as a community. But we're not talking about it at all. I grew up in the ass end of that era when you took care of grandfather, and now people are saying goodbye years before he actually dies. You hear people say, we quit having birthday parties eight years ago."

It's an interesting concept, coming from an undertaker: socialized euthanasia, as in Christopher Buckley's novel *Boomsday*, which imagines, once the boomers hit retirement age, a social security system on the edge of collapse. An influential blogger comes up with the solution: encourage senior citizens to off themselves in exchange for tax benefits.

"That's where I want to be if the cancer comes back," Neil said, "on the fast track. My kids will have no problem with this."

The collective kids at Aubrey and the Factory, meanwhile, are taking the opportunity of a slump in business to crank up the interpersonal sniping. Richard's peeved at Eirik for unilaterally stocking Colonial caskets in the showroom, which Richard considers his turf. A detente's been declared on the issue of clothes-cutting, but now Shannon and Eirik are at odds over her prep room techniques, in particular her practice of "wicking" the dead. This involves cutting into the inner thighs and stuffing the holes with cotton Webril, raising the feet, and leaving the body overnight to drain, to counter-act puffiness and edema. Eirik calls it a waste of time and valuable embalming chemicals (Richard suggests putting the body in the retort "on low" instead, but no one's in the mood for gags). Shannon threatened to quit, to take the repeated offers from Chapel Lawn, but Richard, acting on Neil's request, spent half an hour on the phone with her, talking her out of it. Just keep your head down and do your work, he said, same advice he had for Natalie. It's like any zoo. When they're no longer sure where the next meal's coming from, the monkeys turn on one another.

"I've seen this place like a roller coaster," says Richard, "but now the plunges are getting deeper and that part at the top where you catch your breath is too short. Times like this you hang on for dear life."

The truth is, Richard has thought about moving on himself. The province runs a good disaster management program, and if Winnipeg has anything to offer it's the potential for disaster. The Red River floods every spring. The mosquitoes all carry West Nile virus. FedEx planes are always falling out of the sky and crashing into Osborne Village (in fact it only happened once, but I sense Richard's on a roll). Just once, he says, he'd like a family to call and ask for him by name: not for Neil, not for Eirik, but for Richard. *There's been a death. We need Richard.*

In the old days, undertakers had profile and charisma. When Tommy Cropo walked the centre aisle of the church, his arms out, palms turned down, parishioners would touch the tops of his hands, as if he were God's second son. Cropo always gave free caskets to nuns and priests. "It was about looking good," says Richard, "and helping the Church. He helped build Holy Ghost on Selkirk, he put in the bell at St. Vladimir's, which was Martin Corbin's turf. When the priest at St. Vladimir's died and went with Corbin's, Tommy cut off the relationship." That was how things worked in the north end. Loyalty mattered. Richard drove coach for Cropo and his right-hand *consigliere* Malcolm, and they always fed him breakfast at the Lincoln: bacon and eggs for the long, ninety-minute mass, or coffee and toast for shorter services. When one of his apprentices asked for advice on where to get a mortgage, Tommy bankrolled the house himself. He treated staff and community like family. He had no children of his own, just Malcolm and a dog for whom he'd buy a separate seat on the airplane when they flew to Florida. According to Richard, after Tommy died his brand fizzled. Now owned by a small consolidator out of Brandon, Cropo's is chasing rich south-enders for pre-needs, leaving the working-class Catholics to Corbin's and the Knysh brothers. The joke's on them, Richard says: rich south-enders don't buy big funerals. They want deals. They go to Curly, Larry and Moe. Loyalty's no longer a value in funeral service.

"I had the dream again," he tells me. This time, all he could see was the face of the corpse, like a marble sculpture surrounded by black. It was Neil. Annette was there, but the boys, Jon and Eirik, were not. He reached out to touch the body, but then he woke up. What will happen to this place, he says, when Neil's gone? He's built up a brand based on cremation, ever since his own father died, but when Eirik takes over, what then? Eirik is more like his great-uncle Karl, a casket and burial man.

I've thought about this too, since the day a few weeks ago when Eirik lumbered into the office at Aubrey with a roll of blueprints under his arm. He'd been at the bank with his dad, pitching them on the renovations, which are still up in the air pending the court case with Chapel Lawn.

"We had to hear about the Garden of Memories for the first half hour. The accountant was falling asleep, he's heard about it so many times. Dad wants to fire him."

He showed us the plans: valet parking, a wash bay for the vehicles, a change room for clergy, an office for his mom, and a huge reception hall with a circle in the middle representing the indoor garden.

"He's focusing too much on the scattering garden," Eirik said. "People are going to cemeteries. They want that stone."

Soon enough, as if he wants to keep his hand in the game, Death throws us a gift to occupy our time, but it's wrapped in sad irony. Shannon's uncle has died. At the morning meeting, Richard runs through the details: private interment, reception at the community hall in Dominion City. Cremation is done, opening and closing of the grave is confirmed. Shannon sits at the table in the office at Aubrey in jeans, her feet tucked under her, her hair wet but combed. On the table is a silver-framed picture of her uncle in a white sweater, wearing a boutonniere and a stiff smile. The funeral is Saturday, but she's booked to work at the crematorium on the weekend. Eirik volunteers to cover her shift.

"There'll be an honour guard at the church from the local Legion," says Richard. "The urn is the one with the fish. Did we get a deposit from the family?"

The room is silent. We all look at Shannon, who finally laughs and throws a pencil at Richard.

"I've buried one, two, three, four, five? Six aunts and uncles," he says. "Come Saturday, you'll have to decide: are you the niece or the funeral director?"

Shannon says when her great-uncle passed last year, she did the embalming. Her great-aunt didn't want a stranger to see him naked. She found it therapeutic.

"Even with my uncle yesterday," she says, "my auntie said it gave her comfort that someone he knew was with him at the crematorium. I closed his eyes, set his features, closed his mouth." She asked her aunt if she wanted prayers, and her aunt said no, but called back later and had changed her mind. Shannon went back to the crematorium at six o'clock, pulled the container out of the cooler, said the twenty-third psalm and put him back.

"Do I have to make a purchase order for the urn?" she says.

"If you use toilet paper in this place, you have to put in a request," Richard says. "If you go over the allotted number of sheets you have to give a vivid description of why. Just order it, and send in the paperwork later."

"On the bulletins, can you put a fish?"

"Like a big jumping fish or a fish on a fly-hook?"

"The big dispute last night was over the fish. The American walleye or the Canadian walleye. In the Batesville catalogue the fin is flat on the top, and this is the only acceptable fish, apparently. This one," she says, pointing to a picture in the catalogue, "the coloured fish with the pointy fin? That's American. My family spent half the day on this yesterday."

The day before the service in Dominion City, I set up the chapel for a memorial that Eirik booked weeks ago. Neil's gone to the Factory to change into a suit and Richard's in the office sorting pre-need files (the "not dead yet" files), arranging them alphabetically, because, he says, they die faster that way. Eirik is AWOL. The first family members arrive and I lead them to the arrangement room so they can chill before the service. They ask about cake, there's supposed to be cake. I tell them I'll look into it. They ask about photos, there are supposed to be photo boards, and I tell them I'll look into it. More people arrive so I take my place at the front door, handing out memorial cards. Meanwhile Richard won't budge. This is not my service, he says, this is Eirik's service, and I won't cover for anyone anymore.

Eirik arrives. He takes a quick peek at the chapel and meets with the family before he joins Richard in the office. I can hear them through the door.

"The candles should be out front," Eirik says. "You should have put them out front."

"This is your service, Eirik."

"You could've done that much."

"No goddamn way."

The service begins, and during Shirley's first hymn, the voices in the office get louder.

"I'm not covering your ass again, no more," says Richard, loud enough that a few guests in the back row shift in their seats and pretend not to hear. "You're a fuck-up, and you've fucked up again. I've had it."

I clear my throat, thinking that might help, but it just prompts more people to turn around.

"Remember where you work, Richard!"

"You can't even do a Canada Pension envelope. You're a fuck-up!"

A door slams. The minister begins his homily, a story of the difference between Greek love or Eros and the self-giving love of Agape, as between two brothers.

"A fuck-up!" Richard calls out.

After the service, Richard and I gather flowers. The important thing seems to be to act like nothing happened. The family wants the flowers sent to their mother's care home for the other residents, and Neil, who showed up after the fireworks, tells them he'll take care of it. As near as I can tell, the mystery cake never arrived.

I load the flowers into Neil's car, and we drive off to the Poseidon Centre in silence. It's been snowing all day, but now it's storming. Finally, Neil tells me he knows what happened. And he knows that, during the fight, Richard played a card he's never played before. He told Eirik: I'm more of a son to him than you are.

We turn onto Grant Avenue and Neil says, as if to change the subject, that he's just read a biography of Dietrich Bonhoeffer, the German Lutheran theologian who'd been involved in a plot to assassinate Hitler and who was executed by the Nazis. Even though he knew he was about to die, Bonhoeffer spent his last days learning a few words of Russian from one of his cellmates. The detail, Neil says, haunted him. What was Bonhoeffer doing? Then he thought about his own plans for the new crematorium, how he wants to get it finished while he can, and decided it amounts to the same thing: you do something, anything, right up to the last day, rather than nothing, even if it's pure folly. What happens to the funeral home after he's done is none of his business. At that point it'll be Eirik's business. Maybe, he says, Paul Werschuk has the right idea. Werschuk runs a funeral chapel in the north end and a crematorium in St. Andrew. Tired of battling with deep-discounters and regulators and the fickle consumer, he's getting out of the game and into pet cremations. Little Critters, he's calling the new business. People spend more on pet services than they do for themselves. They love their pets without ambivalence.

We park behind an ambulance at the front of the Poseidon Centre, which is deep with snow. A man in a housecoat pushes his wheelchair backwards through the slush in his slippered feet. "If you could give me a push, that would be the cat's pyjamas," he says, so I do. A woman leans out of the ambulance and points at Neil. "I know you!" she calls out, and he waves and keeps walking. We're buzzed inside by an annoyed attendant who makes us sign a register book and then disappears up an elevator. The lobby smells like steam and potatoes. We put the flowers on the desk and leave.

Outside Neil pulls his coat tight at the collar against the wind and snow, like King Lear in the storm. I'm not sure I understand the play (I get my Edgars and Edmunds confused), but in some ways Neil's story and Lear's seem to match up: he's already lost his Cordelia (Natalie), the most-loved daughter who refused to suck up to her father and was cast out, and I'm doing my best to play the Fool, even knowing that it doesn't end well (hanged to death: act 5, scene 3). But what's *Lear* if not a story of parents and children whose motives are doomed to clash? Neil is an undertaker first and a family man second, while Eirik sees it the other way round. Why was he late today? Maybe he took the kids swimming. In any case, Neil and Eirik, like Lear and his daughters, have different ideas about how to run a kingdom, and as much as I can fathom Neil's commitment to the twenty-four-hour always-on-call status of the proper undertaker, Eirik seems intent on breaking a generations-old pattern of disconnect between a father and his children. Each has a commitment to family. Only Neil's commitment is to his customers' and Eirik's is to his own.

Neil and Annette have a house in Gimli, but I know most nights Neil sleeps at the crematorium in a hideaway bed under the wall unit in his office. I picture him there by himself, poring over the blueprints, the statue of Rheinhold's ape on his desk, the pedestal globe beside him. Then, when it's time for lights-out, he sleeps in a drawer, same as the morgue drawers at the Victoria General Hospital, his only company the embalmed corpses down the hall in the dressing room, wrapped in flannel, everyone warm from the retort heat. This is his life. He didn't pick it, but he's been living it ever since he was twelve and he first helped his father dress a grave.

This isn't my life. For me it's a project. I can walk away. Not so for the families who are stuck with their grief, or even the family undertakers who are stuck with one another.

On Saturday Shannon and I get lost on the way to Dominion City. I follow her Jeep in the big black Dodge, but just before we hit the U.S. border she turns around and pulls to the side of the highway. The back of her Jeep is filled with flowers. Her uncle's in the seat next to her, in the fish urn. She consults a map. Dominion City is where she grew up, but she's not used to the highway. She only knows the back route through the Roseau River Anishinabe First Nation. Once she sorts it out, we're back on the road, and at length we arrive at a crossroads: a snowy street and a railway track, with a hotel on one corner (GOOD FOOD, says the sign), and across the street, a giant fish on a pole. This turns out to be a full-sized replica of the famous Dominion City sturgeon, 15 ½ feet and 406 pounds, caught in Roseau River in 1903. The town also has one grain elevator, where Shannon's uncle used to work before the company closed it.

The United church is down the street from the fish. There we set up flowers on the stage next to a Christmas tree, and Shannon's uncle is placed on a table beside the piano. Two hundred people show up, too many for the chapel, so some have to be sent to the basement where they'll hear the service on speakers. The Legion honour guard stands by the door with their flags, awaiting the family. When they arrive I hear a thundering bellow as if an aircraft is landing on the roof of the church, but it's just a train, grain hoppers and cattle cars, roaring by close enough to hit with a rock. No one else is alarmed; they've seen trains before.

Three of Shannon's aunts (she seems to have many) give quiet eulogies. They talk about their brother's liver transplant, how he was sure he got a lady's because all he wanted to do after surgery was talk and talk. They tell us about the "horrible day when Jesus took him."

"Please stand, those who are able," Shannon says, and they sing "Shall We Gather at the River?" On her cue I hit the CD player for Vince Gill's "Go Rest High on That Mountain," and next to me one of the cousins, a young man with a shaved head, weeps and weeps.

At the cemetery, Shannon makes the sign of the cross on the urn and reminds her family, gathered around the grave, that this would have been the week of their annual Christmas supper. Her voice breaks as she lowers the velvet pouch. When we go back to our cars, the cousin with the shaved head stays behind, standing over the grave. Through the trees I can see the backhoe, waiting for him to leave.

At the community hall, long tables covered in kraft paper are laid with food for the funeral lunch. I sit across from an aunt, who passes me egg and tuna sandwiches, orange and maple cake squares, and tells me that Shannon was a good swimmer as a child.

"So you're a Bardal," she says.

"No, but I work for Neil Bardal."

"Isn't there a Bardal son who owns a funeral home in Portage?"

"There's a Bardal son who works at Neil's funeral home on Portage Avenue in Winnipeg."

"That's what I said."

Women in Christmas sweaters bus tables, emptying coffee dregs into an ice cream bucket. A man with a sixteen-point buck on his jacket scoops sandwiches to take ice fishing. We're joined by yet another aunt, and I'm introduced as Neil Bardal's son. The aunt says she lived in the city once, but didn't much like it. The steam radiators made her sneeze. All the time, I'm watching Shannon as she works the room, shaking hands and hugging cousins. I meet her father and little brother, who work together in the same Winnipeg plant. Father puts his arm around little brother's neck, and Shannon stands behind them, her hands behind her back.

"It's late now," I say. "Time to get the car back to Winnipeg."

"My father's never seen me in my new job," Shannon says, walking me to the door. "This is the first time."

"Congratulations," I say, the wrong word for the occasion, but she smiles.

A week ago she was ready to quit over a cotton-stuffing dispute, but today she's come out to her family, who see her now not just as a niece and daughter but as a professional undertaker. Richard was wrong. She didn't have to pick one role over the other. In the end what we got was no Celebration of Life with its showbiz and murky mission. This was a funeral.

I've told Neil that Dominion City will be my last call for a while. I'm off to California and Vegas, the twin meccas of the future of death-care. There's a trade show in Vegas, at the Mandalay Bay casino, and San Francisco is ground zero for the do-it-yourself funeral movement. In Mill Valley, across the bay, there's a cemetery that's branded itself as a green alternative: no embalming, no vaults, no caskets, just a shroud and a hole in the ground under a tree, with a rock to mark the spot. In Graton, just up from Mill Valley, there's a gallery that deals exclusively in cremation urns designed by artists. Of course, the Bay area was also home to Jessica Mitford, patron saint of the alterna-funeral, a good-enough reason for a pilgrimage. If the industry is going to change, the seeds of change will come, like organic millet, from the American West Coast.

Fifteen

DEATH IN VENICE BEACH

Like any North American town with indoor plumbing, Mill Valley has its Starbucks. I had trouble finding the Fernwood cemetery so I stopped there for directions. Outside, a woman in leather chaps and dreadlocks, wearing snowboard goggles as sunglasses, danced along the edge of a railroad-tie planter and talked at her cell phone in some chirpy local dialect. I managed to make out the word *armoire*. There's money in Mill Valley. The local high school looks like a Spanish cathedral.

"No idea," the barista said, when I asked about Fernwood.

"It's the famous green cemetery," I said. "They wrote about it in *The New Yorker*."

He shrugged.

For most people cemeteries and funeral homes are invisible, just like old folks' homes and landfills: blind spots. San Francisco was doubly odd. It had no cemeteries to ignore, just the historic columbarium. All the city's founding dead had been dug up and shipped, evicted in fact, to the suburbs in the early decades of the twentieth century, to a town called Colma, which now had 1,500 living residents and 1.5 million dead. Old headstones were dumped in the bay, or used to build breakwaters for the Aquatic Park and the St. Francis Yacht Club. San Francisco is penned in on three sides by water, every square inch of property matters—and cemeteries were deemed a waste of commercial potential.

Lately there'd been a fight over a new crematorium the Neptune Society* wanted to build in Richmond, an industrial, low-income, mostly black neighbourhood north of Oakland. The old crematorium in Emeryville couldn't handle the volume, the three or four thousand bodies a year they expected in the upcoming body boom. Plus, Emeryville had grown and gentrified. Pixar had its animation studio there. So they looked to Richmond. But the people of Richmond fought back. "We don't want dead bodies spewing over our community," one activist said. "What goes up must come down." And that included mercury from thousands of dental fillings, and whatever else came from the factory combustion of the white upper-middle-class San Franciscans who presumably made up the bulk of Neptune's clientele. When I spoke to Jimmy White, a Richmond resident, he told me the protest had as much to do with the gap between the rich and the poor as it did with what

---

* Neptune Society of Northern California, that is, owned by Stewart Enterprises, not to be confused with the Neptune Society, owned by BG Capital, which also owns a majority stake in the Clearly Canadian soft drink company. Both base their brands on direct cremation followed by scattering at sea, and neither seem quick to iron out the confusion because the brand is so strong. The original Neptune was founded by Charles Denning, who was known, because of his goatee and homespun charm, as "Colonel Cinders."

came out of the chimney: we've got their oil refineries, he said, we don't want their dead too. "We have enough death in Richmond as it is." In the end the town council voted to keep the Neptune Society crematorium out.

Fernwood meanwhile pitched an eco-friendly burial, where each "tree, flower, songbird, boulder and butterfly becomes a memorial to a loved one and a hope for the future." It was owned by Tyler Cassity, the closest thing the death-care industry had to a poster boy. Charismatic, handsome, a technical adviser to HBO's *Six Feet Under*, he'd bought both Fernwood, an old Portuguese burial ground, and the rundown Hollywood Memorial in Los Angeles, and given them elaborate makeovers. Hollywood Memorial became Hollywood Forever: he was the one who cleaned out the ponds, brought in white peacocks to stroll the grounds and showed movies at night on the wall of the mausoleum. Cassity was known for hiring ex–porn stars and –sex workers to run the cemetery and funeral chapel (to give them a fresh crack at "legit" commerce), and he told *The New Yorker* that when he died, he wanted to be buried at Hollywood Forever in "a circular island of Carrera marble in the lake, beneath which is a submerged sarcophagus, atop which is a statue of a naked Narcissus on all fours, staring at his reflection."

He had even bigger plans for Forever Fernwood.* The original idea was to bury people without chemicals in shrouds or pine boxes or biodegradable caskets like the Ecopod, a form-fitting sarcophagus made of recycled paper and starch plastic—or my dream casket, the Capsula Mundi, an Italian-made acorn with a living tree sprouting from one end, in which the body is meant to curl in the

---

* Unrelated to the 1977 television spinoff of *Mary Hartman Mary Hartman* starring Orson Bean and Shelly Berman also called *Forever Fernwood*, a coincidence.

fetal position. At the same time they'd conserve land, maybe link it to the nearby Golden Gate National Recreation Area. Cassity was a sharp businessman: if people will pay a million dollars to be buried in a family mausoleum, he told *The New Yorker*, what will they pay to be buried under a three-hundred-year-old oak tree? Green didn't mean a pauper's burial, and green didn't mean cheap.

The main building at Fernwood is under construction, so I meet the manager, Gary McRae, in a trailer, the makeshift office, where they keep a wall of GPS gizmos to help visitors find graves in the green section of the cemetery. I also meet Owen, the company dog. Owen yawns and goes back to sleep.

Before Fernwood, Gary had been a homicide detective at New Scotland Yard for eight years. "This is more peaceful," he says, driving us up a hill to the cemetery in a Prius. In my head I had expected a rustic burial ground with shade trees and a white fence. I'd heard about burial forests in the United Kingdom where people were buried under mature trees and the land, instead of being manicured and drowned with sprinklers, was left to grow thick and wild. But Fernwood hadn't got there yet. As we get out of the car, Gary points out the old Portuguese cemetery. Like Brookside in Winnipeg its stone monuments are weathered. Tall grass and scrubby shrubs grow between them. Here they still bury in the traditional fashion: vaults, caskets, the body embalmed if you want—pleasant, and properly spooky. Then, beyond a sharp "no embalming past this point" line marked by a stand of eucalyptus trees is the green burial ground: a bare open meadow with a few Charlie Brown saplings tied to stakes and a couple of rocks. It has a knockout view of the Tennessee Valley, and Gary explains how they're pulling down the eucalyptus trees, basically weeds, and putting in native California plants and grasses, wildflowers and irises to turn the land back into coastal prairie.

But it still looks like an oversized, neglected suburban front yard. The point of Fernwood is fantasy, a dream of pushing up giant redwoods from below, feeding them with your own hard-won carbon atoms, the afterlife as compost. People want to be trees: that's the pitch. But like a lot of things in life, the place doesn't quite match the fantasy. No crime, but frankly the Web site looked a lot prettier.

Gary shows me the work-in-progress, a crematorium and reception space, a cement bunker with skylights where they also have a working prep room, although Gary says they've only done three embalmings in the last year. They use a trade embalmer from Monte's Chapel of the Hills in San Anselmo named Dead Ed who rides a bicycle and embalms in his Lycra shorts and likes to charm local women by bringing them to the morgue. "The reason funeral homes can't make a connection with their community," Gary says, "is not that the community is scared to talk about death, it's that the funeral home is scared to talk about death. That's why funeral homes embalm people, put makeup on them and pretend they're alive. Here we're very realistic. Dead people should look dead."

The crematorium has a kitchenette with an espresso maker. I make a note to tell Neil: a Committal to the Flames with a fresh latte would be a marketing lever even Starbucks can't claim (yet).

The retorts are spotless. I can see my reflection in the green enamel. Still, there's an odd tension at Fernwood: the mission is to reclaim the rite of burial by disposing of the earth-unfriendly bric-a-brac and toxic chemicals, but to make it in death-care you've got to have a retort, even though the crankiest environmentalists

like to point out that each human cremation uses up the equivalent of 16 gallons of gasoline, which is what an SUV burns over a
186-mile trip.

Then there's the mercury, which the U.S. Environmental
Protection Agency pegs at around 278 pounds a year from retort
stacks, based on an average of seven amalgam fillings per baby
boomer—peanuts compared to heavy industry, but a factor for anyone who takes her ecological "footprint" seriously. The Germans
have been experimenting with a solar crematorium, a concrete con-
traption with a big concave mirror, like something Wile E. Coyote
might build to fry the Roadrunner, but it, too, is a work-in-progress.

Before I leave Gary gives me a price list. An "interment right"
(which is what they call a grave) in the green upper meadow,
where butterflies live and make more butterflies, costs $7,000—
$13,000 if you want a tree. The "Family Grove," two full-body buri-
als, four cremation spaces and a boulder in among the oak trees, is
$68,000. They also do a Jewish *tahara*. I ask Gary how many natural
burials they'd had last year. He pauses. "Fifty," he says, then
changes it to forty. Chapel Lawn in Winnipeg probably did forty a
month. I pat Owen, who groans, and head back to the city.

Not long ago I spoke with Joe Sehee. Joe had been a partner at
Forever Fernwood, and ran public relations for the Hollywood
cemetery, but quit to start the Green Burial Council and his own
burial ground near Santa Fe, New Mexico. There'd been an ideo-
logical split. It came down to the definition of *green*. Joe thought
there was more to it than burying people al fresco in shrouds and
pine boxes, although that was a good start: he wanted to give
Fernwood, the land, to an independent steward to create a conservation easement, a legally binding roadblock against future

development. Then the trust would grant Fernwood interment rights, the way protected lands cede mineral rights, only instead of drilling for ore, they'd be planting dead humans. By buying a plot, you contributed directly to the protection of habitat. But the idea never flew at Fernwood. So Joe went his own way.

There should be standards, Joe said. If you open a cemetery and let it grow wild or plant trees like they do in the United Kingdom, that's fine, call it cheap burial or natural burial, "but you're not conserving land. In the U.K. those tree farms look like bad hair transplants."

In New Mexico he had fifteen acres, tall grass prairie, gnarled juniper and pinyon trees growing out of the rock, managed by a non-profit conservancy for "sustainable burial." That meant the land wouldn't be over-corpsed. Marking individual graves was optional: Joe was interested in a different kind of memorial.

"Who says a rock with your name on it is the only way to go? You come to the place, you get to look at this majestic panorama. It invites you in. Half the proceeds go to protecting a thousand acres. That's the memorial." In a way it was like the Catholic trick with the casket pall. In life you may be an avid golfer, but in death, you're part of a bigger whole. "Edward Abbey says the most spiritual thing about the desert is it doesn't give a shit," Joe said. "I've seen it. Close. People can't name it. They're not looking for a wicker casket and a plot, but something more spiritual. It's like they're trying to befriend death."

For an industry that sold glass-front niches in heated indoor mausolea, all this is tough to swallow. Ron Hast, death-care's elder statesman, and one of the pallbearers at Marilyn Monroe's funeral, put it this way: look outside any airplane window and see how much land they say we're running out of. Saving land isn't the job of death-care, but remembering a life, marking a permanent spot, is.

Joe thinks the industry is spending more time arguing with the market than listening to it. "Don't debate whether land needs protecting," he said. "If someone wants their last act to contribute to acquiring and restoring a natural area, just help them do it." His mantra, and advice to funeral directors: make green burial available to your families or someone else will.

Underneath the green concept is a rich myth of a secular afterlife. In his book *Darwin's Worms,* Adam Phillips argues there's no need to despair just because God is dead and the promise of life everlasting, the whole point of religion, went with Him. So you're not the apex of creation, but rather some piece of a mystical, probably pointless evolutionary chain: good for you. Nature has a place for you, and all your organic bits and pieces, in perpetuating itself. It may not give a shit, but nature isn't anarchic, there's order, all run quietly and damply by worms. Darwin, Phillips says, "replaced a creation myth with a secular maintenance myth." Destruction and death made more life possible. "What would our lives be like if we took earthworms seriously, took the ground beneath our feet rather than the skies above our heads, as the place to look, as well, eventually, as the place to be? It is as though we have been pointed in the wrong direction." I confess I have not taken earthworms seriously.

As a myth the Christian afterlife has better visuals, Tintoretto and that crowd. But the message is the same for both: the individual is absorbed into the whole. Darwin's myth is noble enough, a busy, working death. When it comes to evolution and nature's cycle, we, all of us, control the means of production. It just sounds a bit exhausting—a death ritual with an ideology.

Harsh cornflakes, too, for the vault manufacturer. Wilbert, the leading vault maker, puts a sixty-five-year warranty on its Venetian, with the claim it will "resist" water and worms, or they'll replace it (which raises the question: how do you check?). Though, the United States and Canada still sell more Wilbert vaults than green graves by a long shot. Why? Because we are permanence junkies. Karen Leonard, a consumer advocate who once ran the Redwood Funeral Society in northern California, says the United States is the only country that still believes in a forever. The myth that the vaulted body lasts forever is hard to shake, and the idea of dissolving into a conservation easement, no matter how beautiful the view, is still too much like going ovo-lacto: only a few have the taste for it.

Will this change? On *Six Feet Under*, Nate, the lead character, was buried in a green cemetery. Once pop culture gets into the debate, anything can happen. Growth may be slow but even the people I talk to in Winnipeg are inherently drawn to the idea: yes, that's what I want. Availability is the problem. There's one green cemetery in the works in British Columbia and another planned for Guelph, Ontario, but if you die today and want to go green, you'll have to buy an airplane ticket.

This idea of post-mortem self-expression brought me to Graton, in Sonoma Country, not far from the ocean and Bodega Bay, where Hitchcock filmed *The Birds*. Graton has the kind of small-town charm that comes only from pride and great heaping wads of cash: flags on the main street, antiques shops, a general store that sells original artworks and Persian rugs and Japanese furniture. I believe the gas station sells art too. The place smells of linseed oil and apples and real estate agents. The Funeria gallery in Graton deals in "personal memorial artworks," original works that were also designed to hold the standard 200 cubic inches, or at least a keepsake smidgen of ash: art urns. The owner, Maureen Lomasney, hopes to attract the collector who'd be interested in showcasing a piece at home, before climbing into it for all eternity. I'd seen pictures on her Web site of something called a Zen Spaceship Vessel, a gourd-like jar made of mica clay and bronzed grapevine twigs; the one that grabbed me was the Urn-A-Matic, made from a vintage vacuum cleaner that projected home movies and played a loop of Terry Jacks's "Seasons in the Sun" over and over and over. I pictured this one in the Aubrey showroom, the music driving Richard bonkers until one day he'd go at it with a baseball bat. If it was art, it was art I thought I could grasp: whimsical, allusive, but dark and ambiguous too. Like a painting of dogs playing poker.

I park in front of an old wooden warehouse. There are sawdust drifts on the street, and a wild turkey steps out from behind an SUV and coughs. At the far end of the building, over a door, hangs a banner of Anubis, the jackal-headed Egyptian god of embalming and the underworld. Maureen Lomasney meets me, dressed in black: art school black, not funeral black. The space, she says, was an apple-drying warehouse and a martial arts dojo before she hung track lights and turned it into a gallery.

It's unlike any funeral home showroom I've seen, far from Gothic, cheery in fact: there are curious bowls made out of maplewood that look like African drums, a lidded vessel with a finish like a dry, cracked lakebed. "I had a woman," Maureen says, "her husband and daughter died. Separate times, but sadly they died. She said this one felt like coral, which was perfect, because he was very crusty and she was a wild child." I look for the Urn-A-Matic, but no luck. Maureen has shipped it back to the artist in Seattle after a big show in New York. To me, this is like going to Disneyland and finding Mickey is away on stress leave. Still, I find lots to play with, including an oversized pop-arty cigar propped on its ash end, with a band that said *La Vida Buena*. "It's a functional humidor," Maureen says, lifting off the top half, "lined with Spanish cedar, so you can use it to store cigars . . . prior." People like to look inside her urns, she says, "because they're curious about the view, which is sweet."

"I've become much more comfortable with death in the last few years," she says. "We all die, but art lasts well beyond us. Why not have something beautiful that stands in for us?" At home she had two pieces of her own, shaped like boats. "No one else needs to know what they are but me." Like Victorian memento mori and hair brooches, they're happy daily reminders of her own mortality.

Maureen's been working with funeral providers to market her artists, "but I can't say it's been comfortable." The undertakers see themselves as the keepers of the ritual, and their version of "personalization" comes in the form of laser-etched fly fishermen, very literal. And funeral directors don't trust their own taste. They rely on manufacturers' taste, and their market research.

At Aubrey, Richard stocked classic cloisonné urns but not brass dolphins, because people bought cloisonnés and not brass dolphins. It was that simple. It didn't matter if it was a self-fulfilling prophecy, in the funeral world I knew, aesthetics and economics were like two mathematical dimensions that never met.

"I'd like to see funeral homes transform themselves into event centres and art galleries," she says. "I'd like to see them get rid of anything that is ugly and manufactured, tacky stuff." Ever since Martha Stewart entered Kmart, design had progressed. Architects were now designing teapots.

It's one of my weaknesses to want the thing called "taste" while still wearing, as I did more than once at Aubrey, a brown belt with black shoes. A tasteful death feels like another opportunity for me to underachieve, not that the coral bowl wasn't pretty. But how would it hold up sixty years from now, when I'm still dead but the aesthetic goal-posts have shifted, compared to a Harpswell slate urn with a lighthouse on it, which may end up with the same kitsch appeal as a Monkees lunch pail? It's a gamble, betting on taste when eternity's in play.

Two women come into the gallery. They flip through a brochure, whispering.

Maureen introduces herself. She shows them a few showcase pieces, a delicate glass jar, "too small for an adult, maybe for a child or a cat," and something that looks like a Sumerian wick lantern. They're curious about a sculpted puppy's head hanging on the wall near the entrance.

"What's this about?"

"It's an urn," Maureen says.

"You're kidding."

"No, you can suspend the ashes inside his head in a velvet bag. The artist does wonderful figurative work. She does these rolling playful dachshunds."

"Totally nice."

There's a clay piece they like, inlaid with leaves and little white figures dancing in a circle. Maureen turns a knob on top and it spins. "It's a Tibetan prayer wheel. The prayers and wishes go inside and get shared with the universe."

She lets them browse.

"See," she whispers to me, "they're cheerful. There's nothing glum about it, it's a shopping trip."

One of the browsers spins the prayer wheel again.

Maureen leads me behind a room divider to her office, to show me a sketch for an outdoor installation by an artist who'd done large-scale land art. It was going to be a bunker made of unglazed clay boxes that would hold cremated remains as well as messages written on bits of paper, personal histories and prayers crammed into holes like in the Wailing Wall. The whole piece is designed to fall apart over time, to dissolve in the rain. The ashes would get blown or washed away. Deliberate impermanence. The art isn't finished when the artist is done building it, it's finished when it's ruined by time and the elements.

New works are due from a European artist named Nadine Jarvis who makes birdfeeders out of seeds and beeswax and cremated remains. The birds eat the seeds, the ashes get "distributed." Jarvis also makes wood pencils with human lead, on average 240 per cremated body, and teardrop-shaped eggshell vessels that hang from tree branches. The string will eventually break, and the vessel falls and shatters on the ground, and that's how you're scattered. Coincidence and gravity, the artist's collaborators, decide when and how.

I like the pencils. Each one is embossed with a name and dates (birth and death), like a headstone. Once again, a working death: you could become a doodle, or a tax return, or the answers to the

LSAT. It was out of your hands and literally in someone else's, although it's significant the pencils have no erasers.

But is it art? John Dewey says art "renders men aware of their union with one another in origin and destiny," and by that measure the big cigar and the pencils qualify: we're all doomed to be ground out or worn to stubs.

Driving back over the Golden Gate Bridge (the most popular place in the United States to commit suicide), I think about green burial and birdfeeders and wonder what it would take for mainstream death-care truly to warm up to them. The problem is that the industry craves safety and sameness. Even the Celebration of Life, where each service is unique, has as its blueprint the traditional chapel funeral. In the funeral, the body's embalmed. In the Celebration, the life story's embalmed. But burying a body in a desert or feeding the ashes to starlings and cardinals is wild, chaotic, against all the undertaker's instincts for order. For him, the cloisonné urn is a comfort, like a pop song he's heard a thousand times. The alternatives are atonal noise, and they make him change the station.

Now there are new beta technologies for dealing with human remains in the works: promession, a Swedish innovation, freeze-dries the body like camping food and then pulverizes it into a pink powder that can act as a fertilizer wherever it's buried, preferably in a biodegradable cornstarch box. "In the beginning," says Susanne Wiigh-Masak, the biologist behind the prototype, "a wild animal found you dead in nature and saw you as something edible. They tore you apart and spread you around, and you became soil." Promession just cuts out the wild animal factor.

Resomation, meanwhile, involves putting the body in a silk bag and then into a hot bath of water and potassium hydroxide, which dissolves the flesh through alkaline hydrolysis. What's left are bones, teeth and a small amount of green-brown liquid which can be poured into a grave or scattering garden with the other pulverized remains. It's cremation without the fire and fossil fuels, another eco-friendly alternative, according to the company that pitches it. We'll see if the boomer market, which enthusiastically recycles its glass and plastics, will drive any of the new technologies.

Built on the old Odd Fellows cemetery downtown in the nineteenth century, the columbarium was the last stand for San Francisco's dead; the rest had been deported to Colma after burials in the city were banned in 1919. Inside is a huge marble rotunda, lit by a lead-glass dome, and three storeys of niches along circular walkways. Climbing the stairs, I follow the music, Ella Fitzgerald singing "It's Only a Paper Moon" from a portable CD deck on the top level. I stop at a niche with two Elvis busts cheek to cheek. Some of the older niches hold brass urns tarnished blue and green and salty white by the sea air. Cookie jars are popular: rabbits, harlequins, Indian chiefs. Mardi Gras beads hang from the flower vases. It's all very democratic: kitty-corner to a portrait of a stern, unsmiling European couple is a G.I. Joe lunchbox and a set of handcuffs. Not as literal as the niches I'd seen at Chapel Lawn, these are more cryptic and playful. Next to G.I. Joe is an urnless niche with a camera and a pair of pink ballet slippers. Farther down, someone has propped plastic tomatoes on a pair of brass vases. And it's hard to miss the number of rainbow flags and rainbow ribbons: plenty of the dead were young men, born in the '40s and '50s, dead in the '80s and '90s, when AIDS hit San Francisco fast and hard.

On the main level I come across a man on a ladder measuring a niche. His name is Emmitt, and he's the caretaker.

"Some of these older apartments got ten, some got twelve people all dumped in the same container. Whole families, generations," he says, then comes down the ladder to say hello. "People come for weddings and birthdays. One lady comes every Thursday at 10:20. The fellow I call the Storyteller, he came every single day until he died. I give people nicknames, like the Tomato King."

"I think I saw the Tomato King," I say.

"Him and his wife used to grow tomatoes. Those ones, they're plastic. I put them there. Because I knew that's what he would want."

The lady who loved baseball has a ceramic baseball urn, and a hand-painted crowd scene behind her. Emmitt says if I look close I'll see Santa Claus and Batman watching the game. He's rigged a gizmo to turn on a light inside the niche, "since Miss Lily didn't like the dark."

His hands are white from plaster and paint.

"People are already so sad, they don't need more to be sad about. I say you can bring some life and air to death, some personality. I look at you, you look at me, we contribute to society," he says. "Then we die."

He glances over my shoulder to the front door.

"There's my ride," he says. And with that he's gone.

Colma is, at first blush, just another suburb. It has more car dealerships than seem necessary for a town with a thousand times more graves than people, but Colma is where San Franciscans buy their SUVs, when they're not burying their dead. According to Pat Hatfield, who runs the local historical society, they'd just built a card room called Lucky Chances Casino on property leased from one of the Jewish cemeteries: between the car lots and the Texas Hold 'Em, Colma was doing fine, despite any new social trends vis-à-vis burial. In fact, they ran a surplus. If you lived in Colma, you got free cable TV.

I wander up the hill to Cypress Lawn, to a stone proscenium at the entrance of the cemetery. In front of me is San Bruno Mountain, and to my right, past a plastic orange fence, what we'd call a snow-fence in Manitoba, was a nine-hole golf course. It used to be eighteen until the cemetery, in need of more real estate, cut a deal to build more grave plots. Sunlight sparkles on the stone columbaria. On either side, as far as I can see, the land's overrun with headstones and palm trees. Behind me is Woodlawn, SCI's piece of the action, and to the right, the Jewish cemeteries tucked next to the huge Catholic Holy Cross. Scattered round about, according to my map, are Japanese and Chinese and Serbian and Russian cemeteries, and somewhere, the pet cemetery where Tina Turner buried her dog wrapped in a fur coat (the dog, not Tina). According to Pat, the pet cemetery is the most visited spot in Colma.

It used to be, as far back as the late 1800s, that funeral homes in San Francisco or nearby Daly City did all the prepping and casketing, and families would come to Colma by procession or on special black trolley cars, fifty cents per mourner, a dollar to transport the body, the most popular trolley being the swank *El Descanso* with its black leather armchairs and separate parlours for Ladies and Gents. That separation of labour, between undertaker and cemeterian, continued until Cypress Lawn put up its *palazzo* of a mortuary, riling their former business partners. As I walk across the parking lot the building seems to recede, getting farther away the closer I get to it, like Kafka's unreachable castle, a trick of the eye or the climate or something weirder. The head of a red carnation and a Kleenex blow across the pavement in front of me.

I wait in the lobby, at the foot of a spiral staircase, under a cupola, while a woman at a black marble desk whispers into a telephone. Soon a gentleman in a blue suit and red hair skitters down the stairs, hand outstretched. His name is Martin, communications director for the cemetery. I had an appointment with Ken Varner, the CEO, who's just back from a trip to China, Martin tells me, and can't make it. I can speak to him later by phone. In the meantime, Martin offers a quick tour. He whisks me past the chapels, the Cypress Room, the Rose Room, the Laurel Room, all bright and white and palm-frondy, and introduces me to a series of smiling women with clipboards. They hold regular lecture series (next month it's "Body Disposal Through the Ages") and genealogy seminars and a popular antiques appraisal show-and-tell like the one on PBS. In the showroom are caskets I've only ever seen in catalogues: a hand-carved mahogany Marsellus President, just like the one JFK was buried in, and a bronze Promethean full-couch (meaning a single lid, without the split in the middle, so mourners can view the whole body) with mirror finish otherwise known as a "James Brown," the same casket in which the Godfather of Soul lay in state at the Apollo Theater in New York and then, for months after, in an air-conditioned room in his home on Beech Island, South Carolina, while his family argued over the estate. Cypress Lawn also carries *dzi-dzat*, the miniature paper houses and paper cell phones and paper plasma TVs that Asian families use in burial rituals, which Martin calls "Chinese burning things."

"Sixty percent of our families are Asian," he says. "I mean, my *wife* is Asian!"

Ten years ago Cypress Lawn was losing a million dollars a year in operations and had at most a decade's worth of cemetery land left. Later I talked to Ken Varner, and he said he'd had two choices: "Put up our horns, and go into maintenance mode, or expand." So they bought half the golf course, and went hard at the Asian and Filipino consumers with "specific needs." On the model of the Greek and Romanesque family mausolea in the old section of Cypress Lawn, where the great dead white nabobs like William Randolph Hearst are entombed, they built "cremation estates": private sarcophagi with space for ten, twenty or thirty cremated remains, generations' worth, plus elaborate memorials, dragons or Foo dogs, whatever a family might want to mark its one reliably permanent spot on earth (in Shanghai, he said, the cemeteries have their own staff sculptors). Feng shui masters were brought in to redesign the cemetery and iron out the chi, and they hired Asian and Filipino sales teams to work the phones. "Every day," he said, "we go out and tell people they have a problem and that we have a solution."

"What problem is that?"

He paused, generously, to give me time to figure it out. I didn't.

"That they're going to die someday," he said.

Pat told me her favourite spot in town was the children's section of Woodlawn cemetery, where parents decorated the graves with toys and birthday cakes. There used to be a sculpture of Snow White and the Seven Dwarfs, she said, until vandals smashed it. I drive in circles, past the bilingual sign (English, Chinese) with the familiar droopy-tree Dignity logo, and finally come upon a stone slab with what looks to be half a dwarf, possibly Sneezy, just his hands and knees and feet rooted to the slab, the rest of him gone, like he'd stepped on a landmine. Behind him is one of Snow White's slippers. According to Pat, Woodlawn wanted to rebuild the sculpture, but Disney preferred they didn't. "I believe it had something to do with money," Pat said.

Before dark I stop at Molloy's, an Irish pub near Holy Cross. Inside it's pubby and bleak, crammed with pictures of old Colma. "Roosevelt Is Dead!" says a headline in a framed newspaper. The bar is worn smooth from decades of proper use, and behind it, a triptych of silver-backed mirrors barely remembers how to reflect what little light there is. Owen Molloy is behind the bar too. Two regular customers argue about other regular customers who aren't here. In the early days Molloy's was a roadhouse and hotel. Owen tells me gravediggers and monument makers used to drink here, but that the companies have all cut back, "now it's just one guy with a backhoe." Most of his customers are families in need of drinks or a nosh after burying their dead. He lives in Colma and likes it; he has a view of the mountain with no threat that someone will build a skyscraper in front of it.

I ask him, with seventeen cemeteries in town, most of them filled or filling with Bay Area "commuters" and come-from-aways, what happens to local people when they die.

He leans in towards me.

"I got three, four customers cremated in liquor bottles in the crawl space behind those mirrors," he says. He looks around as if someone might be listening.

"Shirley lived up the street," he says. "She drank gin, we put her ashes in a fifth of Tanqueray. Eddy, his ashes are in a fifth of vodka, and Knut, he was a longshoreman, he lived in the trailer park next to us here. Norwegian. He's there too."

One of the regulars, a tall, thin man with a knit cap, gets up from his stool. "He used to sit right over there," he says, pointing to the bar stool next to me. "Ka-nute." He pronounced it as two syllables.

"He was a customer here since I was a little kid," Owen says.

"He shake," the man continues, in a thick Italian accent. "After a few drinks, he no shake no more."

Owen pours the man more red wine. His name is Franco.

"He say, I'm going to stop living when I'm seventy-five," Franco says. "One day he got all dressed up, Father's Day."

"His favourite bartender had moved back east," says Owen.

"When I come in, Knut is here, and he show me, he has a gun. I got shocked. I feel so bad, because the next day . . ." and here Franco makes a pistol gesture at his temple.

Franco is known as the Memory Artist. "I paint my village from my memory," he tells me. He comes from Pontito, in Tuscany. When he moved to California, he was haunted by vivid dreams of his boyhood town, so real that when he woke he found he could reproduce them, in frantic detail, on canvas, even though he had no artistic training. In his mind, he could follow scenes in three dimensions, turn his head to look around buildings and church doorways, even hear sounds. Later I saw pictures of Franco's paintings and photos of Pontito online, and his realism was chilling.

"Yeah, Knut," the Memory Artist says. "This is a shame."

He holds up his glass for a refill.

"I'm seventy-three next month," he says.

———

I walk the beach by the San Francisco Zoological Gardens looking for old headstones from the purges, but no luck. Of course, the Pacific is even more popular than Colma as a place for what some call the Mitford Method of final disposition, even with, as Robert Pogue Harrison wrote, the sea's "irresponsibility, its hostility to memory, its impatience with ruins, and its passion for erasure." You can't mark the sea like you can mark the land, it won't let you, and if it matters to know where your dead are, the sea responds with a wet salty question mark. I couldn't think of anything more cold and terrifying.

Karen Leonard, who lives in Willits, deep in Northern California's granola and redwood belt, wrote me to say, "Out here, we have the Russian River meeting the ocean, at a place called Jenner-by-the-Sea. It's beautiful, and the park rangers swear that the building up of the sandbar near the mouth of the inlet is due to cremated remains." Willits was farther than I wanted to go on this trip, but Karen and her husband Steve invited me to come up and stay the night, camp on the futon. It made sense for my twisted pilgrimage: Karen was, after all, a link to death-care history. She'd been researcher and right hand to Jessica Mitford, helped her write *The American Way of Death Revisited* in the late '90s, just before Mitford died and was herself scattered at sea.

Willits is a toy-train village in the mountains. Lumber trucks roar through it, and proto-hippie kids with canvas backpacks hitchhike into it, then stand in the mist outside Burrito Exquisito looking authentic. It takes three tries and an act of faith to get my rental van up Karen's steep driveway, just before it starts to snow.

She welcomes me, puts on a fire. On the wall above her desk in the living room is a poster-sized black-and-white framed picture of Jessica Mitford playing Scrabble.

Karen tells me her parents were Southern Baptist. "They talked about sex before they talked about death. With them there was a right way to die and a wrong way to die. I'm sorry," she laughs, "I've always found that hysterical." As a young activist she toured funeral homes, undercover, as a fake mourner. Some undertakers made their living on one customer a week, she says, and she wanted to figure out how they did it.

At the time she met Mitford, "my icon," in the '90s, Karen wanted to join a memorial society, the consumer groups that fight high industry prices and monopolies, but Mitford shook her head: eggheads and Quakers and old farts, she said, you don't want anything to do with them. So she hired Karen to help with the book. For Decca, as Karen calls her, you waged war against the enemy directly, you didn't sit in a church basement and chat about it.

"It's a show," she says of the American funeral, "and the undertakers, I used to refer to them as 'godshead waiters,' as if you have to book passage through these guys to get into heaven." In Willits they prefer a Home Depot approach: gather the materials yourself, build your own box, wake the body in its own bed, and then, once the ritual's done, call the undertaker to take care of the cremation. There is nothing illegal about tending to your own dead. You keep the body cool by packing pillowcases with dry ice (the fabric keeps the ice from sticking to the body), wash it, chant, pray, let the kids decorate the box with Magic Markers. Some people drive the body to the crematorium themselves, in a station wagon or pickup. "But you're talking about people that bake their own bread," she says. "One of the wealthiest places in America, and I hear people say they don't use hot water. This is the land of the fruits and the nuts and the flakes. But absolutely every cultural trend starts here first."

Just like do-it-yourself home renovation. Turn on Slice channel, you see half the schedule given over to people covered in their own drywall dust. It sounds empowering and meaningful and I could practically smell the incense—but did people really know what it meant to handle a dead body?

Pros: it's a very intimate, tactile way to say goodbye.

Cons: the dead will shit, piss, purge gastric muck from the nose and mouth, clench up with rigor mortis, and tumble off tables. Their tongues dry out and their eyes sink like bad grapes.

"It's not for everybody," she says. "You need a community or a strong family." And the same people who take care of their own while they are alive, feed them and clean them and change their adult diapers and wash their soiled clothes, will tolerate a bit of purge when they are dead.

I ask her about Jessica Mitford's memorial. I'd read there were horse-drawn carriages, and that some critics, and she had plenty, found it curious that the queen of the quick disposal had what sounded like a big fancy funeral.

In fact there were five memorials, Karen says, including one in London and the family event in San Francisco. And a memorial, unlike a funeral, is not the property of an undertaker. The industry's end of it was less than $500 for cremation and sea scattering at Pacific Interment. On Decca's request they sent the bill to Robert Waltrip at SCI in Houston, in exchange for all the ink she'd given him in her lifetime (they never got a reply). It's true, six black plumed horses pulled a hearse, followed by a twelve-piece marching band: they couldn't resist. It was a standing Mitford family joke to give her a ridiculously overproduced send-off (Decca had also said she wanted to be embalmed, "since it would make her look twenty years younger." She wasn't). The hall was packed. Maya Angelou spoke. Everyone was welcome. It was held at Delancey Street, the halfway house for addicts and ex-cons that Decca and her husband Bob Treuhaft had founded. Delancey Street is across the parkette from my friend Peter's condo, where I'm staying while in San Francisco. I go to the coffee shop every morning. I wondered why the baristas had so many jailhouse tattoos. Now I know: they're Decca's people.

"What would she have made of the teddy bear urn?" I say.

"Oh my God," Karen says, "she would've just loved it. I'm sorry she never lived long enough to see one."

Most states have loose and untested laws about DIY; almost all of them require a licensed funeral director to at least sign a form (for a fee) when the body is picked up or buried. In Manitoba, when the medical examiner releases a body, he releases it to the family. In theory it's the family's choice whether to use an undertaker. All the province cares about is that someone with legible handwriting fills out the paperwork at Vital Stats. Then, if you want, you can back up the station wagon to the hospital for pickup. "My bet," Neil told me, "is anyone who does it will call us next time."

I'd once helped Adina with a body, one of Reg LeClaire's frail little French ladies. We washed and dressed her but did not embalm her: she belonged to a small, clubby Christian sect and they wanted her at home, for prayers, before they buried her. When Neil found out, it was as if he'd swallowed a wasp. It's visceral, for an undertaker, the idea of civilians handling the dead: you may as well take out your own appendix with a butter knife. B.T. Hathaway, the Massachusetts undertaker who'd crunched the numbers on boomer mortality, told me it was fine, the home funeral, for the 5 percent who have money, time, resources, education, and political and emotional will. "But the average consumer is not so well equipped," he said. "It's poetic, but the truth is, I don't know that many poetic families. And it's as much a question of time as anything else—people are *on the clock*. They call on other people to take care of them." This of course is the same argument for why people eat at Pizza Hut instead of milling their own wheat and breeding their own pepperoni cattle: why make it hard on yourself?

Most don't. But what worries the industry is how easy cremation has made it for other hospitality providers—restaurants and hotels and banquet halls—to rip off their trade: if there's no body to drag around and all you need is space for a party, what makes a funeral home any better than a Best Western or a Casa Bonita?

While I was in California, I had the chance to attend a funeral at the Cocoanut Grove Ballroom on the beach in Santa Cruz for Robert Anton Wilson, the writer and conspiracist and friend of Timothy Leary. I didn't know Robert Anton Wilson, except that he'd written thick paperbacks with pictures of pyramids and cats on them, *The Illuminatus! Trilogy* (co-authored with Robert Shea) and other head-scratchers that were big with math majors and stoners and the depressive dystopians I used to drink with in university. You didn't have to know Robert Anton Wilson to go to his funeral: the family sold tickets online, $15 each including parking.

So I went. I got there early and sat in the van outside Cocoanut Grove, eating ice cream and watching the swinging pirate ship on the midway, waiting for the box office to open.

The man's fans were loyal. They followed a kind of arch religion called Discordianism, also called "Zen for round-eyes," that said chaos was just as important as, and more interesting than, order, if you could teach yourself not to be afraid of it. They were happy he'd lived to his seventies, that he'd got a good ride from his "vessel."

The crowd was split into two camps: hippies in fringe vests and pinched straw cowboy hats and feathered white hair; and young hippie wannabes in The Residents "eyeball" T-shirts, striped red and black stockings, squid tendril dreadlocks and stick-on face jewellery. There were top hats in both camps. Inside, I found a table under the mirror ball and ate a quesadilla wedge, while a girl dressed as a Renaissance maiden played Leonard Cohen's "Hallelujah" on a harp. A woman on stage said, "I'd like us to be on the same wavelength a moment." She had a message from Robert Anton Wilson, who'd written his own brief eulogy before he died: "'I no longer claim to know anything,'" she read, "'but I still have some persistent suspicions. Do not dare mourn me.'" The crowd roared. The party had begun.

"Today is my birthday," a young woman told the crowd. "It just seemed right to celebrate life and death together. We read *The Illuminatus! Trilogy* in Dallas, and whenever a character smoked pot, we smoked pot. Thank you for being a light in a very dark place!"

People told me Wilson should have been more famous than he was, that if not for him there'd be no Internet, no *Da Vinci Code*, no TV show called *Lost*, but they weren't angry about it. They weren't angry about anything. They blew into Chinese noisemakers and rattled Chinese rattles. The dead man's ashes sat at the foot of the stage in a wooden box with a gold apple on the lid, the central image from one of his books. We were invited to line up and touch it. I asked a man in a "They Might Be Giants" T-shirt what he thought of this kind of funeral.

"Is that what this is?" he said.

A young woman took the stage. "Hi, I'm Cathy," she said, "and I'm an alcoholic."

"Hi, Cathy," the crowd called back.

Soon, the author's daughter took the urn and the harpist to a boat, moored at the pier, to scatter her father's ashes at sea—to join his wife and, I was told, dolphins from other planets. From the ballroom window, we watched the boat pull away in the long, late-afternoon light.

A man in a fez told me he worked in the field of "quantum tantra." Soon, he said, we'd find ways to contact nature directly, without instruments, and achieve peak experiences through physics the way drugs worked through chemicals. We'd connect with trees and furniture and other people, and of course the dead. He told me his wife had been cremated, and that since then, he'd scattered her in Dixie cupfuls in different places that held meaning. Apparently Robert Anton Wilson's last wish was to have his ashes scattered on Pat Robertson.

"You guys are all defective," a woman told us from the stage. "You're not conforming, you're not doing it the right way. And I love you."

In time the event had the feel of a good party gone on a bit too long. A drunk man hit on the harpist. ("My life's super complicated," he said, spilling beer, "but I gotta say you're beautiful. You're a princess.") While some of the wannabes danced, most left: there was a pagan convention in San Jose and it was getting dark. I'd been well fed, the company was weird and friendly, and if the point was to congratulate a man for having lived rather than dwell on his death, I suppose they pulled it off.

In the corner I saw a handful of older guests, the only ones who seemed to remember why there'd been a party in the first place. These were the veteran soldiers of the counterculture, the real Berkeley rebels from the '70s. From across the ballroom they were the elder statesmen in Birkenstocks, but up close, slouched in their chairs, not talking, just stirring ice in their cups, they looked exhausted, as if they knew the revolution was long over and all that was left was to wait for their turn on the scattering boat.

"I'll see you next lifetime," the drunk told the harpist as I left.

Sixteen

THE MYTH OF PERMANENCE

Normal people go to Los Angeles to see Beverly Hills and the Strip. I get a room at the Holiday Inn in Manhattan Beach and spend two days crawling through cemeteries. Following directions given to me by Lisa Burks, a local "grave hunter" (one of a community of people who hang out in cemeteries, stalking the graves of the famous to take pictures, like post-mortem paparazzi), I pass what should be Hollywood Forever, on a seedy stretch of Santa Monica Boulevard. It takes three loops to find the entrance, which is next to an auto repair shop surrounded by red rusty puddles. Past the gates, it's a huge estate of white-marble headstones and mini-mausolea and cypress trees, bordered on one side by the Paramount studio lot. Behind me are the hills, and the famous HOLLYWOOD sign. I sit to rest on a marble bench, which turns out to be Tyrone Power's grave. Dee Dee

Ramone's black headstone is lipstick-kissed in red and yellow and purple, and pilgrims have left offerings: votive candles, a plastic harmonica, a pair of lady's pumps (also kissed). Across the pond is the Cathedral Mausoleum. Inside it's chilly and dim with banks of crypts like marble filing cabinets. My shoes squeak on the stone floor. Every few steps reveal a familiar name. Here's Peter Finch, already dead and walled into this spot when they gave him the Oscar for *Network*. And here's a treat: David White, who played Larry Tate, Darrin's long-suffering boss on *Bewitched*, in a glass niche with a life-size bronze bust of his head. With the other niches around him, it's as if he's a guest on an afterlife version of *Hollywood Squares*. Farther down I see a piece of paper rolled and stuffed into a bronze vase on one of the crypts (nobody special). Looking around, I pull out the paper, a page ripped from a book. Maybe Scripture? It's from *The Big Book* of Alcoholics Anonymous, step eight, in which you repent to those you've wronged: "We can now commence to ransack memory for the people to whom we have given offence."

I'd read about a Los Angeles couple, Bernardo Puccio and Orin Kennedy, who'd bought pre-need property at Hollywood Forever. They commissioned a neo-classical monument in Carrera marble for themselves and their cat Cristal, had it draped in white and purple silk, and held an unveiling for friends, including fashion maven Mr. Blackwell, at which they served wine and played Johnny Mathis singing "The Twelfth of Never." "Tyrone Power's is minuscule compared to mine," Puccio sniffed to the *Los Angeles Times*.

Forever, as part of its pre-need packaging, sells tribute videos: interviews with family members, photographs and music cut in a professional edit suite and screened at the funeral (released thereafter on DVD)—the fifteen minutes of fame Andy Warhol promised us all, according to one of the producers. This is their brand: the illusion of fame, and an entree into celebrity culture for no-name chumps like me who are willing to pay to be installed in the same theme park as Cecil B. DeMille and Mel Blanc (whose headstone in the Jewish section reads: *That's All Folks!*). You get a piece of Forever: the word's on the letterhead, and the company logo is the sideways figure-eight, the infinity symbol.

So why does the cemetery feel so lonely and abandoned? The tourists are all on the Boulevard, at the Disney store. There's no one else here, except a man in a pith helmet watering the mausoleum wall with a hose. It's hot, and the grass is dry in spots where the thumping sprinklers can't reach. A threadbare white peacock pads by, pecking at something. He looks like a long-tailed pigeon. The reflecting pools in front of the Douglas Fairbanks tomb (both Senior and Junior are there) are green with moss and algae muck. As much as they've tried to embalm sixty-two acres of what used to be desert, fixing its features and combing its cypress hair, nature fights back, as it does in any cemetery. The idea of forever works as a sales tool, but in reality, of course, it's a myth. The writer Geoff Dyer says the ancient Roman city of Leptis Magna in Lybia became interesting only when it fell to ruins, when history was done and all that remained was the scattered evidence of time. The only permanence is impermanence.

Lisa takes me to Grand View Memorial Park in Glendale. Grand View has a few silent film stars, but most of its dead are immigrants and Hollywood journeymen: directors and designers and focus pullers and character actors who'd bought the L.A. promise of fame and big movie money, and had to settle for steady gigs making two-reelers, like the working-class toilers in Nathanael West's *Day of the Locust*. Forest Lawn and Hollywood Forever have superstars. Grand View has the support staff.

Now Grand View is in trouble. The gates are locked. In 2006 the state suspended the cemetery's licence. The state's Department of Consumer Affairs accused Grand View and its principal shareholder, Marsha Howard, who lived in a house in the cemetery, of mishandling remains and embezzling money from the perpetual care fund. The state alleged that bodies were being disinterred at night, that 4,500 sets of cremated remains, some decades old, were stacked in storage rooms, spilled on the floor or dumped in Dumpsters, and that Grand View had been burying remains in plots previously sold to other people (according to court documents, Howard admitted that she'd been reselling graves: "I'm fucked . . ." she's quoted as telling investigators. "You might as well write I'm fucked on that paper"). This being America, the next step came briskly: families of those buried at Grand View launched a class-action lawsuit against the cemetery. Then, in a final twist, Marsha Howard was found dead in her house, of natural causes, which left her business partner, the minority shareholder, to deal with the mess.

Without a licence, Grand View had no cash, and without cash they couldn't pay for upkeep and insurance, so the city of Glendale shut them down, calling the place a hazard: the grass is tinder dry and the trees are shedding heavy palm fronds.

Lisa and I visit on a Sunday, and the gates are open. Twice a month the city opens Grand View for brief supervised visits, staffing it with volunteers who hand out maps and water bottles, making sure no one smokes or burns incense. The visitors are mostly local Armenians who have family in Grand View and are used to tending their graves daily, like gardens. They've been on local TV, weeping and cramming flowers into the padlocked gates, building a shrine, breaking people's hearts. So Glendale came up with this bimonthly compromise. Only the mausoleum remains shut, by court order.

"I talked to people who jumped the walls so they could see their families," Lisa says.

I watch a family carry milk jugs full of water to a grave, to feed the dry plants. The grave had been decorated with white gravel and a chandelier hanging from an iron brace. Others rake their plots and sweep them with brooms. Two women sit in lawn chairs and trim flowers.

Paul Ayers, one of the lawyers in the suit, sits at a card table under a tree, so families can sign up for a piece of the class action. Two days ago, he says, he and a handful of lawyers acted as pallbearers for a court-ordered interment in the mausoleum. Nothing is allowed to come into or leave the cemetery now without a judge's okay: everything that isn't already buried (and some things that are) is considered evidence. "One lady," Lisa says, "she brought in her mother's headstone on a dolly. The rangers made her take it out. They were like, sorry, but you can't do that." The lady's mother had been the last to be buried before the gates were locked.

The Armenian markers are polished black marble, many with laser-etched pictures of the dead, as sharp as photos. Behind a shed I come across an unfinished headstone, with a woman's face partially carved into the marble. She has glasses but no eyes, a face but no mouth.

We cross the cemetery to the mausoleum, the thick cover of dry grass crunching like cornflakes under my feet. I'm slick from the heat. We come upon an old woman in black, holding an umbrella against the sun, sitting in front of her husband's grave on an overturned bucket. She speaks to us in her own language, pointing at the face on the black headstone, crying into a hankie. Lisa gives her a fresh bottle of water.

The mausoleum, a stucco fortress with a terra cotta roof, covers a full Glendale city block, spanning the western edge of the cemetery. When it was built in 1924 they called it the "Huge House of the Silent." It's locked now, but through a curtained window in the door, I can see the dark staircase where the inspector found the thousands of cremated remains. It's not known if the remains were left here over the years by families who never came back to get them, or why they were stockpiled instead of buried. I suppose it's a kind of perpetual care, keeping thousands in storage-room limbo for decades, but it can't be what they signed up for.

I turn around to find a woman standing behind us. Her name is Melinda, she says, and she's the great-grand-niece of Edna Purviance. Lisa is thrilled. I confess I don't know who Edna Purviance is, or was. It turns out she was a silent film star, Charlie Chaplin's favourite leading lady, who appeared in more than thirty of his films, including *The Kid* and *A Jitney Elopement*, and she's been a resident of the Grand View mausoleum since 1958. Some of her fans have recently launched an online campaign to get her out of the troubled cemetery and into a more stable community, maybe Forest Lawn. "People live on if they're on film," Melinda says.

But not forever.

In Japan there's a design concept known as *wabi-sabi*, or humble beauty. An object worn by time and weather and use, like a rough, handmade tea bowl, has *wabi-sabi*. The point is to value transience and built-in impermanence, to appreciate the flawed and the doomed because, like you, they're not going to last. So a paper lantern, a clay pot, a knit shawl, the ruins of Leptis Magna, and fading jailhouse tattoos all have *wabi-sabi*, but a Twinkie, iPhones, Ikea furniture, Swingline staplers and Hello Kitty do not. In the funeral world there's no patience for *wabi-sabi*. Decay is bad for the brand and runs counter to the promise of "perpetual care." But Grand View is crawling with *wabi-sabi*. This is at the heart of the class-action suit: families had been promised perpetual care and maintenance of their graves and crypts, it was in the contract, and now instead of forever they got wild, unkempt and chaotic *wabi-sabi*. In 2007, the cemetery settled with the state by admitting to three of the fourteen accusations. The owner agreed to reimburse $50,000 to the endowment care fund and to sell the cemetery within three years. It may still be for sale. Check eBay.

If the illusion of permanence is a North American vice, like tummy tucks, hair weaves, rust protection and TV series starring Tony Danza, a promise with commercial appeal, it's one bound to be broken by gravity, weather, water, wind, failing memories and time. Chapel Lawn is challenging Neil over his rose garden because he can't guarantee forever. How long is forever in cemetery time? Fifty years? A hundred? A thousand? Or until the survivors themselves die and there's no one to visit or launch lawsuits anymore? In 2007, workers in Granite Falls, North Carolina, uncovered fifty-one graves dating back to the 1700s. The remains were moved to make room for a Walmart. In the late '70s, developers acquired an old, overrun Orthodox Jewish cemetery in Yonkers, agreeing to move all 250 bodies to Jerusalem. Due to a logistical mix-up, the remains of 135 children were left behind, and now rest under a

Home Depot, Costco and a two-storey parking garage. And where are the dead of nineteenth-century San Francisco? In Colma. When measuring forever, it's important to factor in human progress and shifting priorities.

Craving some noise and light, I drive out to Hollywood Boulevard to see the legendary freaks, but what I find instead are chubby happy families with fanny-packs taking pictures of one another with *Star Wars* Wookiees and Spider-Mans outside Grauman's Egyptian Theater. Winnie-the-Pooh has a star on the Walk of Fame. Edna Purviance does not. One of the most durable myths of pop culture says that Walt Disney, who died of cancer in 1966, was cryogenically frozen and locked in a chamber under the Pirates of the Caribbean attraction at Disneyland where he'll await science and his own team of Imagineers to thaw him, cure him and send him back to the world like a god in a Wagner opera. This too is a myth: he was cremated, had a private family service and is interred at Forest Lawn in Glendale.

I drive to the Hollywood Hills. At the bottom, pink in the sunset, are the towers of Walt Disney Studios. In Robert Stone's novel *A Flag for Sunrise*, an American anthropologist has too much to drink and, like Khrushchev at the UN banging his shoe on the desk, warns a roomful of Central American diplomats: "In my country we have a saying—Mickey Mouse will see you dead."

Sean Dockray, an artist and teacher at UCLA, wrote a peculiar paper about the American funeral home, which I'd found online a few months before I got to California: he argued that the modern funeral was a performance art, a kind of mass entertainment that owes more to Hollywood than it does to religion. Consider the funeral chapel, the chairs in rows, and up front, the lid of the casket propped open like a movie screen. "The windows are traditionally blocked by curtains so that little or no natural light enters," he wrote, "allowing the funeral director absolute control over the lighting of the environment, preventing unflattering natural light from reaching the skin of the deceased, and allowing the visitors to leave the outside world behind," as at a Cineplex. With makeup and wardrobe and special effects (arterial embalming), the "director" orchestrates a production with a central tragic hero and a strong but simple narrative: life goes on, and he's in a better place. The end. The mourners leave, having spent a short time in suspended disbelief.

"I'm fascinated by people who have total control over their space," he tells me when I meet him on campus for a coffee. He's thin and fidgety, easily distracted by birds and shiny objects as we sit in an outdoor parkette. "We all have control of our own space," he says, "but we let it go, it gets dusty and cluttered. Time takes its toll." But a mortuary, he says, is like a perfect diorama. They vacuum it every day. No one does that in their own home.

He leans over the table, hands around his cup like a priest at mass.

"Are you familiar with the experience economy?" he asks. "The experience is what you buy," like at Disneyland or Starbucks, not the thing, not the cup of coffee. You could buy a chicken at the grocery store, or get someone to cook one for you in a restaurant, or you could go to Medieval Times where they wrap a narrative around your chicken and you pay $50.

"I think the funeral industry is ahead of the curve," he says. "They're at the level of Disney."

Disney was selling experiences in the 1950s, at the Anaheim theme park. They produced not things, but memories. Funeral homes were hitting their stride around the same time, and as Jessica Mitford pointed out, their product was not the casket or the embalmed body so much as the "beautiful memory picture" the two combined to create.

"You know what's next?" he says.

I do not.

"Transformation economy," he says. "You are changed and improved. Vegas is an experience, you go to Vegas to see a pyramid and eat, I don't know, lamb. But a transformation is more like yoga. You don't take a memory away, you become a different person."

This, he says, might be the future of the funeral trade: change how people understand death. Like religion used to do.

Seventeen

THE SPOOKIEST TRADE SHOW IN AMERICA

The Tropicana casino in Las Vegas has been slated for demolition, but not, the clerk assures Annie and me, while we're staying here. This is how the Vegas strip works: at the first sign of *wabi-sabi* in a hotel or casino, they get out the dynamite and blow it up, then build a new one the next morning and act like nothing ever happened. Bartenders at the Mirage were suing the hotel and their union for age discrimination: they'd been fired for looking too old, they no longer fit the Vegas brand. History and tradition matter in Vegas, but not if they are more than a few weeks old.

Our first night I dozed with the TV on, half watching Steve Lawrence in a tuxedo talking about the new Vegas. "You used to have to dress to go to the casinos," he said, "it used to be all mom-and-pops, until Circus Circus opened up." Now the casinos are all corporately owned, there are no more high-rollers, just families and shrimp buffets. I woke up thinking, I've heard this all somewhere.

We walk the Strip, packed with the same pudgy families I'd seen on Hollywood Boulevard, golf jackets and hoodies from mid-western colleges tied around their waists, drinking glowing green Hurricanes and Slurpees. My feet stick to the sidewalk from sugar. Toddlers toddle, wee zombies buzzed on the light and colours, and the only signs of sin in Sin City are the "porn slappers" who press hooker cards into our hands as we pass. But they're families too: mothers and grandmothers and teenage boys, migrant workers from Mexico.

The next morning we hit the International Cemetery, Cremation and Funeral Association trade show at the Mandalay Bay casino. ICCFA: "Guardians of a Nation's Heritage." The hall is packed with vendors, hawking burial vaults and retorts and caskets and memorial gizmos: trippy glass tombstones and fake hollow tree stumps and rocks for cremated remains. The gift shop sells little wooden casket key chains and toy hearses. I tell Annie how to spot an American funeral director: a man with no neck, or a woman who looks like Mary Tyler Moore, only thinner and more authoritative. The vendors are desperate to make eye contact, to talk up such things as the benefits of granite. Across from Ace Caskets, with its new spring hardwood line, a man in a tie-dyed lab coat offers us a chance to win a Cherokee child's casket: the casket, the size of a beer cooler, is the raffle box.

"Why the lab coat?" I ask, filling out a card.

"Because I don't have a personality," he says. "The coat gives me a personality."

Two delightful young men show us their innovation: Shiva Shades, paper blinds for Jewish families, to cover mirrors during the seven days of shiva. The paper unfurls like an accordion and sticks to the glass with an adhesive strip. "No more cumbersome bedsheets," they tell us.

Funeral directors and cemeterians walk the aisles, shopping. A salesman offers Annie a ride in the Body Scoop, an electric lift for moving corpses. I take pictures while he lowers Annie into a casket. She claps with joy, but I feel ill, the image now burned in my head.

In a room off the main exhibition hall, an undertaker from Louisiana draws a red line on a dry-erase board and labels it *Cremation*. "This is a warning sign," he says. People take notes. *Warning sign*, they write. "And death won't bail us out." He has a preacher's gift for the long, telling pause. "The Centers for Disease Control keeps getting better and better, and it's sixteen years until the baby boomers get here," he says. "Now, what if they're all cremations?" He taps his red line. "We are in the *hole*, brothers and sisters!" What he's pitching are video terminals, like the confession-cams on reality TV shows. People sit in a booth and record their memories of the deceased. The clips are cut together and burned onto a DVD, which can be shown at the service. It's added value, a tool to keep cremation families from taking their business to a hotel or restaurant.

"This is what we own, ladies and gentlemen: the ceremony, the gathering," he says. "When people are on their deathbed, what they want is to make sure they're not forgotten." The concept's been focus-grouped and his pre-need sales are through the roof.

Next door, John Earle, of the Arbor Group Earles (father of Andrew, the manager at Chapel Lawn in Winnipeg), hosts a bull-session on food as a "revenue replacement program" for funeral homes. Clear out your casket showrooms, he says, and build reception halls. People eat after funerals. Why watch them drive to the mall when you can feed them on site, and not just with snacks and carrot sticks but with hot meals? Chapel Lawn, he says, has a full-time cook ("Thirty hours a week, her name is Barbara and she's a college graduate"), and a patio for barbecues. "This little gal has personality," he says, flashing a picture of his hostess on the PowerPoint screen. "She's comfortable around deceased human remains. That's important.

"And don't be afraid to put in bright yellow umbrellas. It says patio, it says food, it says entertainment."

At $1,220 for a catered event for fifty people, your profit margin is $795, a better markup than on caskets. Chapel Lawn does eight, eight and a half receptions a week. "If you don't have a fool managing your business and you love your families, you cannot go wrong, folks," he says. "But you need to value-add, and you need to revenue and cash-flow replace." The group applauds.

John Earle made me hungry. Back in the trade show hall, I line up at the lunch buffet for nachos and fajitas. Annie's gone to look for the Liberace museum, so I take my food and sit at a table by myself near the Matthews booth. Matthews has dolled up its set like a cremation garden and columbarium. Laid out like graves are brass markers, all of which bear the name *Matthews*, as if there'd been a bus crash on the way to the show and the whole family was wiped out and buried in the floor of the expo hall, among red wood chips and a bird bath filled with hard candies.

A couple sits down with me. They're husband and wife, from the Gardens of Gethsemani, a Catholic cemetery in British Columbia.

"Deals deals deals," says the woman, breathless. She's just bought a set of rubber tracks to keep the tractors from digging up the cemetery grass, and has her eye on a stone eagle statue. "If you wait till the end," she says, "you'll get a good deal on statues. The dealers don't want to have to carry them all the way home again." She yoo-hoos across the hall to another woman, who joins us with news of a discount on religious statuary.

"What's so special about it?"

"I don't know, blessed by the Pope or something."

Off they go, leaving me and the husband behind. He stares at his empty paper plate.

A big crowd gathers in one of the session halls for the two men who run Eternal Hills, a cemetery–funeral combo in Klamath Falls, Oregon. Eternal Hills is famous for having no salaried staff: everyone works on commission and bonuses. They sell package deals on the following model: If you offer a man a balloon release, he'll tell you he doesn't want one. If however he needs a graveside service with forty chairs, and the forty-chair package includes both a balloon release and a Thumbie, a gold pendant with the impression of the deceased's fingerprint, he'll take the package. The arranging directors have a credo:

> We know the family has shut down mentally.
> We know they are still at the hospital in their mind holding
>   the deceased's hand.
> We know we need to move them from anger to love.
> We know with enough repetition they will see value in one
>   of the items in the packages—Funeral . . . Cemetery . . .
>   Crematory—three times to say no.

Who says "no" three times?

They drill their staff on arrangement techniques like a football team, until, in their words, not only do they get it right, but they can't get it wrong.

Eternal Hills may have solved a modern puzzle in death-care: what to do about RTFs, or return-to-familys, the cremated remains that walk off the cemetery property before they have a chance to contribute to the revenue stream. For this crowd, with their love–hate relationship with cremation, it was like solving the Fermat's Last Theorem.

"Are your families saying 'We just want cremation,' and do they really know what that means?" they ask. Eternal Hills offers a guarantee: they sell glass-front niches with a two-year cooling-off period. If, during the two years, the family decides to take the ashes home or scatter them somewhere special, the cemetery refunds the money for the niche. A bit like negative-option billing for cable television: we keep the ashes unless you decide otherwise. In effect they're gambling on human behavioural inertia, that most people will leave well enough alone. It works. In eight years they've had only one customer take them up on the offer and remove the remains.

In fact, the manager of Eternal Hills tells us, his best friend and fishing partner, a teacher, who died suddenly of a heart attack while on a school trip, came close to being scattered in the North Umpqua River in Oregon, which, according to his son, was what he'd always wanted. It was a favourite fishing spot. But the family agreed to leave him in a niche at Eternal Hills until they could sort out the logistics. "That was in 1999," the manager tells us. "My best friend is still in the glass-front niche." The Eternal Hills guarantee had saved a soul from the oblivion of scattering.

The big product companies, Matthews and Batesville, hold the prime spots on the floor. Steve, the Batesville rep, gives me a crushing handshake and shows me a cremation hybrid casket that looks like a Shaker blanket box. I ask him about Chinese knock-offs, what they're doing to Batesville's market share, and he tells me a story about a two-hundred-pound woman who fell through the bottom of a Chinese casket in front of her family at a funeral. He tells me too about a badly embalmed body that dripped as it was carried down the aisle (and here he makes the sound of a dripping body: *pup, pup, pup*) through a poorly welded knock-off. "Twenty-eight percent of your business is gone in a lawsuit," he says. "Now, will you pay the $400 premium for a Batesville?"

Next booth over, David, from House of International Inc., sells Chinese caskets: cherrywoods with stained glass tops. His brochure says, "We provide much styles and sizes and looking forward to service you." I ask David how it feels, working so close to Steve all day. "Pressure, pressure, pressure," he says with a sigh. Then he tells me he's heard tell of a woman who fell through the bottom of a Batesville casket in front of her family at a funeral (the saga of the two-hundred-pound woman is an apocryphal industry fairy tale— it never happened, but this is a competitive racket and fear sells).

Ed sells clocks, and Toni sells greeting cards. Toni has choppy blonde power hair and sad, ebony eyes that follow me, like those in a painting, so I stop at her booth. They've exiled her to the back of the hall with the other indie entrepreneurs and the John Deere lawn mower enthusiasts who drink iced tea and talk loudly about sod. Her company, called A Touch From Beyond, sells Hallmark-style cards. I pick one off the table and open it.

"You meant a lot to me and I appreciated knowing you," it says.

I read it again, noting the past tense. The idea, she says, is you sign and stamp the cards before you die. Then, after you're gone, someone mails them out to friends, co-workers, caregivers and family. Posthumous thank-you cards. She got the idea when her husband died, just three years after she lost her father.

"Are you married?" she says.

I tell her I am, but not really. We just live together. Well, not "just," we've been together for years, and now she's somewhere out on the Strip looking for the Liberace museum, but anyway, I say, I suppose I'm missing the point because I think I'd probably say goodbye to her, you know, in person, rather than send a card.

The cards are for people who "don't have the words," she says. She hands me a few more samples.

Our shared lives were
comprehensive
and fulfilling

and you gave more than
I ever requested
or required.

Thank you for all you did.

They have a certain businesslike charm, like a well-crafted memo ("comprehensive and fulfilling"). After all, we buy cards to mark other life transitions: birthdays, bar mitzvahs, graduation, Secretary's Day. But I think about people I know in Newfoundland, who aren't so much superstitious as practical about omens, who would spend a day and a night at the Basilica of St. John the Baptist with a rosary if they ever got a greeting card from beyond the grave. "Stay in Their Memories Forever," the pamphlet says. Who could forget such a card? I thank Toni, but I know she knows I don't get it.

"Until you go through it," she says, "you don't understand."

The words, and her eyes, give me a chill.

Ed's clocks are urns, or his urns are clocks. Some clocks are set into pen-holder desk sets which are also urns. They are, I would say, conceptually busy. Am I supposed to reflect on the tyranny of time or the transience of human communion through the written word, or is it just a clock and a pen holder? The desk set with the clock set into a golf ball is even more work. I'm growing tired of everything being packed with cryptic meaning.

"Is this working?" says Ed.

I don't know what he means. I'm not wearing a watch, so I can't tell him if his clocks are running on time.

"Do people want this?" he clarifies. "I mean, you probably know about these things."

Richard calls them pot-and-pan salesmen and Neil calls them carpetbaggers, entrepreneurs aiming to elbow their way into the funeral market with gadgets that have no inherent meaning except as vessels for ashes. Take an object, a paperweight or a model boat, carve out a space big enough for a capsule: whammo, a $675 memorial keepsake. But I feel bad for Ed. He's in a near panic. He seems to sense that his clocks lack something, a necessary gravity. All I can think to tell him is what I've learned today: that if you don't have a fool running your business and you love your families, you cannot go wrong by value-adding, and revenue- and cash-flow replacing. Instead I tell him to hang in, that the marketplace is a rich tapestry.

The casino beckons. I sit down at an *I Dream of Jeannie* slot machine and feed it a dollar, but it can't even muster the energy to play me like a fish, so pathetic is my bet. It just eats the dollar and chirps, beckoning someone who knows how to play. I'm lost in here, like I was in the exhibition hall. I remember what Sean Dockray said, that Vegas is a managed experience: playtime for families who seek the fantasy of living in a pyramid or medieval castle for a weekend, to escape the chaos and discord of their real lives. They don't come to win, they come to experience the *possibility* of winning, on the next turn of the slot machine barrels, which never happens but that's not the point. The target customer in Vegas does not lose his shirt nor does he win the jackpot. He's simply delivered through time, distracted. For this he and his family will pay, and buy the T-shirt and eat shrimp in buckets. This, in a way, is the goal of the funeral trade too: to divert your attention long enough to get the body into the ground or the retort. Every funeral is a gamble that through some combination of product and ceremony, greeting cards and clocks and barbecues, you'll feel better, not transformed or changed but carried, dazed, over the hump. Is that enough? Is it better than nothing? I don't know, but neither does the industry, and it occurs to me as a dreamy revelation that death-care is playing the Vegas game too: blowing itself up and rebuilding in a panic, hoping their invented traditions will stick this time and draw a crowd.

I pass a craps table and a twenty-ish man in a porkpie hat and plaid shorts, with a beer in one hand and the dice in the other, calls out, "Who's feelin' it, because I'm not feelin' it." He looks at me. "Is anyone feelin' it?" Vaguely depressed I go back to the expo.

A small group has gathered across from the Shiva Shade boys. Perhaps, I think, a knife fight has broken out between Batesville and House of International Inc. But I look closer and see that the crowd is huddled around a dog, a golden Lab. Undertakers are patting him behind the ears and making clucky tongue noises at him. The dog's name is Derek, and he's a canine therapist. He wears a vest. Derek belongs to Tom Flynn, who owns a cemetery in Hermitage, Pennsylvania. His son, John, runs the family funeral home. Tom's philosophy on death-care is elegant: adapt or perish.

"For me," he says, cupping my elbow, "it came down to pets or vets. We got a lot of Catholics where we are, but Catholic cemeteries get them all. With veterans, Catholic or Presbyterian or what-have-you, they still identify as vets."

"But people will spend more money on pets," says John.

So pets it was.

They cremate pets, bury pets, host 150 pet funerals a year ("We had one family spend $800 on a guinea pig!" John says, as if he can't believe it himself), and once they got the okay from the city of Hermitage, they branched into burying pets and people together, Dad and Spot in the same grave. "We pre-need like crazy," Tom says.

"At first I was terrified," John says. "I thought we'd have people dragging their dead dogs in the front door of the funeral home."

Tom puts it this way: His cemetery has 25 percent of the local market (human, that is) and the funeral home gets 20 percent. But two-thirds of all homes have pets, and as the only pet death-care provider in town, that gives him a 66 percent share, plus most people own seven or eight pets in a lifetime. And satisfied pet owners buy pre-needs for themselves and their families too: for most people, burying a pet is their introduction to the death-care industry. Meanwhile, thanks to cremation, other, less diversified funeral homes are down to twenty funerals a year. How do you make a living on twenty funerals a year? By jacking the unit price, which only drives people to find cheaper cremation elsewhere, and the wheel keeps turning. "The whole world's changing," he says.

Attendance is sparse for the mainstage event with Dave Norton of Stone Mantel, an "insights consultancy" that counsels business on building "meaningful branding experiences." The crowd is attentive, if distracted by the crew in the back that's setting up coffee urns and baskets of muffins. Dave strides onto the stage. "Yours is a highly experiential industry," he tells us, "but you're treating it as a service: you offer to memorialize my loved ones for me so I don't have to." Meanwhile what people are looking for is an experience that matters, what he calls "cultural capital," whether it comes from art, spirituality or family life. Our lives are plastic: look around you, the city you're in, a fantasyland, and people are tired of fantasy. They're simplifying their lives: couples are scaling down, selling the SUV, or one of them, and living on a single income, eliminating economic premiums in favour of meaning—more time with family, more time for spiritual growth.

"Do they go around saying, 'I gotta have that latest casket'? They do not," he says.

They're hungry for products and experiences with high cultural value. The Body Shop does it by linking a story, of human and animal rights and fair trade, to shampoo and soap. Boomers have money to create a legacy, not because they care about status but because they want their lives, in the end, to have mattered. Look at the rise in volunteerism, and geo-tourism: they're taking their vacations in India and Guatemala, building housing and wells for clean water, reading to local kids, not sitting on the beach.

"Take a stand," says Dave. "What is soap?" he asks. (No one puts up his hand to hazard an answer.) "It's a product that takes a position: it's against dirt. People say, I'm against dirt too."

The man to my left is asleep, leaning on his cane, head resting on his hands. A woman at the front applauds lightly. The rest line up for coffee. I feel like I've seen and heard something important but cryptic, and this is the trouble with consultants. Like prophets they lead you to the edge of redemption and leave you to find God's grace on your own. What does he mean, "take a stand?" I suppose if pressed to choose one way or the other I'd have to say I'm against death. But what he's after is deeper fish. It's not enough to be against death; I need to face up to its absurdity, find meaning in the mess. How? Through some mystical "premium cultural experience." No wonder the industry crowd is ambivalent. In a way he's telling us to strip it down and start again, that the impulse to fix grief through shopping is giving way to the hunger for substance. How do you put that on a General Price List? What's the funeral equivalent of Body Shop shampoo? Then it comes to me: I've already seen it. A simple act, without the artifice of embalming or baroque funerary product. Just a direct application of body to ground where it's left to contribute to the great cycle: ashes to ashes and all that, back to Mother Earth in a shroud and a plain wooden box. Instead of deflecting a confrontation with death through commerce, you face it, fill the hole by hand, and then get on with the hard work of mourning, knowing that instead of passively choosing an object from a catalogue and subcontracting the ritual to someone else, you've acted, taken a stand, not against dirt, in fact, but *in favour* of it. An act with meaning.

At day's end I meet Annie for supper, at a real restaurant that serves food on plates delivered by waiters, with none of the wheelbarrow shrimp or deep-fried salad of the casino buffet: an authentic experience for our last night in Vegas.

"I have seen the future," I tell her. "And it's Jewish."

Eighteen

One Less Undertaker

The ground in front of the Factory has been dug up and graded. A backhoe sits perched like a vulture over what used to be the rose garden, now a hole ten feet deep and lined with concrete. The steel girders were sunk a week ago, marking the boundaries of the new reception centre. During construction, Neil says, one of the front-end loaders pierced a gas line. They could smell it in the crematorium. All they could do was evacuate the building, then hurry the bodies from the cooler into the removal van and drive them to a safe distance and wait for the fire department. Though the retorts were shut off, the two corpses inside continued to burn on their own fuel. Neil stood across the street and waited for his dream, now finally realized and halfway to being built, to blow up. But the firemen arrived in time to shut off the gas.

The evidence is in front of me: Neil won his court battle with Chapel Lawn, and the judges awarded him costs. The rose garden, they said, is a private matter on private property. If Neil wants to let people scatter their ashes and charge them a fee, that's his business. Cremated remains, they said, are not human remains. A scattering garden is not a cemetery. With the lawsuit out of the way, the bank fed him the cash for the building expansion, and a ribbon cutting is scheduled for next September. Chapel Lawn will not appeal, and is presumed grumpy.

But with the victory came a sour trade-off. After a twenty-year battle to see a paper idea turn into concrete and steel girders, he's lost half his staff. Adina was the first to go. After graduating from embalming school she took a job at Glen Lawn, one of the Arbor Group homes in the east end. Shannon followed soon after, to Chapel Lawn. It was their third shot at cherry-picking her and, as she told Neil, they weren't likely to call a fourth time. So she accepted their offer. Of course there were long-standing grievances, the clashes with Eirik over technique, but as far as Neil can tell, it came down to work–life balance.

"She got that if you give your all to a family in mourning, that it's worth something," he says. "The part she didn't get is you have to have flexible time." People die at night and on Sundays, Christmas and Easter. Bodies are cremated on Saturday so they can be scattered on Monday. Undertakers who expect to work according to a fixed schedule can't manage for long in a place like Neil's: there are some things for which you can only count on family. Staffers won't get up at 4 a.m. to see a grieving widow, but family will. If you spent your childhood in a funeral home, you already know your time isn't your own. Eirik understands this,

Neil says. He's a work in progress, but he knows what it means to "grow up funeral."

After Shannon left, Glenn handed in what was to be the last of his many resignation letters. He's now the night manager at Pasta La Vista. But Eirik and Richard have smoothed over their conflicts, and in the new building they'll share an office.

The fate of the downtown chapel is still pending. Neil would like to see it used for other functions. Richard's doing the research. He's reaching out to the gay and lesbian community, pitching same-sex weddings in a funeral home. Meanwhile, Neil's law-firm model for funeral service has been stashed away in a drawer for now. It might've worked with Natalie and Shannon on board, but Richard, he says, is too old and stubborn to buy into it, so the status quo will have to do.

Six months have passed since my American junket: six months of procrastination and writing, trying to figure out what I've figured out, if anything. When I got back from Las Vegas I spent three weeks in Richard's care at Aubrey Street and it was as if I'd never left: chairs needed stacking, coffee cups needed bussing, mourners had to be aimed at washrooms and parking spaces. Like an explorer bringing back exotic spices from the Orient, I tried to get Richard excited about the art urns I'd seen in Graton, but as predicted he just yawned: they'd never sell in Winnipeg. A spinning prayer wheel? Please. We have a hard-enough time getting people to pick flowers, he said. We don't need to stock the showroom like it's Toys "R" Us.

Green burial was another matter. There'd been talk from the city about building a green section at municipally owned St. Vital cemetery, but with red tape still to be cut and numbers to be crunched, no one at Neil Bardal Inc. expected it would happen in their life-times. Still, Richard has his eye on new products: biodegradable caskets made of wicker and shaped like sarcophagi, the same caskets Neil's grandfather used to carry at Sherbrook Street before anyone had dreamed of saving the planet through better dying.

The last service I worked with Richard was a sparsely attended affair. Sunlight marked the church floor purple and red where it shone through the stained glass windows. The organist played "What a Friend We Have in Jesus."

"I think it's the only one she knows," said Richard.

The dead woman's pre-teen great-grandson gave the eulogy. "She seemed to be proud of me," he told the small crowd. "She said, 'You're a good boy, Keenan, and you have a good speaking voice.' She used to knit sweaters. I wish she'd knitted more of them. Goodbye, Grammsie."

Richard and I sat at the back of the church. He put his feet up on the empty pew in front of us, and I did the same.

"You got to admit," he whispered, "it's a good way to kill an afternoon."

Now, months later, the crematorium is a construction site.

"Where are all the people?" I say to Neil, staring down into the empty hole that used to be the rose garden.

He leads me to the back of the building. There, under a pair of blue and orange tarps secured with rope and cinder blocks, is a pile of dirt. It will all go back into the Garden of Memories once the building is done. Someone's left a flower on one of the tarps.

There have been visitors, Neil says, though the physical remains are long gone, leached into the deep soil and groundwater, dissolved and cycled through nature. But the place, the spot on the earth where the last act took place, has meaning. It's still charged with the families' memories of the people who've been scattered.

I had always had trouble figuring out the appeal of the rose garden. Why here? Why would I scatter my loved ones by the airport, two doors down from Two Amigos Moving and Storage, when I can scatter anywhere, create my own meaningful last act? But now I see it's the act that counts and not the place. Neil's just providing an option, somewhere with washrooms and plenty of parking, free of the oppressive (and expensive) baroque theatrics of the cemetery. Scatter where you want, bury where you wish, but do something with intent, don't be passive and follow what commissioned pre-need salesmen consider the norm. Use your imagination, balance your own spiritual beliefs with guesswork, but do the work: accept that we know nothing about death, take a leap of faith, and have the courage to act anyway.

I once asked Neil the question directly: What's the right thing to do when someone dies? He thought about it, then said, "I don't know." Not the answer I wanted, but after a moment he added, "I think you have to struggle with it."

When his father first showed signs of what Neil calls "emotional trouble," he asked Neil to move him to Deer Lodge Centre, where his friends, the other Hong Kong vets, enjoyed a certain institutional clout. He had learned from the Japanese prison camp how to live in a restricted space, and he wanted to stay in Deer Lodge until he died. Promise me you'll let me do this, he said, and Neil promised. The rest of the family, his aunts in particular, popped a collective gasket, and overruled the decision.

"As we were leaving the hospital, my dad said to me, 'You know, boy, I really thought I could trust you this time.'"

Sometime later, Njall Sr., after spending a few hours writing letters, announced to his son that he was dying, that in fact he'd be dead by six that night. He asked to be taken back to Deer Lodge, and Neil drove him there, expecting the same outcome as last time: his father would stay for a while and then Neil would take him home. But by six Neil's father was dead. He'd suffered an aortic aneurysm. The doctors said he'd been filling up with blood for hours, and he must've known it. As Neil had already told me, his father had asked to be cremated, but Neil had other plans.

The casket was oak, the vault donated by the manufacturer. Viewing was at the Sherbrook Street funeral home, and the service followed at St. Stephen's. Neil said it was a $15,000 funeral by today's market, and the stone cost ten grand.

"I knew we'd keep 30 percent," he said. "But if we cremated him like he wanted, that's $3,500 all in, and we'd keep 20 percent. I had to ask, what am I doing to my own profession?

"Everything told me I was doing the right thing as a businessman, but none of it was meeting my needs as a son. I'd betrayed him twice," he said—first by taking him out of Deer Lodge, then by burying him against his wishes. "But I decided if we're going to show what we do, let's show it in its fullest form, let's have the casket and the viewing, the whole ball. Now I walk past his grave and say, 'Sorry, Dad.' It never left me. When I started to think about it I came to the conclusion: the simpler the act the better."

His father's death forced him to go back to first principles. What is an undertaker? Is he a product salesman? No, he deals first with the body and then helps the family work out a ritual with meaning.

It's hard, maybe impossible, to know what has meaning, and the impulse may be to seek the comfort of the casket showroom or the customs of the Church. But if you struggle with it, Neil said, you'll come up with an idea. For him, getting the body from bed to retort to ground with no sold product in between, except for the cardboard container, is an act with meaning.

But then so is burying a man with his favourite shoes and a can of Pringles chips. If modern living means there's no code of conduct except for what you devise yourself from shreds of religion, a few of the more hard-core Commandments, common law, taste and the basic rules of collaborative society (don't jump the queue at the ATM), then deciding what has meaning is a matter of personal choice. Oh boy. I have a hard-enough time choosing toothpaste: wintergreen, peppermint, cinnamon, apricot, anise, ginger or tea-tree oil. Please, someone, tell me what I want; advertise me into a decision.

Maybe this is why the corporates will never lose by pitching the full-fig package, with a balloon release, a gold Thumbie and a two-year guarantee on a columbarium niche. Predigested meaning is oddly liberating: it frees me of the responsibility to decide among a sea of choices I have neither the skill nor the experience to navigate. Doing nothing is an option too.

But somewhere in between everything and nothing I'm left with my own unreliable instincts. In the past these instincts have led me to bad choices, to buying T-shirts with ironic sayings that I no longer understand. How can I trust them in the face of death? Maybe by following Neil's example, and the examples of the families I've met on this weird journey: by interrogating my beliefs. If your belief is that the Canadian walleye is superior to the American walleye, then have the Canadian fish etched on the urn. This is not a trivial detail. It's a human response to an absurd event.

As Neil did after his father died, let's break it down to first principles. Here's the body. You have to do something with it. The hospital wants it out of the morgue, fast, to make room for fresh ones. What are your options? Until promession and resomation find the right investment and branding opportunities, they're off the list, as is Tibetan sky burial, in which the corpse is left in the treetops to be devoured by carrion birds. Basically you have two choices: burn or bury (or both).

Too simple? Of course. The choices are fraught with a powerful need to find meaning in what otherwise is an act of disposal. Maybe you believe in the myth of permanence, the need to control the wild and absurd through human ingenuity. So the body is skilfully embalmed, made to look serene, and buried in a "sealer" casket and vault. Or, it's cremated and inurned, placed on a shelf, an heirloom-to-be for future generations to match furniture and drapes against. The cemetery promises perpetual care: six hundred years from now a college student will still be cutting the grass over the grave, with some laser doodad. The myth of permanence is seductive. In a way it's no different from religious faith, with its promise of immortality. It's a reasonable, socially sanctioned reply to an unreasonable demand, and gives you the tools to deflect a confrontation with real, putrid, worm-crawling death. Zygmunt Bauman and Ernest Becker and Sheldon Solomon all agree that this is the supreme human accomplishment: the ability to deny that death will someday happen to you. By controlling it you rob it of its power. It's a war, and we fight it one managed corpse at a time.

Maybe you believe the opposite, that the answer to death is to embrace the chaos, to see the body dispersed rather than managed and packaged. So you cremate and scatter, or bury the ashes loose in the soil, or if you can find a cemetery that doesn't insist on a vault or concrete liner (good luck) you can bury the body as is, in a shroud or a simple wooden box. The green burial fits a desire for a different kind of immortality: the perpetuation of the carbon cycle, rebirth through the organic efforts of Mother Earth. Yes, it's a secular variation on the Jewish rites, which I'm convinced can be pitched to baby boomers as an experience with high cultural value: brand it as *tahara*, the Hebrew term for purification of the corpse through washing and prayer. It has enough of a Japanese ring that it speaks of the value of decay, of *wabi-sabi*. We used to fear decay, and the industry played on that fear, using it as a sales lever to pitch embalming and protective caskets, but now rot is a value. We compost our carrot tops. I have friends who keep earthworms in Tupperware containers and feed them coffee grounds and egg-shells as if they were pets. The modern *tahara*, an ancient, meaning-ful ritual (stripped of its emphasis on the God of Abraham, Isaac and Jacob for the sake of marketability) where the body is washed, wrapped in linen and buried at once, might appeal to the same crowd that recycles its cat food tins and buys twirly light bulbs: current practices are unsustainable. It's a sin against nature to bury veneer hardwoods and steel. Go pre-modern, like your dreadlocked neighbours who wear only hemp. Joe Sehee's grand, ambitious green burial grounds, where the goal is to preserve and conserve, call for a near-religious faith in political action even after death:

you can take up space in a cemetery or you can contribute to sustainable land management. It's a meaningful act.

But my impulse, inspired by Neil's bed-to-garden philosophy, is to keep it simple and modest. The Tahara brand could be hooked to the development of small, rural cemeteries, like the burial ground in Starbuck: no-embalming zones that are left to grow wild. Invest in property now, register it with Joe's Green Burial Council. I smell the equivalent of the condo boom.

Having stood at enough open graves by now to feel the seductive pull, I can understand why my grandparents wanted the piece of real estate above all else: the body belongs in the ground, in whatever form—ashes or whole, marked with a stick or a bronze plaque or nothing at all. Robert Pogue Harrison says that "to be human means above all to bury."

Which leaves us with the ceremony. I see no difference between the Celebration of Life and the rite of Christian burial. Both use storytelling to take the sting out of death. One praises the life that was, the other the life that follows. Death is simply the trigger for a crafted narrative, where the bad bits are edited out. The dead man may have been a dick or a sinner, but for one day (one day!) we can forget all that and commit his soul either to memory or to an everlasting communion with God: our choice, it's a ritual of deliverance either way. But it doesn't have to happen in a funeral home or a church. Gather more than two people in a room with a photo album and a bottle of wine and it's a wake. The advantage of the funeral home is that it's bookable on short notice, and provides access to parking and potable water. The disadvantage is that, for the most part, the funeral home is still stuck in a decades-old Home Shopping Channel aesthetic, with its porcelain-figurine and airbrushed-pony-painting kitsch-charm. A graduate student I met did her thesis on funeral home design and concluded that the modern ritual is best served by a blank canvas, a space without emotional expectations and predigested signifiers: in other words, a white room.

I saw this white room by accident one night, walking on Queen Street West in Toronto. I came across a store that hadn't been dressed yet with product, whatever it was the vendors intended to sell. The walls were lined with white bunting and beautifully lit. The space was deeper than it was wide, and my eye was drawn to a focal point at the back, where I imagined the shrouded corpse or an unglazed pottery urn or the ashes loose and sprinkled in a ring with a candle or stone pot of burning sweetgrass in the middle. Instead of pews the mourners would be issued yoga mats. A bald Asian man in an orange sarong would ring a tiny brass bell. The guests would be encouraged to reflect on time and decay in some private manner. They could nap if they wanted to, or hold hands with a stranger, or murmur the Kaddish, which could be projected on the wall like surtitles at the opera. For a line of Tahara outlets in suburban power centres, next to the LensCrafters, all I'd need is a bazillion dollars in start-up. But with 75 million souls hungry for transformative experiences, name me a safer investment. The industry has appropriated Christian imagery long enough: it's time to steal grapes from another great religion.

The fantasy evaporated when a sales clerk hustled out to tell me to stop taking pictures, that I was presenting a security risk. I carried on down Queen Street, stopped into The Body Shop and bought a bottle of ginger shampoo in order to save the planet and untold cosmetic-lab bunnies. Body Shop would be a good name for a funeral chain too, but it's taken.

Still, I was left with the image, a space stripped of commerce, and in my head Neil's mantra: the simpler the act the better. Fantasy aside, how do you find simplicity in an industry so committed to baroque product and ceremony? The same way you find the right dentist or hairstylist: by shopping around. There are undertakers like Neil who believe that their job is to deal with the body, and to deliver a ritual with meaning. It takes work to tease them out of the Yellow Pages herd, but two questions might do it. Can I visit the body without having it embalmed? Can I sit with it at the crematorium while it's in the retort? Even if you intend to do neither, the answers will tell you what kind of funeral director you're dealing with.

I started this trip, my head full of Mitford, thinking funeral directors were, at best, well-meaning crackerjack salesmen whose answer to the madness of loss was to dress it up, package it and perform a kind of ad lib voodoo, leaving the real work of grief to the families after the cheque had cleared. Instead I found a community trying hard, if not always succeeding, to carry their customers from confusion to clarity, and at times helping them to confront real death in a genuine way. They have more to offer than product: they listen, and they don't treat grief as a communicable disease. Neil and his family bury and burn the dead, and although it's not their job to deliver the souls to a better place, they can and do deliver the living to a better place: to the comfort of a meaningful rite, religious or secular or invented on the spot.

———

The churchyard in Dacotah is all yard and no church. The building was moved years ago, leaving a bald patch on the grass next to the cemetery. The Scandinavian Lutherans who used to worship here now go to the church in nearby Starbuck. But the cemetery is still active: the stones, some old enough to be covered in orange lichen, bear names with more consonants than vowels. A few people have gathered for the burial, overdressed for the summer heat. Two men in wraparound sunglasses stand over one of the old graves. The headstone has toppled off its pedestal and they push it back into place, promising to come back later with contact cement to fix it properly.

"That's his sister there," one of the men says, wiping his hands on his trousers. "She died in '53, in that train accident."

"I thought it was suicide," the other says.

"It was, but everyone says it was an accident."

The pastor calls us to a spot under a tree for today's interment. In one hand I'm holding the late Mrs. Q. in an urn that looks like a Russian peasant's jewel box: folk-arty flowers on black lacquer. Uncommonly pretty for a commercial urn. In the other I'm holding the urn vault, a small plastic tub with a lid, like a hotel ice bucket. After the pastor's blessing I place the urn in the vault and secure the lid with Testors model-airplane glue. Strands of glue blow in the breeze, and a woman beside me picks some out of her hair. Neil hands out single roses to the guests, who then place them, one at a time, in the grave.

Hands are shaken, and the small crowd is released to their cars. Service will be in Starbuck, at the same Lutheran church where Neil and Richard and I once buried the farmer with a sheaf of dried wheat on his casket. The gravedigger arrives in his pickup. He is in fact the backup gravedigger (filling in for someone named Mitch), a hobby farmer from "exactly three miles east," he says.

"I'm amazed how dry the hole is," he says as he fills it. "I expected the earth to be clumpy but it's bone dry." He picks up a handful as proof.

Leaving him to his work, I join Neil in the van. On the way out of the cemetery, I can see the backup gravedigger sticking each rose stem-first into the earth over the grave, like a birthday candle. They keep falling over and he keeps standing them up. It's hopeless of course, but all the more moving in its futility and the fact that he doesn't know I'm watching. That's all it takes, I think: a simple, private human gesture.

After a quick lunch at the Starbuck Hotel, at which the same man behind the counter offers us the same ham sandwiches on defrosted hamburger buns (end of the week: no bread), Neil and I attend to the guests at the church. Men whose pants still have creases from the clothes hangers where they've hung since the last funeral let their wives sign the guest book for them. Their necks and ears are sunburned, their bald spots white. They wipe their feet on the way into church. The pianist plays a plunky "Ode to Joy."

During the service, Neil and I stand outside in the sun. It occurs to me I never did have Richard's dream about the dead man who sits up in the prep room, which I take to be a reverse omen, a sign from the undertaker gods that it's time to move on. When I think back on what I've learned—how to find a man's femoral artery by touch, how to put a blouse on an old woman whose elbows are locked, how to bake and sort a human skeleton, how to jam 300 cubic inches' worth of meat packer into a 200-cubic-inch container—I see that I'm left with a very peculiar new skill set, but also, I hope, some new instinct for knowing what to do in the face of death. It calls for a gesture, that's all, as simple as jamming roses into the earth. But I won't know for sure until it happens. You can't pre-need the struggle.

"I've been studying Buddhism," Neil says.

Perfect, I think, for a man who wants to shake his material attachment to caskets and other funeral-ware in an industry where permanence is just an illusion anyway. He has also looked into the new technologies. Resomation sounds interesting, he says. He can imagine some kind of fountain arrangement in the Garden of Memories where the liquid remains are channelled back into Mother Earth. Until someone comes up with 100 percent cremation, there'll always be a remainder. Our mission is to do something interesting with it.

"But that's for the future," Neil says. "What matters most now is family, and those old dears at St. Stephen's who take care of me . . ."

He turns his head. From the church I can hear the closing hymn, "Take My Hand, Precious Lord," the last in the order of service.

When my life is almost gone,
Hear my cry, hear my call,
Hold my hand lest I fall.

"I'll take family over everlasting life," he says, and before I can respond, he's gone.

The hymn is our cue to lead the congregation from the church. There'll be plenty of time for shop talk and theology later—a lifetime, whatever that may be. For now we have work to do. I follow him into the chapel.

Acknowledgements

$\mathcal{E}$ xcept for the parts you didn't like, for which I take full responsibility, this book was a collaborative effort. Thanks to my friends and narrative counsellors at the CALC round table at the Artful Dodger for their advice, and for enduring my cockeyed obsessions with death and ritual. Thanks to Christine who loves a good Catholic funeral like a kid loves funnel cakes, and to Cheyenne who was the first to ask: why death, when you could just as well write about chocolate and puppies? Next time.

My friend Paul Wilson and John Pearce, my agent at Westwood Creative Artists, were the twin godfathers of this project. I'm grateful for their guidance and patience. Without them this would still be a pile of notes scribbled in a mortuary bathroom. Thanks to Jim Brown and Sharon Cavanagh for reading the first formless draft of the manuscript and making it better, and to my mom, my role model, for transcribing interviews and for teaching me how to listen.

Thanks to all those in the business, and their critics too, who cared enough about the subject to answer my naive questions: Karen Leonard, Joe Sehee, Ron Hast, Thomas Lynch, Gary Laderman, Paul Ayers, Gary McRae, Mark Krause, B.T. Hathaway, Josh Slocum of the underfunded but invaluable Funeral Consumers Association in the U.S., to members of the Winnipeg death-care community and especially the families who, through the machinery of fate, wound up doing business at Neil Bardal Incorporated in the months I was there. To protect their privacy, I've used only initials or pseudonyms in recounting their stories.

Thanks to Lisa Burks who pokes around troubled cemeteries not for the gruesome kicks, but to remind us that we are who we bury, and to Katherine Isaac for imagining a funeral home without the signs, symbols or cheesy post-colonial furniture of the standard North American mortuary. Funeral directors: read her thesis at the University of Manitoba, and if you can drop the addiction to embalming too, we'll all join you come the revolution.

Thanks to the Manitoba Arts Council. They paid for the ramen noodles and black funeral socks consumed and worn during the writing of this book. Thanks to Ray Fennelly and Beth Oberholtzer for further feeding, watering and spiritual care while I was on the road.

Big heartfelt shout-outs to my editors Kendall Anderson and Anne Collins, and everyone at Random House of Canada, for giving shape and architecture to my scatter-brained notes. Anne Collins is a gift to all writers lucky enough to work with her.

To Eirik Bardal, Jon Bardal, Jean Bardal, Annette Bardal, Richard Rosin, Janice Dryden, Adina Vogt, Shannon Jackson, Natalie Ricard and Glenn Menge, who let me into their workplace and lives, and to Neil Bardal, my friend and mentor, I'm grateful for your honesty and trust.

Finally, with love and apologies for the years I disappeared to find my own inner undertaker, and to live inside a Joy Division song, this book is for Anne Gregory.

TOM JOKINEN is a radio producer and video-journalist who has worked on *Morningside, Counterspin* with Avi Lewis and *Definitely Not the Opera* as well as many other CBC shows. In 2006 he took a job as an apprentice undertaker at a Winnipeg funeral home. He has also worked as a railroad operator and an editorial cartoonist, and spent two years in medical school at the University of Toronto. He dropped out, but not before dissecting two human cadavers.